DISCOVERING
SEATTLE PARKS

DISCOVERING
SEATTLE PARKS
A LOCAL'S GUIDE

LINNEA WESTERLIND

MOUNTAINEERS
BOOKS

For my dad, Pete, who loved to walk and explore

MOUNTAINEERS BOOKS

Mountaineers Books is the publishing division of The Mountaineers, an organization founded in 1906 and dedicated to the exploration, preservation, and enjoyment of outdoor and wilderness areas.

1001 SW Klickitat Way, Suite 201, Seattle, WA 98134
800.553.4453, www.mountaineersbooks.org

Printed in China
Distributed in the United Kingdom by Cordee, www.cordee.co.uk

First edition, 2017

Copyeditor: Rebecca Jaynes
Design and layout: Jen Grable
Cartographer: Bart Wright, Lohnes+Wright
Photography: Linnea Westerlind
Cover illustration: Jen Grable

Library of Congress Cataloging-in-Publication Data
Names: Westerlind, Linnea, author.
Title: Discovering Seattle parks : a local's guide / Linnea Westerlind.
Description: First edition. | Seattle, WA : Mountaineers Books, 2017. | Includes index.
Identifiers: LCCN 2016039824 (print) | LCCN 2016056876 (ebook) | ISBN 9781680510010 (pbk.) | ISBN 9781680510027 (ebook)
Subjects: LCSH: Parks--Washington (State)--Seattle--Guidebooks. | Outdoor recreation--Washington (State)--Seattle--Guidebooks. | Seattle (Wash.)--Guidebooks.
Classification: LCC F899.S43 W47 2017 (print) | LCC F899.S43 (ebook) | DDC 917.97/77204--dc23
LC record available at https://lccn.loc.gov/2016039824

ISBN (paperback): 978-1-68051-001-0
ISBN (ebook): 978-1-68051-002-7

Contents

City of Seattle Map 8
Introduction 9
How to Use This Book 11
10 Fun Facts about Seattle Parks 18
The Rich History of Seattle Parks 21

DOWNTOWN SEATTLE & THE INTERNATIONAL DISTRICT

1. Olympic Sculpture Park.............. 25
2. Myrtle Edwards and
   Centennial Parks 27
3. Lake Union Park........................29
4. Cascade Playground 31
5. Denny Park................................. 32
6. Tilikum Place 33
7. Regrade Park 35
8. Victor Steinbrueck Park 36
9. Waterfront Park.......................... 38
10. Freeway Park 40
11. City Hall Park 42
12. Pioneer Square...........................43
13. Occidental Square 45
14. Kobe Terrace 47

MAGNOLIA & QUEEN ANNE

15. Discovery Park 51
16. Lawton Park 56
17. Magnolia Manor Park................. 57
18. Ella Bailey Park...........................58
19. 32nd Ave. W. Boat Launch 61
20. Smith Cove Park 62
21. Kinnear Park................................64
22. Parsons Gardens 65
23. Kerry Park....................................67
24. Counterbalance Park 68
25. Ward Springs Park 69
26. Bhy Kracke Park 70
27. Trolley Hill and
    MacLean Parks 72
28. Thomas C. Wales Park............... 73
29. Mayfair Park................................74
30. West Ewing Mini Park................76
31. Soundview Terrace......................77

NORTHWEST SEATTLE

32. Carkeek Park 81
33. Llandover Woods Greenspace ... 85
34. Northacres Park............................86
35. Licton Springs Park 88
36. Greenwood Park 89
37. Green Lake Park........................... 91
38. Meridian Playground 94
39. Gas Works Park........................... 96
40. Woodland Park............................97
41. Fremont Peak Park....................100
42. Hiram M. Chittenden Locks.....102
43. Ballard Commons Park............104
44. Ballard Corners Park................ 105
45. Kirke Park 106
46. Sunset Hill Park 108
47. Golden Gardens Park 109

NORTHEAST SEATTLE

48. Warren G. Magnuson Park........113
49. Laurelhurst Playfield 118
50. Belvoir Place 119
51. Ravenna and Cowen Parks 120
52. Ravenna-Eckstein Park 123
53. Dahl Playfield 124
54. Maple Leaf Reservoir Park........ 127
55. Pinehurst Pocket Park 128
56. Little Brook Park 130
57. Matthews Beach Park................131

CAPITOL HILL & THE CENTRAL DISTRICT

58. Washington Park Arboretum.....135
59. Madison Park........................... 139
60. Howell Park.................................141
61. Homer Harris Park 142
62. Madrona Park 144
63. Powell Barnett Park 145
64. Leschi and Frink Parks.............. 147
65. Flo Ware Park............................149
66. East Portal Viewpoint 150
67. Judkins Park and Playfield 152
68. Firehouse Mini Park 154
69. Harborview Park 155
70. Plymouth Pillars Park 156
71. Cal Anderson Park 157
72. Volunteer Park and
    Conservatory 159
73. Interlaken Park........................... 162
74. Streissguth Gardens................. 163
75. I-5 Colonnade............................ 165
76. Lynn Street Mini Park 166
77. Rogers Playground 168
78. South Passage Point Park 169
79. Montlake Playfield 170
80. East Montlake Park................... 172

BEACON HILL & SOUTH SEATTLE

81. Seward Park 175
82. Pritchard Island Beach 179
83. Beer Sheva Park and Atlantic
    City Boat Ramp 180
84. Chinook Beach Park...................183
85. Kubota Garden........................... 184
86. Othello Park 186
87. Oxbow Park.............................. 187
88. Jefferson Park............................ 188
89. 12th Ave. S. Viewpoint 191
90. Dr. José Rizal Park..................... 192
91. Daejeon Park..............................194
92. Atlantic Street Park 195
93. Seattle Children's PlayGarden 196

94. Sam Smith Park 198
95. Mount Baker Ridge
    Viewpoint 200
96. Colman Park 202
97. Mount Baker Park 204
98. Genesee Park and Playfield 207

WEST SEATTLE & SOUTH PARK

99. Lincoln Park 211
100. Solstice Park 215
101. Lowman Beach Park 216
102. Ercolini Park 217
103. Emma Schmitz
     Memorial Overlook and
     Me-Kwa-Mooks Park 218
104. Alki Beach Park and
     Playground 221
105. Schmitz Preserve Park 223
106. Hamilton Viewpoint Park 225
107. Jack Block Park 226
108. Camp Long 228
109. Cottage Grove and Greg
     Davis Parks 230
110. Herring's House and
     Terminal 107 Parks 232
111. Duwamish Waterway Park 234
112. Westcrest Park 236
113. Roxhill Park 238
114. Fauntleroy Park 240

BEYOND SEATTLE: GREAT REGIONAL PARKS

115. Forest Park 243
116. Shoreview and Boeing
     Creek Parks 244
117. Saint Edward State Park 247
118. Marymoor Park 249
119. Luther Burbank Park 252
120. Gene Coulon Memorial
     Beach Park 254
121. Ed Munro Seahurst Park 256
122. Point Defiance Park 258

Resources 261
Acknowledgments 263
Index 265

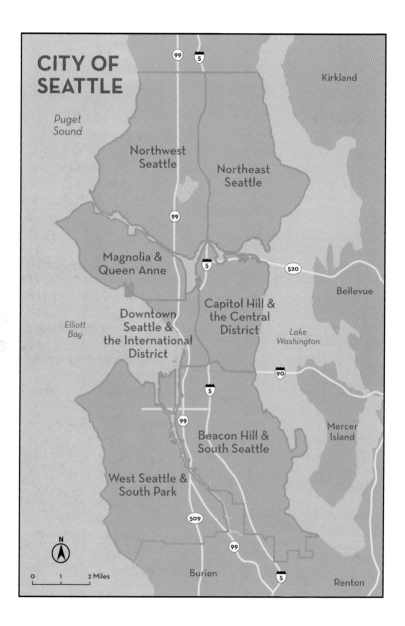

Introduction

In 2009 I set out on a warm August morning with my six-month-old son tucked into an orange jogging stroller, a pair of brand-new walking shoes, my camera, and a handful of Google Maps printouts. My destination was Seward Park, and it was the first day of my ambitious quest to visit all the parks in the city of Seattle in one year. I spent a glorious day walking the trails of Seward Park, stopping at every sign to read about the park's fascinating history, and taking dozens of photographs of the views of Lake Washington and Mount Rainier along the way.

As I crisscrossed the city with my maps, I learned about the influence of the Olmsted Brothers, discovered interesting tidbits about Seattle's founders, and relished the gorgeous viewpoints, walking trails, and peaceful greenspaces I'd found.

One year eventually stretched to four as I realized I had underestimated the extent of Seattle's always growing parks system—more than four hundred existing parks and a handful of new ones built every year—and my little family grew from three to five with the arrival of twins.

As I trudged out in all types of weather to every corner of the city (now with a blue double jogging stroller), my appreciation for my hometown's amazing parks grew. I loved coming across tiny pocket parks and hidden lookouts in neighborhoods I'd never set foot in before. As I read placards about natural history and examined interesting art pieces, my kids played on playgrounds and tested out spray parks.

Not every park left me amazed. Some have worn-out amenities and others look a little neglected. I puzzled over why the city owns several parks that are nothing more than a triangle of grass alongside a busy road. But I continued on, especially enjoying the times when I stumbled upon a wonderful little-known park.

The West Point Lighthouse at Discovery Park was the first manned lighthouse on Puget Sound when it was built in 1881.

In 2013 I finally completed my mission to visit all the city's parks. But instead of feeling the huge sense of accomplishment I'd hoped for, I itched to share my favorite parks with other urban nature lovers.

This book is for you: resident or visitor, urban walker, explorer, biker, swimmer, dog owner, parent, nature lover, or even couch potato. I hope you will tuck this book into your pocket and let it inspire you to explore. Seattle surely has one of the best parks systems in the country. This book will help you find the captivating viewpoints, hundreds of miles of hiking, walking, and biking trails, acres of accessible public shoreline, neighborhood dog parks, thrilling playgrounds, and many wheelchair-accessible spaces that make Seattle such an incredible place to live.

In this digital era it is more important than ever that we get outside and play. Go and enjoy.

How to Use This Book

Living in a city with hundreds of amazing parks, I found it agonizingly difficult to narrow down the list to the most interesting, appealing, and worthy of visiting for this book. But the task had to be done, so consider the parks in this book to be, in my view, the best of the best of Seattle parks.

This book is divided into seven chapters based on large geographical Seattle neighborhoods to make perusing easy, plus a chapter of parks outside the city but within the Puget Sound region that are worth the journey.

It is a snapshot in time for Seattle parks, and the city is adding new parks and upgrading older ones every year. In particular, playground equipment is replaced regularly. So a park may appear different on your visit than it was on the day I explored it.

WHAT THE ICONS MEAN

Kid-friendly

Dog-friendly

Barbecue grills

Views

Beach or waterfront

Spray park or wading pool

Unpaved trails

Paved paths

Historic significance

Accessible

Public art

Gardens

Kid-Friendly These parks have a playground, skate park, or other attraction designed for play.

Dog-Friendly This icon designates an official off-leash dog park. Many additional parks are excellent places to exercise your dog on a leash, especially

Flowers bloom in spring against dense green foliage at Parsons Gardens on Queen Anne.

the parks indicated as good for hiking. Keep in mind that it is prohibited to have dogs on playgrounds, playfields, or beaches in the city of Seattle.

Barbecue Grills We are lucky in Seattle that virtually every park has a bench or table that would make a nice picnic spot. Harder to track down are places to barbecue, so this icon indicates parks that have charcoal barbecue grills for anyone to use. Bring your own charcoal, and note that some grills may be reserved as part of a shelter or picnic table reservation. You can make a reservation through the city's parks department at www.seattle.gov/parks.

Views These parks have exceptional views of water, mountains, or city skyline.

Beach or Waterfront Many of our parks have waterfront property abutting Puget Sound, Lake Washington, the Duwamish River, or other major bodies of water.

Spray Park or Wading Pool These places are designed with kids and summer in mind. You'll find either a spray park or a wading pool, open during summer months. Sometimes the city closes certain wading pools for the year due to funding issues, so check online before you visit. Hours vary, and poor weather can prompt a closure.

Unpaved Trails Dozens of our parks are great for urban hiking. I've listed the total mileage of trails for each park where hiking is possible. In some parks it is possible to do a loop, and in others you may need to hike out and back. In places where official trail lengths are not available from the city, I estimated their length using online mapping programs. So consider my trail lengths a rough estimate to use as a guide in planning your outing.

Paved Paths These are parks with flat paved paths that are good for strolling or kids on bikes.

Historic Significance Seattle's parks showcase our city's rich history. This icon points out parks that have a significant historical element, such as the site of an important event or the former property of a city founder.

NOTE: The information in this book is based on the research and expertise of the author. It is incumbent upon readers to confirm park details, such as hours, fees, facilities, or transit access, and to be aware of any changes in public guidelines, jurisdiction, or other city, county, or state regulations. The publisher and author are not responsible for any adverse effects or consequences resulting from the use of any of the suggestions presented in this book.

Accessible for Wheelchairs and Strollers With this icon you'll find parks that are the most accessible for wheelchairs and strollers. Some of these parks still may not have ideal conditions for those with limited mobility, but most are accessible from the parking area. For example, these are parks with designated disabled parking and flat paved pathways inside the park. Not specified are playgrounds with ADA play equipment, as more than 115 parks in Seattle already have this and more are upgraded to meet this designation every year. Parents of kids with disabilities often say that even ADA-approved playgrounds pose challenges for their kids, and some parks work better than others. Consider this icon to be a starting point for determining accessibility to our parks.

Public Art More than 130 pieces of art add color, shape, and inspiration to our parks. This icon designates parks with more than one piece of art or a truly iconic piece by a well-known artist.

Gardens This icon highlights our best publicly accessible gardens in the city.

OTHER NOTES

These notes cover the location, size of the park, amenities, and tips on how to get there.

Location This category lists the street address for the park or the closest major intersection. In some cases the park boundaries or the nearest cross streets have been added for clarity. The neighborhood—or city in the case of the regional parks—is also listed.

MAP LEGEND

————	Road	**P**	Parking	⊢——⊣	Railroad
– – – –	Trail	🛈	Restroom	▬▬▬	Park
ⅢⅢⅢⅢⅢ	Steps	🛝	Playground		
		🚌	Bus stop		

An exquisite variety of Japanese-inspired plants and trees frame a spring-fed pond at Kubota Garden in South Seattle.

Acreage This information gives you a sense of the park's size.

Amenities In addition to the icons, the major amenities for each park are included to give you a quick reference for what to expect. Note that some amenities, including restrooms in some parks, are open only seasonally.

Getting There These directions are subdivided into sections on driving, transit options, and cycling options, wherever applicable.

By Car This section gives driving directions to each park, beginning at major roads or freeways. There may be a quicker route for you depending on your starting point.

The Seattle skyline shines in the distance from Hamilton Viewpoint Park on the northern tip of West Seattle.

By Bus Also noted are the closest major bus stops to each park, but there may be more stops within a reasonable walking distance and there may be more routes. OneBusAway (http://pugetsound.onebusaway.org) is an excellent tool for planning your trip. You can also check out Metro's website for updates or to confirm routes: http://metro.kingcounty.gov.

By Streetcar This means the South Lake Union Streetcar, which runs from Westlake Center (5th Avenue/Olive Street) to Fred Hutchinson Cancer Research Center (Fairview Avenue North/Aloha Street) or the First Hill Streetcar, which runs from Occidental Square (Occidental Avenue South/ South Jackson Street) to Capitol Hill (Broadway Avenue East/East Denny Way). Noted are the closest stops. Check www.seattlestreetcar.org for route maps and schedules.

By Light Rail This indicates Link light rail operated by Sound Transit, which currently runs between the University of Washington and Angle Lake just past

With your purchase of this book, you also get access to a comprehensive list of the 300-plus parks (hundreds more than we could include in this book) throughout Seattle. • Go to our website: www.mountaineersbooks .org/SeattleParks. Download the PDF. • When you open the document on your computer, enter the code "p@rkL15T" when prompted. Offering this bonus feature is our way of thanking you for supporting Mountaineers Books and our mission of outdoor recreation and conservation.

Sea-Tac Airport. The closest stops and distances from each park are included. Consult Sound Transit's website for detailed maps and schedules: www .soundtransit.org/link.

By Bike This is mentioned in places where there are major bike trails close by, but many parks without nearby trails are still readily reached by bike.

By Ferry The closest ferry terminal and route is noted when a ferry stops immediately inside or adjacent to a park.

Extend Your Visit These are easy add-on walks or bike rides to another park or attraction nearby.

A WORD ON SAFETY

Seattle's parks are generally safe. That said, it's always smart to take simple precautions. It's best to avoid parks after dark—and always respect official park hours (generally 4:00 AM to 11:30 PM but check signs). Hiking with a buddy is a good idea in the large parks that have more isolated, forested trails. Avoid wildlife and never feed little critters.

Consult a trail map before heading out for a hike. One trick I use if a park doesn't have hard-copy trail maps is to take a photo of the map at the information board with my camera or phone that I can consult later if I get confused.

Many of our parks with pools and waterways are staffed by lifeguards during the summer. It is best to swim only when lifeguards are on duty. Never swim alone. Parents and caregivers should watch children—both swimmers and nonswimmers—carefully on beaches and in pools and wading pools.

10 FUN FACTS
ABOUT SEATTLE PARKS

1 Discovery Park is Seattle's biggest park at 534 acres.

2 Fifteen parks within the city are bigger than 100 acres.

3 There are more than 150 parks smaller than 1 acre, including many that are the size of a small square of lawn. And several contain nothing more than a square of lawn.

4 Seattle has an astounding amount of public land: 6,200 acres representing 11 percent of all land in Seattle. That includes 24 miles of public shoreline.

5 Seattle's oldest park is Denny Park on the northern edge of downtown. It was dedicated in 1884 and honors city founder David Denny.

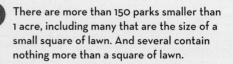

6 The world-renowned Olmsted Brothers firm had a role in the planning or design of more than 50 Seattle parks and boulevards, including the Washington Park Arboretum, Seward Park, and Volunteer Park. They also recommended the development of another 30 parks. Their goal was to have a park within a half mile of every Seattle home.

7 The term "P-Patch" originated in Seattle and isn't short for "pea patch." It actually comes from "Picardo," the family who farmed a 20-acre plot in the Wedgwood neighborhood. Part of this land became the city's first community garden. Today there are more than 80 P-Patches in Seattle.

8 Several of our parks are named after Seattle sister cities, including Kobe, Japan; Tashkent, Uzbekistan; and Be'er Sheva, Israel. Some sister cities have reciprocated with parks or markers named in our honor. It's fun to think that in the future there could be a "Seattle Park" in more places around the globe.

9 Many Seattle parks are named after notable Seattleites, including David Denny, Louisa Boren Denny, James Colman, Henry Yesler, and Powell Barnett. A tour through our parks is like taking a tour through Seattle history.

10 Many parks feature public art installations by local and international artists. In addition to pieces at the Olympic Sculpture Park, other art worth checking out includes Douglas Hollis's *Waterworks* at Cal Anderson Park and Doris Chase's *Changing Form* at Kerry Park.

The Rich History of
Seattle Parks

*Parks are the breathing lungs and beating hearts of great
cities... and in them are whispers of peace and joy.*
—James Ronald, Seattle mayor, 1892–1894

A fantastic way to learn more about our city's origins is through its parks. Many Seattle parks sit in historic places—the setting for battles or the original homesteads of our founders—and others are named after famous people from Seattle's history.

It's important to mention that we would know much less about Seattle history if one former parks employee hadn't dedicated years to preserving precious paper files. An engineer for the Seattle parks department for more than two decades, Don Sherwood enthusiastically took on the enormous assignment of compiling and recording historical information for three hundred parks—an incredible feat. You can learn much more about each of these parks by accessing his helpful notes on the parks department website, www.seattle.gov/parks.

The founding of Seattle's first parks dates back almost as far as the official establishment of the city. But the Duwamish tribe likely used land in and surrounding the city for recreation for many years before our first park—Denny Park—was designated in 1884. It's difficult to imagine our city without the sweeping greenspaces that make it such a wonderful place to live, but parks are not an inevitability in a young city, and we can thank the foresight of the citizens who valued nature, open space, and recreation more than a century ago.

OPPOSITE: *Looming seventy-five feet high, the historic water tower dominates the scene at Volunteer Park on Capitol Hill. Its observation deck holds a fascinating display on the history of Seattle's parks system.*

The sun rises above the pagoda at Daejeon Park on the north side of Beacon Hill.

Several factors helped shape our parks and our city into what they are today. As Seattle grew in the 1880s, developers began to plan housing tracts in neighborhoods outside the downtown core, reachable by a new system of trolleys and cable cars. In order to attract buyers to these new "far-off" neighborhoods, developers either built private parks (often with amusement rides, zoos, restaurants, and other extravagant amenities) or pushed the city to designate land for parks in these areas. Madrona Park, Madison Park, Alki Beach Park, and Leschi Park were originally elaborate weekend recreation areas.

Two key figures in our parks' history were R. H. Thomson and George Cotterill, city engineers—George later became mayor—who together with volunteers built 25 miles of bicycle paths (part of what's now Lake Washington Boulevard, Interlaken Boulevard, and Magnolia Boulevard) to meet demand for a new bicycle craze in the 1890s. These paths became the starting point for a plan to develop a network of boulevards and parks across the city. And it's at this point in our history that the name Olmsted enters the picture.

In 1903 the city made a crucial and brilliant move in hiring the Olmsted Brothers firm—famed for New York City's Central Park—to create a plan for Seattle parks that included greenbelts, playgrounds, ball fields, and scenic drives. Land was acquired, funds were raised, and the Olmsteds ultimately designed, influenced, or made recommendations for more than eighty parks or boulevards that still grace our city.

The timing of the Olmsteds' work was key because Seattle was set to host the Alaska-Yukon-Pacific Exposition in 1909, an event that would bring more than 3.5 million people to the city. John C. Olmsted designed the fairgrounds at the University of Washington (which still bears their mark) to take advantage of views of Mount Rainier, Lake Washington, and Lake Union. Many other parks projects, most notably Woodland Park and Volunteer Park, were planned to show off Seattle at its best during the expo.

Another important factor in the development of our parks was the Great Depression in the 1930s, which prompted the federal government to create the Works Progress Administration (WPA) to provide jobs to the unemployed. The WPA undertook numerous public works projects, many of which are still visible in Seattle parks, including many of the structures at Camp Long, the stone cottage and lookout shelter in the Washington Park Arboretum, and the Green Lake wading pool.

Seattle has a long history of citizen support for parks. King County's $118 million Forward Thrust bond proposition in 1968 was one of the biggest bonds in support of parks and recreation passed in the country at the time. That thumbs-up by voters led to dozens of new amenities in Seattle, including indoor swimming pools, playfields and playgrounds, tennis courts, small neighborhood parks, and the Seattle Aquarium. Over the decades that followed, with few exceptions, voters have continued to back the maintenance and development of our parks system.

Today Seattle parks are evolving to meet modern desires for recreation and greenspace in the midst of a fast-growing urban region.

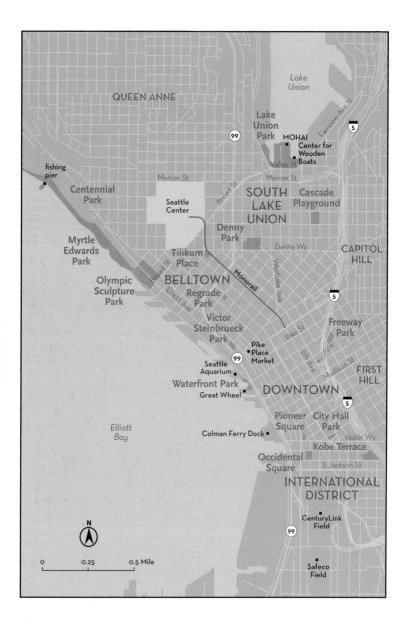

Downtown Seattle & the International District

1 OLYMPIC SCULPTURE PARK

Alfresco art museum lives up to international acclaim

Location: 2901 Western Ave.; Downtown
Acreage: 9
Amenities: Restrooms, seasonal café (hours vary), wheelchair-accessible parking garage with elevator, 0.5-mile gravel path, benches, chairs

GETTING THERE

BY CAR From downtown Seattle, take Western Ave. north through Belltown. The park is at the corner of Western Ave. and Broad St. Paid parking is available in the wheelchair-accessible garage on Broad St. **BY BUS** Elliott Ave./Broad St.; 1st Ave./Broad St.; Denny Wy./Queen Anne Ave. N. **BY BIKE** The Elliott Bay Trail runs along the park's western edge.

A remarkable experience for locals and tourists, this outdoor museum makes art fun and accessible for everyone, while elegantly linking the city with its waterfront.

Olympic Sculpture Park features more than twenty works of art by internationally acclaimed artists in a spectacular outdoor setting.

Conveniently situated between the Space Needle and Pike Place Market, this park has become one of Seattle's major tourist attractions since it opened in 2007. Unsurprisingly, it has won numerous national and international awards.

Its design by Weiss/Manfredi and Charles Anderson Landscape Architecture makes clever use of a former industrial fuel storage site. As you wander the park, which is shaped like a large Z, art of all sizes and shapes pops out of the landscape to greet you. Children will enjoy exploring this easily walkable park, and several of the pieces are especially fun for kids—although you may need to remind them about the "hands-off" rule.

This public park is operated by the Seattle Art Museum (SAM). SAM donors and volunteers helped make the park possible, including a $30 million gift from Mary and Jon Shirley to kick things off. It's clear that people in Seattle care about art.

Begin your visit at the top near the café (a great place to grab lunch or a snack in the summer) and follow the gravel path. Veering to the right leads you down toward Richard Serra's famous *Wake*. Signage provides information about each work of art, and you'll also spot plaques that give the names of native plants and trees in Lushootseed, the language of many Puget Sound tribes, and explain how they were used by our region's first inhabitants. (Bearberry, for example, was used as an astringent for cuts.) Each part of the park reflects a different Pacific Northwest landscape, from meadow to shoreline.

You'll barely notice that you cross above Elliott Avenue as you approach the iconic orange sculpture by Alexander Calder called *The Eagle*. Pull up a seat here on one of the bright orange chairs and take in fantastic views of the Olympic Mountains, Bainbridge Island, West Seattle, and even Mount Rainier on a clear day. Or continue south along the path, crossing the railroad tracks, to the colorful *Seattle Cloud Cover* by Teresita Fernández that seems to defy our gray skies. The path zags again down a steep slope to the waterfront, where several more pieces of art sit near the shore along a paved walking path. Here you'll find Louise Bourgeois's *Father and Son*. Watch as the two figures disappear and reappear in a fountain as the water rises and falls.

Even if you aren't an art buff, visit the park to run or walk, a particularly attractive option given the park's easy access to Myrtle Edwards Park at the shoreline. Or picnic on one of the benches along the waterfront. For a different view of the sculptures and more solitude, plan a visit for the early morning or evening. The park opens thirty minutes before sunrise and closes thirty minutes after sunset.

2   MYRTLE EDWARDS AND CENTENNIAL PARKS

Spectacular waterfront stretch creates paradise for runners, walkers, and bikers

Location: Myrtle Edwards Park: 3130 Alaskan Wy.; Centennial Park: Pier 86; Downtown
Acreage: 15.8
Amenities: Restrooms, benches, drinking fountain, 1.4-mile paved biking and walking path, fishing pier, exercise station

GETTING THERE
BY CAR From downtown Seattle, take Western Ave. north through Belltown and turn left on Broad St. The entrance to Myrtle Edwards Park is at the intersection of Alaskan Wy. and Broad St. Paid street parking is available on Alaskan Wy.
BY BUS Elliott Ave./Broad St.; 1st Ave./Broad St.; Elliott Ave. W./4th Ave. W.
BY BIKE The Elliott Bay Trail runs through these parks.

One of Seattle's most scenic stretches of waterfront is essentially a marriage of two parks—one managed by the city's parks department and one by the Port of Seattle. Sitting side by side, Myrtle Edwards Park and Centennial Park combine to create nearly a mile and a half of flat paved paths perfect for running, walking, and biking.

Myrtle Edwards (the parks department's responsibility) begins just north of the beachfront section of the Olympic Sculpture Park, where a small area of sand and gravel beach littered with driftwood provides a fun place for kids to play. The park is named after the former city councilmember and council president who helped secure the land for Gas Works Park and was a big proponent of public open space.

Head north along the winding path, which splits: one trail for walkers and runners and another for bikers—a wise move by the park's planners as bike commuters zip by at high speeds. Benches are placed throughout the long stretch of park to capture the best views of West Seattle, Magnolia, Bainbridge Island, and the Olympic Mountains. As you wander, you'll come across large sections of lawn that make great places to picnic while you watch giant container ships come and go in Elliott Bay.

Slow down near the small brick building or you'll miss the artwork by Laura Haddad, at the center of which are five mirrored steel pipes sticking up from a stormwater outfall site. True functional art, the pipes help release air as water comes through the pipes below. A fascinating etching along the wall below interprets what's happening underground. The art piece continues as a swale etched with words and waving lines cuts through a stone plaza to where the underground pipes empty into the Sound.

Continue along the trail a little farther to a wide lawn where you'll find a cluster of giant boulders, a climbable work of art by Michael Heizer. A black metal bridge here connects to 3rd Avenue West, linking Interbay and Queen Anne with the waterfront. Kids will also enjoy watching trains pass below the bridge.

Shortly after the bridge, you enter Centennial Park, which celebrates the Port of Seattle's centennial in 2011. A stone beacon sponsored by the port, maritime unions, and the Coast Guard memorializes men who died working at sea.

Quieter than Myrtle Edwards, Centennial Park is worth exploring. You'll find more picnic tables, a thirty-two-foot Tlingit totem pole, and an exercise station with chin-up bars, parallel bars, and a bench for sit-ups. Wander through the lovely rose garden, or pull out your binoculars near the shore for excellent bird-watching. After you pass under the enormous grain-terminal elevator, you'll reach the public fishing pier that has built-in stools, sheltered benches, and fish-cleaning stations. A small bait shop near the pier sells lunch and snacks, and across from it are restrooms.

EXTEND YOUR VISIT

Centennial Park officially ends just north of the fishing pier, but the **Elliott Bay Trail (Terminal 91 Bike Path)** continues north to connect to Magnolia. Follow the path north and after 0.4 mile, you'll pass under the Magnolia Bridge. The trail then follows a dull section of chain-link fence and wraps around port activity, ending after an additional 1.6 miles at **Smith Cove Park**.

3   LAKE UNION PARK

Cornerstone waterfront space connects us to Seattle's maritime history

Location: 860 Terry Ave. N.; South Lake Union
Acreage: 12
Amenities: MOHAI café and restrooms, CWB boat rentals and classes, historic vessels, beach, seasonal spray park, model boat pond, hand-carry boat launch, 1 mile of paved walking paths, benches, chairs

GETTING THERE

BY CAR From downtown Seattle, take Westlake Ave. north through South Lake Union. Turn right on Valley St. Turn left immediately into the parking lot. Some of the spots are paid public parking; read signs carefully to avoid reserved spots. **BY BUS** Westlake Ave. N./Mercer St.; Fairview Ave. N./Valley St. **BY STREETCAR** South Lake Union line to Valley St./Terry Ave. N. **BY BIKE** Westlake Ave. N. Cycle Track.

For thousands of years the Duwamish people lived in this area, building canoes from a dense forest of old-growth cedars. Those were the first boats on this lake, which today sees kayaks, rowing skulls, sailboats, and yachts. Be sure to check out the fascinating pillars you'll see as you enter the park, each packed with photos and lessons on the origins of Seattle. Learn about Thomas Mercer, the site's first white settler, the birth of the airplane industry on these shores, and the park's naval history.

Anchored by the regal white armory building that is now home to the Museum of History and Industry (MOHAI), Lake Union Park is a fantastic urban space with walking paths, an interesting waterfront, and great views of the lake.

The 1942 armory building at Lake Union Park casts its reflection in a pond where kids float model boats in the summer.

In the summer, kids will be unable to resist the fountain that squirts water up from a long, narrow stretch of pavement near the parking lot. Parents or caregivers can rest and watch the action from a row of benches. People who work in South Lake Union often take advantage of the bright orange chairs and bistro tables nearby for a lunch break in the sun.

Paved walking paths lead in gentle, curving patterns through the lawn and past boat-shaped planters toward the water. Wander the waterfront and piers to get a close-up look at several historic ships that dock at Lake Union Park, including one of the country's oldest tugboats still afloat. Check the signs on each pier—the boats often admit visitors for free. Sunday ice cream cruises also set sail from one of the piers. Don't miss the twenty-foot-tall ornate Carroll's clock built in 1913, one of the finest antique clocks in the city, or the upside-down steel-and-aluminum boat, a sculpture by Peter and Sue Richards that plays acoustic tricks.

Around the corner you'll find the Center for Wooden Boats (CWB), made up of several floating wooden buildings and a network of docks where rowboats and sailboats await their turn out on the lake. Both members and non-members can rent boats here year-round. On summer weekends kids can rent their own model boat to launch on the large pond on the southwest side of MOHAI. More benches ring the pond.

Walk around the southern end of the bay or cross the pedestrian bridge to reach a flat gravel beach with a hand-carry boat launch. This is also a great place to watch the seaplanes that land and take off at this end of the lake.

Public restrooms are available inside MOHAI during museum hours and at the CWB boathouse.

EXTEND YOUR VISIT
Looking for a half-day of urban exploring? Walk, run, or bike the 6.2-mile **Cheshiahud Lake Union Loop**. For a clockwise loop, begin at Lake Union Park, set off north along Westlake Avenue North, and follow the shoreline to the northwest. Cross the Fremont Bridge and turn east toward Wallingford, then cross the University Bridge and head south through Eastlake. A map at Lake Union Park shows the route and describes many points of interest along the way, including street ends with waterfront views. Look for signs on the route with a call-in number to access an audio tour of the loop.

4 CASCADE PLAYGROUND

Outdoor play space encourages visitors to linger in growing neighborhood

Location: 333 Pontius Ave. N.; South Lake Union
Acreage: 1.9
Amenities: Restrooms, playground, picnic tables, benches, half basketball court, P-Patch

GETTING THERE
BY CAR From downtown Seattle, take Westlake Ave. north toward South Lake Union. Turn right on Thomas St. and continue four blocks. The park appears at the corner of Minor Ave. N. Paid street parking is available on adjacent streets.
BY BUS Fairview Ave. N./Thomas St.; Fairview Ave. N./Harrison St.; Eastlake Ave. E./Stewart St.

South Lake Union has transitioned from a sleepy industrial neighborhood into one that is bursting with new tech companies, bars and restaurants, and condo towers. Set among all the bustle is Cascade Playground, the neighborhood's outdoor living room.

South Lake Union residents and workers wander through the park on fair-weather days to get fresh air or eat lunch on one of the many picnic tables and benches. The northwest corner of the park is particularly pleasing for a lunchtime stroll, with short dirt paths that wind among native trees and shrubs and cross a little wooden bridge.

The park's two separate play areas draw families with young kids. A small structure, sized for toddlers, sits between two large sandboxes. Older kids will love the big climber that features a small zip line, several slides, and a climbing wall. A panel describes how to play the game "hot lava" by crossing from one end of the play area to the other without falling into the wood chips below. A nice bonus of this park is that most of it is fenced, providing a little peace of mind for parents and caregivers.

A stroller- and wheelchair-friendly paved path circles the large grass playfield. You'll find a half basketball court and restrooms in the northeast corner, and a P-Patch with quirky garden art in the southwest corner. Adjacent to the P-Patch is the Cascade People's Center—a neighborhood center operated by the Y (formerly the YMCA), in partnership with the city's parks department, that provides programs and classes for youth and adults.

5   DENNY PARK

Oldest Seattle park
provides tree-filled oasis

Location: 100 Dexter Ave. N.; South Lake Union
Acreage: 4.6
Amenities: Playground, off-leash dog park, 0.3 mile of paved paths, benches

GETTING THERE

BY CAR From downtown Seattle, take Westlake Ave. north toward South Lake Union. Turn left on John St. After one block, the park is on your left. Paid street parking is available on John St. **BY BUS** Dexter Ave. N./Denny Wy.; Aurora Ave. N. (Highway 99)/Denny Wy. **BY STREETCAR** South Lake Union line to Westlake Ave./9th Ave.

Designated in 1884, Denny Park is the city's oldest public park and holds the tallest stand of trees in the downtown area. The park sits on land claimed and later donated by early settler David Denny. It first served as a cemetery, but the graves were transferred so the land could become a park. It's hard to imagine today, since the park feels so central, but in its early days visitors had to take a wagon on an unpaved path from Pioneer Square to reach Denny Park on the fringes of the city.

Today a planter surrounded by benches forms the heart of this leafy public space. Eight wide paved paths extend in all directions from this point, creating convenient corridors for people who live or work in the neighborhood. At the southern end of the park you'll find a bust of Reverend Mark A. Matthews, a Presbyterian minister and influential figure in Seattle in the early 1900s.

Towering pines, maples, cedars, cypresses, and dozens of other varieties of trees cover the park in a green canopy, especially in spring and summer. On warm days nearby tech workers are drawn to the park's benches for a shady picnic.

A small playground designed especially for kids under five has a climbing structure, a colorful playhouse for toddlers, and a little net climber that spins like a merry-go-round. Dog owners living in the area use the 4,500-square-foot fully fenced off-leash dog area with a gravel carpet, tire, and playful pretend fire hydrant. There are plans to move the off-leash area to a new location when space becomes available in the neighborhood.

If you're looking for a break from a busy workday, try out the reflection labyrinth made up of concrete pavers on a round patio near the playground.

6   TILIKUM PLACE

Seattle's namesake greets visitors at peaceful plaza

Location: 2701 5th Ave.; Belltown
Acreage: 0.1
Amenities: Benches, tables

GETTING THERE
BY CAR From downtown Seattle, take 4th Ave. toward Belltown. Turn right on Cedar St. After one block the park is on your right. Paid street parking is

This figure of Chief Seattle was the first statue in the city.

available on Cedar St. **BY BUS** Cedar St./Denny Wy.; Denny Wy./5th Ave.; Wall St./5th Ave.

A statue of Chief Seattle greeting newcomers welcomes visitors to Tilikum Place on the edge of Belltown. So it's appropriate that this park was named after the word for "friendly people" in Chinook, a trading language for many area tribes and settlers. Dedicated in 1912, the bronze statue by James Wehn was Seattle's first commissioned piece of public art. It tops a fountain that features plaques commemorating the chief of the Suquamish and the first sighting of non-natives in the Puget Sound. The location of this park is historic as it roughly marks the northern boundary of the first land claims of the Denny, Boren, and Bell families, whose land would later make up downtown Seattle.

After decades of exposure to sun and rain, the statue of Chief Seattle had turned green by the 1980s. A well-meaning resident, in trying to clean it himself, accidentally scratched the surface, and people first thought the statue was ruined. Restorers discovered that the scratches revealed the statue had been painted in gold leaf, and the original layer actually lay beneath. After a thorough restoration, the figure now shines in the sun and is an official city landmark.

Park benches and several small tables are scattered around the park, and a ring of trees provides shade on hot days. A couple of restaurants and cafés open onto the flat plaza, which is easily accessible for strollers and wheelchairs.

THE CITY'S LIVING ROOM

No part of Seattle better represents our social and cultural gathering place than **Seattle Center**. With the city's preeminent landmark, the Space Needle, watching over and the monorail whizzing by, this seventy-four-acre space truly defines Seattle. Although not technically a park, Seattle Center was built as the grounds for the World's Fair in 1962 and now hosts annual festivals, including Bumbershoot, PrideFest, Bite of Seattle, and the Northwest Folklife Festival.

Within this true urban hub, you'll find museums, performance spaces, attractions, and events as varied as the city itself. Some highlights to check out: the International Fountain on a hot day; the Museum of Pop Culture (formerly the Experience Music Project); a playground with a thirty-five-foot-tall climbing tower; a ten-thousand-square-foot skate park; the Pacific Science Center; two giant IMAX theaters; KeyArena, home to the Seattle Storm women's champion basketball team; a winter ice-skating rink; a children's museum; several theater companies; McCaw Hall for ballet and opera aficionados; the KEXP radio station and KCTS TV station; the Chihuly Garden and Glass exhibition; an all-ages music and arts venue; and even an alternative high school. Picnic on one of the many open lawns or grab lunch or dinner or hit up happy hour inside the Armory, a true former armory that now holds a dozen restaurants and cafés.

7   REGRADE PARK

Corner park is urban dog playground

Location: 2251 3rd Ave.; Belltown
Acreage: 0.3
Amenities: Off-leash dog park, chairs, drinking fountain

GETTING THERE

BY CAR From downtown Seattle, take 4th Ave. toward Belltown. Turn left on Bell St. After one block, the park is on your left. Paid street parking is available on 3rd Ave. **BY BUS** 3rd Ave./Bell St.

As the landscape of Belltown has changed, so has Regrade Park. Once a rarely visited, unwelcoming public space, it was transformed in 2004 and is now a busy corner for the hundreds of dogs and their owners who live in the nearby apartments and condos.

Enter the fully fenced park through one of the two double gates at opposite corners. Concrete pavers of varying heights and a few chairs provide seating for dog owners while their pets exercise among the rocks, logs, and a brightly colored agility ramp. Although most of the ground is concrete, two gravel and mulch sections provide a softer footing for dogs with sensitive paws. A spiral concrete statue by Lloyd Hamrol in the northeast corner of the park makes for an unusual dog ramp. Trees and the adjacent buildings provide shade on hot days.

Dog owners will appreciate access to running water to quench their pets' thirst. Lighting also illuminates the thirteen-thousand-square-foot space, making it friendly for evening use.

EXTEND YOUR VISIT

Wander the adjacent pedestrian-friendly **Bell Street Park** from 1st Avenue to 5th Avenue. This four-block tree-lined section has wide sidewalks, planters bursting with cheerful flowers, and bistro tables for outdoor picnics.

8 VICTOR STEINBRUECK PARK

Tourist must-do features buskers and views

Location: 2001 Western Ave.; Downtown
Acreage: 0.8
Amenities: Public art, shelter, picnic tables, benches

GETTING THERE

BY CAR Located in downtown Seattle on Western Ave. at its junction with Virginia St., just north of Pike Place Market. Paid parking is available on Western Ave., Virginia St., and Lenora St. **BY BUS** 1st Ave./Lenora St.; Pine St./2nd Ave.; 2nd Ave./Stewart St. **BY LIGHT RAIL** Westlake Station, 0.4 mile east at 5th Ave./Pine St.

It's urban, it's at times a bit gritty, and it's frequented by all sorts of people, from tourists and wandering musicians to office workers and the homeless.

But there's no better place on a sunny day to get commanding views of Elliott Bay and the Olympic Mountains than Victor Steinbrueck Park. And the park's paved pathway is friendly to wheelchairs and strollers.

Watch the ferries go by from one of the many benches that line the two grass lawns, popular spots for summer sunbathing. Ten wooden picnic tables make the park a great place to enjoy lunch gathered from the vendors at nearby Pike Place Market. A small shelter provides cover on rainy days.

Three pieces of public art add character to the space, including two fifty-foot-tall cedar totem poles carved by James Bender in 1984. *Farmer's Pole* (uncarved except for two figures at the top) is a nod to the hard-

One of the two cedar totem poles designed by Marvin Oliver that grace the skyline at Victor Steinbrueck Park

working farmers who bring their goods to the Pike Place Market.

The heart-shaped stainless steel sculpture and glass plaza designed by Clark Wiegman, Karen Kiest, and Kim Lokan in the northeast corner of the park is titled *Tree of Life* and honors homeless men and women who have died. A closer look at the ground surrounding the sculpture reveals interesting objects beneath the glass surface.

The park was designed by Victor Steinbrueck and Richard Haag. It was named after Steinbrueck in 1985 to honor his role in the preservation of Pike Place Market. Steinbrueck also commissioned the totem poles.

Note: Some visitors are intimidated by the small groups of homeless individuals who congregate in the park, but the risk of being hassled is low.

9   WATERFRONT PARK

Wooden boardwalk connects city and waterfront

Location: 1401 Alaskan Wy.; Downtown
Acreage: 4.8
Amenities: Fishing pier, benches, picnic tables, fountain

GETTING THERE

BY CAR Located in downtown Seattle on the waterfront at the junction of Alaskan Wy. and Union St. Paid street parking is available on Alaskan Wy., University St., and Western Ave. **BY BUS** 1st Ave./Union St.; 1st Ave./University St.; 1st Ave./Pike St. **BY LIGHT RAIL** University Street Station, 0.3 mile east at 3rd Ave./University St.

Wedged between the aquarium and the Great Wheel, Waterfront Park is part of the classic Seattle waterfront experience. The smell of the sea air and the wooden planks of the park's piers underfoot invoke a nostalgia for old-timey Seattle. And in fact, this spot has seen important moments in the city's history. A wharf, built by the immigrant Schwabacher brothers, that once occupied this spot held Seattle's first customshouse, was a key stop on trade routes, and launched the Klondike gold rush when the vessel *Portland* arrived in 1897 carrying gold from the Yukon.

But few visitors know this history, and it's the striking views of the Olympic Mountains, Bainbridge Island, and West Seattle that really stop tourists—and locals—in their tracks.

In the summer the sixteen-foot-tall bronze fountain near the aquarium by James FitzGerald, Margaret Tomkins, and Terry Copple attracts kids who love to watch the splashes up close. Climb the steps to the highest part of the park for a different view of their sculpture, where you'll also find picnic tables and benches. A little farther south is another sculpture, installed in 2010, called *Waterfront Whimsea*, which shows fish, crabs, and an octopus tangled in a web of green kelp.

The park zigs and zags, with several square sections jutting into the sea, as you work your way north along the railing. As you cross the pier, ponder this

The Great Wheel forms a modern backdrop to a historic spot on Seattle's waterfront.

fact—an amazing twenty thousand old-growth trees were harvested to build the original seawall and create Seattle's piers.

The park has plenty of seating areas, including wooden benches built into the concrete walls. Have a seat on one and watch the ferries cross Elliott Bay and the Great Wheel slowly rotate. Or grab a picnic from one of the waterfront seafood take-out restaurants a little south of the park and enjoy it at one of the bright blue tables.

As the Seattle waterfront undergoes dramatic changes with a new seawall and highway tunnel, this park will surely continue to evolve, strengthening the connection between the city and the sea.

10 FREEWAY PARK

Architectural urban maze is a well-kept secret

Location: 700 Seneca St.; Downtown
Acreage: 5.2
Amenities: Fountains, free Wi-Fi, 0.5 mile of paved trails and stairs

GETTING THERE

BY CAR Located in downtown Seattle adjacent to the southeast side of the Washington State Convention Center. Wheelchair-accessible entrances: from the fourth floor of the convention center onto Ellis Plaza, at 6th Ave. and Seneca St., at 9th Ave. and University St., and at Seneca St. and Hubbell Pl. Note that many sections connect via stairs. Paid parking is available in the convention center parking garage below the park; from Pike St. turn right on 8th Ave., then turn left into garage. **BY BUS** Seneca St./8th Ave.; Seneca St./6th Ave.; Convention Pl./Union St.; Seneca St./5th Ave.; Pike St./Convention Pl. **BY LIGHT RAIL** University Street Station, 0.2 mile west at 3rd Ave./University St.

Hovering over the top of Interstate 5 as it passes through downtown Seattle, dodging office buildings, and reaching into narrow pedestrian passageways, this park transforms an awkward, unused area into accessible public space. One of the first parks in the country to be built over a freeway, its clever design was conceived by renowned landscape architect Lawrence Halprin and executed by his protégé Angela Danadjieva. Also known as Jim Ellis Freeway Park, in honor of the activist who championed the effort to build a park as a lid to I-5, it was realized in 1976.

Despite the park's reputation for being unsafe in past decades, the city has made big strides in improving Freeway Park's safety by installing better lighting and keeping shrubs trimmed. Today it is a popular lunch spot for office workers and convention goers. Nurses, doctors, and hospital staffers on First Hill use the park's pedestrian paths and stairways as a convenient shortcut to reach the business district downtown.

Hugged by the skyscrapers surrounding it, Freeway Park is made up of many small and large plazas connected by paths that make sharp turns, revealing public art, hidden stairways, and tunnel-like walkways around seemingly every corner. The park has several major sections—with 8th Avenue cutting the park roughly in half—and each has interesting features to explore. Take a look at the map kiosks located in several spots to get a sense of the scope of the park and all its nooks and crannies.

Highlights include Ellis Plaza, a large open square surrounded by benches just outside the convention center. The sharp angles of the basalt rock sculpture by Danadjieva reflect the green boxes that make up the convention center's glass atrium. At one end of the plaza you'll find a raised grass platform holding a sculpture by Buster Simpson that shows the

An intriguing maze of water and concrete, Freeway Park's Canyon Fountain was built in the 1970s.

faces of George Washington and Chief Seattle supported by a large tripod and slowly becoming covered with ivy.

Notice the diversity of trees and plants, including hemlocks, Japanese maples, and many native shrubs, set inside concrete planters as you pass the American Legion Fountain and follow the path through the narrow East Plaza that leads to an intersection. Head east up the hill to the Pigott Memorial Corridor and Fountain to get to First Hill or turn west toward downtown and use a pedestrian underpass to reach the other side of 8th Avenue.

The park's biggest feature is the Canyon Fountain at the park's southwest corner, a spectacular waterfall that circulates up to twenty-seven thousand gallons of water every minute in the summer, creating such a roar that little road noise is audible from the freeway. Resembling a collection of children's blocks in a brutalist architectural style, the waterfall is still fun to explore in the winter when you can climb through the narrow canyon without worry of getting wet.

Nearby is another waterfall—the Cascade Fountain—providing a pleasant backdrop to a large plaza where workers from the adjacent buildings can take a break on benches and bright red tables and chairs. Freeway Park is one of the city's Wi-Fi-enabled parks, allowing people to take their jobs outside.

A narrow path on the west side of 8th Avenue will lead you to a series of steps descending to Union Plaza. Near the bottom take note of the 826-pound bell, a gift from a Japanese businessman to symbolize harmony among nations. Climb back up and head north toward the convention center to reach Ellis Plaza again.

11   CITY HALL PARK

Peaceful downtown greenspace has tragic past

Location: 450 3rd Ave.; Downtown
Acreage: 1.3
Amenities: Benches

GETTING THERE

BY CAR Located in downtown Seattle at the intersection of Yesler Wy. and 3rd Ave. Paid street parking is available on Yesler Wy. **BY BUS** Pioneer Square Station; 3rd Ave./James St.; Prefontaine Pl. S./Yesler Wy. **BY LIGHT RAIL** Pioneer Square Station, 3rd Ave./Yesler Wy.

More than a century before the World Trade Organization riots, the original Battle of Seattle happened here when Native American tribes allegedly led by Chief Leschi of the Nisqually tribe attacked Seattle pioneers in 1856. The dispute was over treaties the territorial government had forced upon several Puget Sound–area tribes. Although few white settlers were killed (as opposed to many more Native Americans), their sense of security was shaken, and the battle probably slowed development of the young city. Leschi was executed in 1858 over the protests of many white settlers who believed he was innocent.

He was finally exonerated in 2004. Today the only clue to this park's bloody past is a plaque and small pile of cannonballs.

Before becoming an official park, this open area was used for public speeches and carnivals. In 1911 the parks department transformed it into an elegant public space with a pristine lawn and rows of tidy plants. This must have been a desirable place to relax on a lunch break, as it was the only public park in this end of the city at the time. Today tall oak trees tower over the park, providing shade to three flat patios with benches. Homeless men and women often linger here in good weather, which sometimes deters other visitors, but the park is hospitable and worth a stop for history buffs.

Curious why a park named after City Hall is not located near City Hall? Seattle has actually had a handful of different homes for its central government over the decades, including in the adjacent building, which is now the King County Courthouse.

12   PIONEER SQUARE

Elegant square offers glimpse into Seattle history

Location: 100 Yesler Wy.; Downtown
Acreage: 0.3
Amenities: Benches

GETTING THERE

BY CAR Located in downtown Seattle at the intersection of Yesler Wy. and 1st Ave. Paid street parking is available on James St., Yesler Wy., and 1st Ave. **BY BUS** 1st Ave./Yesler Wy.; 2nd Ave./James St. **BY LIGHT RAIL** Pioneer Square Station, two blocks east at 3rd Ave./Yesler Wy. **BY STREETCAR** First Hill line to S. Jackson St./Occidental Ave. S.

Visiting Pioneer Square feels like stepping back in time in Seattle history. Before becoming a public park, this site was very close to the city's first mill. Today you'll see a bust of the city's namesake, Chief Seattle, holding court near the middle of the park, which is really more of a triangle than a square. Two

Historic letters indicate Chief Seattle, whose bust is displayed at Pioneer Square, was a powerful orator.

large panels by Native American artist Hock E Aye Vi (Hachivi) Edgar Heap of Birds capture the essence of Chief Seattle's 1854 public address in English and Lushootseed, Seattle's native language.

Brick buildings surround the cobblestone park that features curved benches, old-fashioned streetlamps, and an exquisite iron and glass pergola. Built in 1909, the pergola was originally designed to provide shelter for the entrance to an underground "comfort station." At the time this restroom was thought to be the most luxurious underground loo in the country. In 2001 the driver of a semitruck damaged it, and today's pergola is a reconstruction using most of the original pieces.

SEATTLE'S SKID ROAD

Just a block from Pioneer Square near the waterfront, Henry Yesler started the first industry of Seattle when he built a steam-powered sawmill. This provided numerous jobs to both white settlers and Native Americans. Using what is now Yesler Way, men skidded logs down the steep hill from the forest above, leading to the name "Skid Road." Today the term has come to be associated with an undesirable urban area. In addition to serving two terms as Seattle's mayor in 1874 and 1885, Yesler also built the city's first rudimentary water system.

The park's large Tlingit totem pole is a replica of one that dates to the 1790s and was stolen by Seattle businessmen from a Native American village in Alaska. An arsonist then seriously damaged it in the 1930s. The villagers were finally paid just $500 for the burned pole and, amazingly, generously agreed to carve a reproduction for free.

EXTEND YOUR VISIT

Bill Speidel's Underground Tour leaves from Pioneer Square and takes locals and tourists on a fascinating exploration of Seattle history through its underground spaces.

13   OCCIDENTAL SQUARE

Urban square hosts artists, city dwellers, and drifters

Location: 117 S. Washington St.; Downtown
Acreage: 0.6
Amenities: Benches, bistro tables and chairs, bocce ball courts, chessboards, games and information kiosk

GETTING THERE

BY CAR Located in downtown Seattle at the intersection of S. Main St. and Occidental Ave. S. Paid street parking is available on S. Main St., 1st Ave. S., and S. Washington St. **BY BUS** S. Jackson St./Occidental Ave. S.; S. Jackson

With bricks underfoot and ivy-covered buildings surrounding the plaza, Occidental Square is filled with charm.

St./2nd Ave. S.; 3rd Ave. S./S. Main St. **BY LIGHT RAIL** Pioneer Square Station, three blocks northeast at 3rd Ave./Yesler Wy. **BY STREETCAR** First Hill line to S. Jackson St./Occidental Ave. S.

The first of its kind in the country, Seattle's popular Pioneer Square art walk has been taking place the first Thursday of the month since 1981, and Occidental Square is at the center of it all. On a warm summer evening it buzzes with energy as artists and crafts vendors set up booths. The square is often the scene of concerts and food truck gatherings, and the neighborhood's old brick buildings are home to many of the city's art galleries and artist studios.

The rest of the month you'll still find a lot of activity in this park. The large cobblestone square holds several pieces of art, including four cedar totem poles by Duane Pasco and a dramatic memorial to fallen firefighters designed by University of Washington graduate Hai Ying Wu and created by a team of students and faculty from the university. Get a great overview of Seattle's history on the eight placards near the information kiosk, where you can also pick up chess pieces and bocce balls for games when an attendant is on duty.

Although it tends to draw a handful of folks who are homeless during the day because of the number of social service agencies located nearby, there's no reason to be intimidated. Take a seat on one of the sunny yellow chairs in the shade of the dozens of maple trees that ring the park. Old-fashioned streetlamps and ivy crawling up four stories on one of the adjacent buildings add to the atmosphere.

EXTEND YOUR VISIT

Walk one block east on South Main Street to the entrance of the wonderful **Waterfall Garden Park**. The site of the first UPS headquarters, this small park has a rushing waterfall that makes for a soothing getaway for residents and workers in the neighborhood. The park is open to the public during daylight hours.

14   KOBE TERRACE

Peaceful hillside spot showcases gifts from Japan

Location: 650 S. Main St. (accessed from S. Main St. or S. Washington St.); International District
Acreage: 1
Amenities: Benches, P-Patch, 0.2 mile of paved and unpaved paths

GETTING THERE

BY CAR Located in downtown Seattle at the north end of the International District on S. Main St. at its intersection with 7th Ave. S. Paid street parking is available

PARKS EXHIBIT SEATTLE'S SISTER CITY TIES

Seattle has twenty-one official sister cities spanning five continents. Several of these friendships are on display in Seattle parks named in their honor. These include Beer Sheva Park in South Seattle in honor of Be'er Sheva, Israel; Bergen Place in Ballard in honor of Bergen, Norway; Daejeon Park on Beacon Hill in honor of Daejeon, South Korea; Kobe Terrace in the International District in honor of Kobe, Japan; Nantes Park in West Seattle in honor of Nantes, France; and Tashkent Park on Capitol Hill in honor of Tashkent, Uzbekistan.

Many cities have reciprocated by honoring Seattle. In Tashkent you can visit the Seattle Peace Park; in Be'er Sheva, Israel, and Chongqing, China, a Seattle Garden symbolizes our cities' relationships; there's a Seattle Forest in the Kobe Municipal Arboretum; and Nordnes Park in Bergen, Norway, has a totem pole from Seattle that marks that city's nine-hundred-year anniversary.

Early spring brings the first leaves to cherry trees that decorate the hillside of Kobe Terrace.

on S. Main St. and 7th Ave. S. **BY BUS** S. Jackson St./Maynard Ave. S.; 5th Ave. S./S. Jackson St. **BY LIGHT RAIL** Pioneer Square Station, 0.3 mile northwest at 3rd Ave./Yesler Wy. **BY STREETCAR** First Hill line to S. Jackson St./5th Ave. S.

An eight-thousand-pound hand-carved stone lantern greets visitors at the highest point of Kobe Terrace, named to honor Seattle's relationship with its Japanese sister city. The lantern and surrounding cherry trees were a gift from the city of Kobe in 1976 to mark the park's opening.

From the top of the park, follow the paved path down the hillside to enjoy the ambiance of Kobe Terrace. Several benches set among Japanese-style lanterns and bamboo create a quaint picnic spot. Ivy and other plants form a screen behind you, obscuring the fact that the park sits next to I-5. From the park's wooden platforms enjoy views of the International District, the stadiums, and—on a clear day—even Mount Rainier.

Venture lower onto the narrow dirt trails to connect to the Danny Woo Community Garden, a privately owned P-Patch that is open to the public during daylight hours. The garden's eighty-three plots are tended by low-income seniors who live near the park. The Woo family has leased the land for one dollar per year since 1975. Kids will enjoy discovering the chicken coop and its cackling occupants.

EXTEND YOUR VISIT

While you are in the neighborhood, walk two blocks south on Maynard Avenue South to the recently expanded **Hing Hay Park**. The park's beautiful red pavilion, a gift from Taipei, Taiwan, in the 1970s, is a centerpiece to the bustling International District. Planters that curve like a dragon's tail create intimate gathering spaces where community members linger on bright red metal seats that have been perforated with Asian-influenced designs and are lit from within, creating a lantern-like effect.

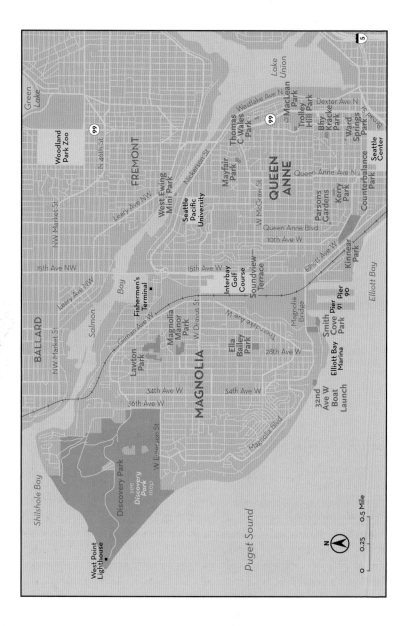

Magnolia & Queen Anne

15   DISCOVERY PARK

Miles of shoreline and prominent bluffs mark Seattle's biggest park

Location: 3801 Discovery Park Blvd. (bordered by 36th Ave. W. and W. Emerson St.); Magnolia
Acreage: 534
Amenities: Environmental Learning Center, playground, restrooms, 7 miles of unpaved hiking trails, 5 miles of paved biking paths, tennis courts, full basketball court, Daybreak Star Cultural Center

GETTING THERE

BY CAR From downtown Seattle take Elliott Ave. W. toward Magnolia. Continue as Elliott becomes 15th Ave. W. Take the Dravus St. exit and turn left on Dravus St. After three blocks turn right on 20th Ave. W. Follow road 1.6 miles as it curves, becoming Gilman Ave. W. and then W. Government Wy. The main park entrance will be straight ahead. Free parking is available at five parking lots inside the park. The Environmental Learning Center, tennis courts, and playground are located near the east parking lot, the first lot on the left after you enter the park. Paved bike paths and the Wolf Tree Nature Trail are best accessed from the north parking lot; continue straight from the main entrance. The Daybreak Star Cultural Center has its own parking lot; from the north parking lot turn right on Texas Wy. and then immediately left on Bernie Whitebear Wy.

A small parking lot at the beach is available with a permit only to wheelchair users, seniors sixty-two and older, and families with children under eight; ask for a permit at the Environmental Learning Center (Tuesday–Sunday), then follow signs for Discovery Park Blvd. The Historic District and bluffs are best reached from the south parking lot, which is the only lot not accessed through the main entrance. From the main entrance turn south on 36th Ave. W., turn right on W. Emerson St., and turn right into the park's south gate. The popular Loop Trail can be easily accessed from the east, north, or south parking lots.

BY BUS W. Government Wy./36th Ave. W. just outside the park near the east parking lot; Illinois Ave./Texas Wy. inside the park near the north parking lot; W. Emerson St./Magnolia Blvd. W. outside the park near the south parking lot; W. Government Wy./33rd Ave. W. outside the park.

With an expansive beach, miles of hiking trails, an Environmental Learning Center, a working lighthouse, and a historic military fort, the city's largest park needs repeat visits to fully explore. At more than five hundred acres of varied terrain, Discovery Park has magnificent trees and plentiful wildlife, including harbor seals, sea lions, coyotes, and more than 270 species of birds. Just a few miles from downtown Seattle you can hike in quiet forest or walk across open meadows to catch outstanding views of the Puget Sound and Olympic Mountains. The park's long shoreline captivates visitors for hours.

Named after Captain George Vancouver's ship, the HMS *Discovery*, which explored the Puget Sound in the late 1700s, the park encompasses the historic Fort Lawton army base. In 1898, hoping to boost economic development in the area, the city gave the US Army the land to build a fort to hold thousands of soldiers and officers. It only received light use, and in the 1930s the army offered to sell the land back to the City of Seattle for one dollar. Remarkably, the city missed the value of this opportunity and declined the offer because they weren't sure how the land would be maintained.

During World War II, Fort Lawton was home to twenty thousand troops at a time, and it was one of the largest departure points for troops and gear headed to the Pacific during the war. More than one thousand German prisoners of

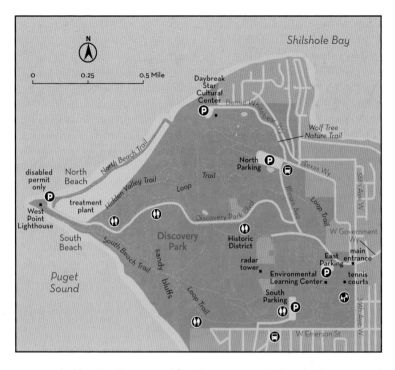

war were held at Fort Lawton and five times as many Italian detainees passed through on their way to be imprisoned in Hawaii.

Most of the military's land was surplused and turned into a park in 1973. The fort was officially closed as a military station in 2012, but its legacy continues to be on display, with beautiful buildings now on the National Register of Historic Places, including officers' quarters, a guardhouse, and a chapel. (Note that some buildings are private residences and no trespassing is allowed. Read signage.)

There's so much to do at Discovery Park, and much of the park is not accessible by car, so the best way to explore is to set off on foot. Begin at the east parking lot and pick up a park map at the Environmental Learning Center (open and staffed Tuesday through Sunday from 8:30 AM to 5:00 PM). The center offers dozens of parks department programs year-round for all ages,

More than a mile of shoreline lures visitors to Discovery Park.

including full-moon walks, storytelling, bird-watching, toddler outings, and nature camps. This is also a great place to escape from rainy weather with environmental displays, benches, indoor restrooms, and a children's play room.

The 2.8-mile Loop Trail is a popular way to tour the entire upper section of Discovery Park. Look for the trailhead near the entrance to the east parking lot. Turn north to follow the path counterclockwise as it meanders through a forest of cedars, poplars, Douglas firs, hemlocks, and bigleaf maples. The trail varies between dirt and gravel and has only gentle elevation changes. Many inviting side paths cross the main trail, offering connections to other corners of the park. After approximately a mile and a half, the trail arrives at sandy bluffs where several viewpoints provide a reason to stall. Benches here allow for a break while you enjoy views of the Puget Sound, Olympic Mountains, and Bainbridge Island. Placards explain the park's geology and ecology. This section of the park resembles a prairie with rolling hills and tall grass. In the distance you'll spot the white dome-shaped radar tower, once a part of our country's missile defense system, and now a backup for Sea-Tac Airport.

Continue along the trail and you'll soon catch sight of the Historic District, which is accessed through trails and a paved path that departs from the Loop Trail to the east. The Loop Trail continues back into the forest and descends, passing the south parking lot. A short while later you'll arrive back at the east parking lot. Explore behind the Environmental Learning Center and find tennis courts, a full basketball court, a playground, and a large lawn for picnicking.

Unless you have a permit to park in the small beachfront parking lot, you will have to walk about 1.3 miles to reach it. Use the Loop Trail to connect to the North Beach Trail from the north parking lot or the South Beach Trail from the south parking lot. Both routes involve steep descents (and steep returns), but the South Beach Trail has wooden platforms with rewarding water views from among the trees, and the North Beach Trail provides more solitude in this busy park.

From either direction you'll arrive to find two long stretches of shoreline, nearly 1.3 miles total, that meet at the westernmost point, like a nose sticking out into the Sound. Dominating the view is the West Point Lighthouse, dating to 1881. Although it is automated today, it was the first manned lighthouse on the Puget Sound.

This is one of the best places in the city to explore tide pools and look for sea creatures at low tide. Watch for slippery rocks as you scamper along the waterfront, especially on North Beach. Discovery Park is also popular with bird-watchers, and keen-eyed visitors can spot swallows, herons, and loons along the shore. Farther inland look for owls, woodpeckers, and bald eagles.

Because the park is such a pristine environment, it surprises many visitors to learn that a large sewage treatment plant is tucked behind a concrete barrier just east of the beachfront parking lot—thankfully, mostly out of sight.

The park's 5 miles of paved roads and paths make it a great biking destination. If you decide to explore on two wheels, keep in mind that bikes are allowed on roads, paved paths, and sidewalks inside the park but not on unpaved trails.

EXTEND YOUR VISIT

While you're in Discovery Park, consider a visit to the **Daybreak Star Cultural Center** at the northern end of the park for an opportunity to connect with this area's more than four thousand years of inhabitation by Native Americans. Run by the United Indians of All Tribes, the facility hosts regional powwows and is also a conference center, Native American art gallery, and preschool. The kid-friendly half-mile Wolf Tree Nature Trail begins behind the center and passes ponds and marshland. It also connects to the park's north parking lot.

16   LAWTON PARK

Playground, playfields, and short trails entice kids

Location: 4005 27th Ave. W.; Magnolia
Acreage: 11.9
Amenities: Playground, soccer field, baseball/softball field, 0.4 mile of paved and unpaved paths

GETTING THERE

BY CAR From downtown Seattle take Elliott Ave. W. toward Magnolia. Continue as Elliott becomes 15th Ave. W. Take the Dravus St. exit and turn left on Dravus St. After 0.3 mile, turn right on 20th Ave. W. Continue for 0.6 mile as it becomes Gilman Ave. W. Turn left on W. Elmore St.; after two blocks, turn left on 27th Ave. W. The park is straight ahead at the end of the block. Free parking is available on 27th Ave. W. and at the south end of the park near 26th Pl. W. and W. Emerson St. **BY BUS** Gilman Ave. W./26th Ave. W.; 30th Ave. W./W. Thurman St.

The hillside play area is the first thing children will make a run for at Lawton Park. Younger tots can investigate a playground with slides, a mini climbing wall, and a small climbing net set over a rubber surface. An upper section with wood chips holds swings, a merry-go-round, and a tree-house-style structure that has plenty of diversions for older kids, including a slide, a climbing rock, and a climbing wall. A couple of benches overlook the play area. Across the paved path is a large playfield set up for baseball or softball games.

The park looks down onto the adjacent elementary school—both are named after the Fort Lawton army base at Discovery Park, which honors Major General Henry Ware Lawton, a decorated US Army officer who served in several wars in the late 1800s.

Follow the path up the hill behind the playground for views of Ballard in the distance. The steep grass hillside is a nice spot for a picnic or—for daring kids—a good starting point for a fast roll downhill. The park's paved paths branch out in several directions, leading you to short dirt trails that are child-friendly in length. To reach the most interesting trail, from the main path at the peak of the hill look east to find a narrow entrance to a trail. In spring a flowering red currant bush marks the spot with its vibrant magenta blooms. Descend on this pleasant wooded trail to reach a marsh with a short looping boardwalk where you can peer into the murky water below. The approximately 0.1-mile trail hits a dead end shortly after. Make a U-turn or follow the sidewalk north along 25th Avenue West; turn left on West Thurman Street and then right on 26th Avenue West to reach another trail on your left that connects just beside the playground.

EXTEND YOUR VISIT

Want to add in one more mini hike in the park? Take the paved path west from the playfield and cross Williams Avenue West to reach another unpaved

Lawton Park's sloping hillside features paths and a lawn for picnics.

trail. This 0.2-mile trail stretches up a gentle canyon among ferns and young cedars and empties out at West Emerson Street and 29th Avenue West.

17   MAGNOLIA MANOR PARK

Accessible dog park allows exercise for all

Location: 3500 28th Ave. W. (between 26th Ave. W. and 28th Ave. W.); Magnolia
Acreage: 2
Amenities: ADA-accessible off-leash dog park, benches, 0.2 mile of paved paths, P-Patch

GETTING THERE

BY CAR From downtown Seattle take Elliott Ave. W. toward Magnolia. Continue as Elliott becomes 15th Ave. W. Take the Dravus St. exit and turn left on Dravus St. After 0.8 mile turn right on 28th Ave. W. Continue for two blocks; the park is on the right. Free street parking is available on 28th Ave. W. **BY BUS** 28th Ave. W./W. Ruffner St.

Sometimes the perfect piece of land for a park is right in front of everyone's eyes. When Seattle Public Utilities moved the Magnolia Reservoir underground, the community and the parks department saw a great opportunity and dreamt up Magnolia Manor Park as a wheelchair-accessible and dog-friendly neighborhood gathering place.

Dogs and their owners take advantage of the only off-leash park in Magnolia in all seasons. The enclosed dog park is fully accessible with a paved path that leads from the street curb well into the off-leash area, making it easier for people with limited mobility to exercise their dogs. The park's attractive wooden fence encircles two separate spaces—a smaller gravel area for little or shy dogs and a larger section with logs and stumps on top of a mix of gravel and wood chips.

The paved path makes it possible to explore the park by wheelchair or stroller, and kids can bike it while staying in view of their parents. A chain-link fence indicates the land that is closed to public use because of the underground reservoir, but the path continues alongside it to reach the park's eastern edge, where you can look out toward Queen Anne and Ballard in the distance. The path was recently expanded to connect the off-leash area to a neighborhood P-Patch at the south end of the park.

18   ELLA BAILEY PARK

Hilltop park with spectacular views captivates for picnics and play

Location: 2601 W. Smith St.; Magnolia
Acreage: 2.4
Amenities: Playground, picnic tables, barbecue grills, half basketball courts, portable restroom

Views from Ella Bailey Park include Mount Rainier, Puget Sound, and the city skyline.

GETTING THERE

BY CAR From downtown Seattle take Elliott Ave. W. toward Magnolia. Continue as Elliott becomes 15th Ave. W. Take the exit toward W. Garfield St./Magnolia Bridge, and keep right to follow signs for Magnolia Bridge. Follow for 0.8 mile as road becomes W. Galer St. Turn right on 28th Ave. W. After 0.6 mile turn right on W. Smith St. The park is at the end of the block on the right. Free street parking is available on W. Smith St. and adjacent 27th Ave. W. **BY BUS** 28th Ave. W./W. Smith St.; W. McGraw St./32nd Ave. W.; Thorndyke Ave. W./ Thorndyke Pl. W.

From its position atop one of the highest points in Magnolia, this park presents unobstructed views of our state's tallest mountain—Mount Rainier—as well as vistas of Elliott Bay, downtown Seattle, and Queen Anne. The park gets its name from the former property owner, a schoolteacher, who sold the land to the city in the 1920s.

With a special parking area and ADA curb, Ella Bailey Park was carefully designed to provide excellent accessibility for people with wheelchairs and

BLUFFSIDE TREE-LINED WALK

The neighborhood of Magnolia and its fantastic pedestrian-friendly boulevard should technically have been named Madrona. George Davidson, a geographer and surveyor who apparently missed his course in tree identification, mistook the gorgeous madrona trees that are the hallmark of the neighborhood for magnolia trees. Despite the error, the name stuck. Today, one of the best walks in the city is a stroll along Magnolia Boulevard, where you'll pass the tall, red-trunked madronas that cling to the bluff. The most scenic section of the boulevard is a 1-mile segment along Magnolia Boulevard West from 34th Court West to West Armour Street. Benches along the route make for great places to rest and enjoy the views. Park anywhere along the boulevard or in the small lot just north of West Howe Street.

strollers. A flat paved path circles the huge grass field, making a fine loop for strolling in the sunshine.

Two climbing structures are sunken into a bed of wood chips in the play area. Designed for kids ages two to five, the smaller has a slide, net ladder, and miniature monkey bars. The larger climber has steep slides and two challenging climbing walls. Between the two you'll find a spinning ring that's fun for old and young.

A swing set sits between the play area and two half basketball courts. The path is also the perfect length for kids to bike, and parents, nannies, and grandparents will appreciate the good sightlines from every part of the park.

Trios of picnic tables were placed to take advantage of the views, and each has a barbecue, as if inviting you to enjoy an afternoon in this fabulous park.

EXTEND YOUR VISIT

Want more playground time? **Bayview Playground** is an easy one-third-mile walk away. Walk two blocks north on 26th Avenue West; turn right on West Raye Street, and continue two more blocks. The park is straight ahead. You'll find a large playground made up of two play structures, a rock climbing wall, and swings, as well as a playfield and restrooms. Alternately, walk 0.5 mile west on West Smith Street to reach **Magnolia Playfield**, which has a seasonal outdoor swimming pool, play area, ball fields, and community center.

19   32ND AVE. W. BOAT LAUNCH

***Secret beachfront
showcases Elliott Bay***

∞ 〰

Location: 32nd Ave. W. and W. Galer St.; Magnolia
Acreage: 0.3
Amenities: Hand-carry boat launch

GETTING THERE

BY CAR From downtown Seattle take Elliott Ave. W. toward Magnolia. Continue as Elliott becomes 15th Ave. W. Take the exit toward W. Garfield St./Magnolia Bridge, and keep right to follow signs for Magnolia Bridge. Follow for 1.3 miles as road becomes W. Galer St., then Magnolia Blvd. W., then Clise Pl. W. Take a sharp left on 32nd Ave. W. and drive 0.4 mile downhill. At the dead end, follow the driveway that curves slightly to the left and is designated with a parks department sign. There is free parking for four to five cars immediately in front of the beach. **BY BUS** Condon Wy. W./W. Crockett St.; 28th Ave. W./ W. Blaine St.

Launch your kayak at this little-known waterfront spot and you're virtually guaranteed to have the shoreline to yourself. The park is made up of a modest stretch of rocky beachfront strewn with driftwood.

On a clear day you'll have views that extend for miles. Located on the south end of Magnolia, the park faces West Seattle, providing an excellent vantage point for observing the boat traffic in Elliott Bay, including massive cargo ships. Turn your gaze left and you can see the hundreds of sailboats and yachts docked at the Elliott Bay Marina nearby. To the right you'll get glimpses of the Olympic Mountains.

EXTEND YOUR VISIT

Twelve-acre **Magnolia Park** sits almost directly above 32nd Ave. W. Boat Launch. You can reach it by foot and via a hidden staircase in a half-mile walk. Head north on 32nd Avenue West until you reach the car overpass. Take the stairs up to the left and cross over the bridge (West Howe Street), heading

Take in sights of a glittering Elliott Bay from this southern perch in Magnolia.

east. Turn right on Magnolia Boulevard West and the park is immediately on your right. Walk across the grass to the bluff and compare views with the beachfront park below. In addition to great spots for picnicking, the park also has swings, restrooms, and tennis courts.

20   SMITH COVE PARK

Peaceful waterfront contrasts with busy marine locale

Location: 23rd Ave. W. and W. Marina Pl. (near W. Garfield St.); Magnolia
Acreage: 7.3
Amenities: Playfield, benches, picnic tables, portable restroom

GETTING THERE
BY CAR From downtown Seattle take Elliott Ave. W. toward Magnolia. Continue as Elliott becomes 15th Ave. W. Take the exit toward W. Garfield St./Magnolia Bridge, and keep right to follow signs for Magnolia Bridge. After 0.2 mile, take a slight right on 23rd Ave. W., following signs for Elliott Bay Marina. At the T intersection, turn left to stay on 23rd Ave. W. The entrance to the park's

waterfront section is at the end of the street. Free parking is available in the lot immediately in front of the park. **BY BUS** No convenient bus service. **BY BIKE** The Elliott Bay Trail (Terminal 91 Bike Path) runs adjacent to the park.

In the shadow of the Magnolia Bridge and wedged next to Smith Cove Cruise Terminal at Pier 91, this park sits on the shores of a small notch in the northern edge of Elliott Bay. Previously little-known and underused, this stretch of waterfront is set to be expanded and improved in 2019, which will surely give it a citywide draw. For now, have a picnic in the shade of a willow tree as you ponder this site's colorful history.

First settled in 1853 by Dr. Henry A. Smith—one of Seattle's earliest white settlers and the cove's namesake—this land has served many purposes during the past 150 years. In the late 1800s the transcontinental railroad ended here, and it was also the launching point for the Pacific Coast's first regular steamship service to Asia.

The Port of Seattle bought twenty acres of land at Smith Cove in the early 1900s and built two piers—at the time believed to be the longest commercial docks in the world. In 1934 a longshoremen strike took place at Smith Cove, which caused intense fighting between workers and police. This became known as the Battle of Smith Cove and eventually resulted in Seattle losing much of its maritime traffic to Los Angeles. The US Navy assumed control of the site during World War II, and thousands of navy personnel left for war from Smith Cove.

In 1992 local residents convinced the navy to transfer the property to the city to create a new park, and in recent years the city, county, and port, with urging from the community, have engaged in a complicated land swap of adjacent parcels, which will allow the community to expand Smith Cove Park. In 2014, during construction of an underground sewage-storage tank sandwiched next to the park, workers unearthed more than 2,400 artifacts, most dating to the 1920s—a significant archaeological discovery.

Cross the parking lot to find another section of the park, which is dominated by a large multiuse playfield. Look up the steep hillside to see one more reminder of the park's history—the graceful Admiral's House, a shining white structure overlooking Smith Cove. Once home to naval admirals and their families, this City of Seattle historic landmark is now a scenic wedding venue.

EXTEND YOUR VISIT

For a lovely walk, continue along the sidewalk west toward **Elliott Bay Marina** and follow the paved path that bends around the harbor. After half a mile, the path ends at a lookout with western views of the Olympic Mountains and Bainbridge Island.

21   KINNEAR PARK

Nineteenth-century park remains popular spot for quiet leisure

Location: 899 W. Olympic Pl.; Queen Anne
Acreage: 14.1
Amenities: Off-leash dog park, tennis court, swings, benches, picnic tables, 0.9 mile of unpaved trails

GETTING THERE

BY CAR From I-5, take the Mercer St. exit and continue on Mercer for 1.2 miles, passing Seattle Center. Turn right on 2nd Ave. W.; go two blocks and turn left on W. Olympic Pl. After 0.4 mile, the park will be on the left. Free street parking is available on W. Olympic Pl. To reach the ADA-accessible tennis courts, instead continue straight on W. Mercer St. and turn right on 5th Ave. W. After one block turn left on W. Roy St. and park for free at the end of the block. To reach the dog park, continue on W. Mercer St. as it becomes W. Mercer Pl.; turn right on tiny W. Roy St. (more like a driveway) at the southwest corner of the park. A free parking lot is available evenings and weekends just before W. Mercer Pl. meets Elliott Ave. W. **BY BUS** Olympic Wy. W./7th Ave. W.; Elliott Ave. W./W. Roy St.; Elliott Ave. W./W. Prospect St.

George Kinnear arrived in Seattle in 1874 and as a savvy real estate investor saw the value of view property. Luckily for Seattle, he was also generous. He sold fourteen acres of his land to the city for one dollar to create Kinnear Park—one of the city's first parks and now a historic landmark.

This wooded hillside park is made up of two separate sections. Begin in the upper section, which still feels like an old-fashioned park, with stately trees, a swing set, and benches set alongside curving gravel paths. The best views of Elliott Bay and the Olympic Mountains are from the brick viewing platform on the roof of the 1920s comfort station. Get a close-up view of the building's engraved stonework from another plaza just below, where you'll also find a pair of benches. Stroll the paths interspersed with large sections of grass that are idyllic for picnicking or games of Frisbee.

It's easy to miss the park's large lower section. Pass the enormous oaks and towering evergreens and look for the wooden stairs at the southeast corner of the park near West Olympic Place and 6th Avenue West. Descend a set of zigzagging stairs to reach a tennis court that is wheelchair accessible from West Roy Street. Follow the paved path to a grassy knoll where a set of picnic tables offers a view of Elliott Bay.

A gravel path begins nearby, leading down through younger forest to a 5,400-square-foot off-leash dog park. Enter through a double gate into the fully fenced enclosure that is covered with wood chips and has logs and rocks for playing. The surrounding trees provide nearly full shade in the summer.

EXTEND YOUR VISIT

If your dog still needs exercise after a romp in the dog park, continue downhill toward the waterfront. Head north on busy Elliott Avenue West and cross at Prospect Street to take the pedestrian overpass into **Myrtle Edwards Park**.

22 PARSONS GARDENS

Secret garden blooms for solace seekers and lovebirds

Location: 650 W. Highland Dr. (bordered by Willard Ave. W., W. Highland Dr., 7th Ave. W.); Queen Anne
Acreage: 0.4
Amenities: Benches

GETTING THERE

BY CAR From I-5, take the Mercer St. exit and continue on Mercer for 1 mile, passing Seattle Center. Turn right on Queen Anne Ave. N. Drive up the hill six blocks and turn left on W. Highland Dr. Continue 0.5 mile; the park is on the

AN ELEGANT, ARCHITECTURE-RICH LOOP

Many of the first houses on this hill were built in the American Queen Anne architectural style, giving Queen Anne its name. For an architectural walking tour that takes you past stately mansions and several historic landmarks, there's no better route than the century-old **Queen Anne Boulevard**. The entire 3.7-mile loop encompasses a handful of streets and circles the top of the hill. The best section begins at Marshall Park (7th Avenue West and 8th Place West) and follows the sidewalk to the northwest. Step back in time as you pass stylish streetlamps and sections of the original Willcox Wall (named after its designer and often misspelled), built in 1913. Take the double staircase down at West Garfield Street for a view of the intricate brickwork.

right. Free street parking is available on W. Highland Dr. and 7th Ave. W. **BY BUS** Olympic Wy. W./7th Ave. W.; 6th Ave. W./W. Galer St.

Parsons Gardens is a lovely spot year-round, but visit in the spring and you'll be treated to a splendid display of flowering plants and trees. Steal away for some quiet time among the colorful blossoms or bring a blanket for a romantic picnic for two.

Entering the park, you'll feel like you're escaping into a secret garden. A gravel trail winds among carefully tended plants, giving you access to every corner of this little park. For peaceful solitude seek out one of the two benches that are placed in quiet corners or spread out your blanket on the large flat lawn. A gazebo covered with climbing vines is a focal point and the site of many summer weddings.

The park was originally the family garden of Reginald and Maude Parsons, whose house was the beautiful Dutch Colonial still standing—and now a city landmark—directly to the east. This duo was a prominent Seattle couple in the first half of the last century. In 1956 their children donated the land to the city in their parents' honor. The park continues to feel like a private garden, with intimate spaces set against a stunning backdrop of dozens of varieties of plants and trees, including hydrangeas, rhododendrons, and magnolias.

EXTEND YOUR VISIT

Parsons Gardens is within walking distance of several Queen Anne parks. The closest is **Marshall Park**, featuring the Betty Bowen Viewpoint, just across the street to the southwest. Enjoy views of the Olympic Mountains, Elliott Bay, Interbay, and Magnolia from one of this park's three benches. Take your eyes off the view long enough to admire the nine works of art set into the sidewalk by local artists.

23 KERRY PARK

Seattle's most popular viewpoint enchants tourists and locals

Location: 211 W. Highland Dr. (between 2nd Ave. W. and 3rd Ave. W.); Queen Anne
Acreage: 5.8
Amenities: Benches, playground, half basketball court, playfield

GETTING THERE

BY CAR From I-5, take the Mercer St. exit and continue on Mercer for 1 mile, passing Seattle Center. Turn right on Queen Anne Ave. N. Drive up the hill six blocks and turn left on W. Highland Dr. Continue 0.2 mile; the park is on the left. Free street parking is available on W. Highland Dr. **BY BUS** Queen Anne Ave. N./W. Highland Dr.; W. Olympic Pl./3rd Ave. W.

You know a park has a special appeal when even on a drizzly day visitors take their time soaking in the views, oblivious to the weather. Kerry Park is a popular stop on the "what to do with out-of-town visitors" tour. Its location on the south end of Queen Anne makes it the perfect spot for views of downtown Seattle, Bainbridge Island, and Mount Rainier. On every visit you will inevitably find handfuls of tourists taking picture after picture of themselves with the Space Needle in the background. But it's always enjoyable as a repeat visit for locals, too. Walkers and runners circling Queen Anne often stop for a rest here on the park's many benches.

Albert Sperry Kerry was a lumber mill owner who was active in Seattle civic affairs. He and his wife, Katherine, donated the land to create Kerry Park in

1927. The large steel sculpture *Changing Form* by artist Doris Chase was a gift from the Kerrys' children.

EXTEND YOUR VISIT

Have kids in tow? Descend the steep stairs on the west side of the park to Lower Kerry Park, recently renamed **Bayview-Kinnear Park**, for some playtime on a playground that includes climbing structures, a large rock climbing wall, and a pair of exhilarating slides built into the park's natural slope. You'll also find a half basketball court, play-field, and picnic tables. While there, look up to see tourists and their cameras lining the railing above, capturing the quintessential Seattle souvenir.

The fifteen-foot-tall sculpture Changing Form *is photographed nearly as often as the Seattle skyline at this classic park.*

24 COUNTERBALANCE PARK

Urban plaza creates neighborhood gathering place

♿

Location: 700 Queen Anne Ave. N.; Lower Queen Anne
Acreage: 0.3
Amenities: Tables and chairs, benches, drinking fountain

GETTING THERE

BY CAR From I-5, take the Mercer St. exit and continue on Mercer for 1 mile, passing Seattle Center. Turn right on Queen Anne Ave. N. and go one block;

the park is immediately on the right. Paid street parking is available on sections of Queen Anne Ave. N. and Roy St. **BY BUS** Queen Anne Ave. N./ W. Mercer St.; 1st Ave. N./Mercer St.

This urban Lower Queen Anne park gets its name from the trolley system counterbalanced by weights that whisked people up and down Queen Anne Avenue from the 1890s to 1940. Today bright yellow bistro tables and chairs invite people who live and work in the area to linger. With flat wooden planks underfoot and trees providing patches of shade, the space feels like the deck of a community backyard.

The park is mostly flat and adjoins the sidewalk so it's accessible for wheelchair users and parents with strollers. On a slightly raised level above, gravel crunches underfoot in the large square plaza lined with a dozen benches. The best time of day to visit is in the evening, when a fantastic display of neon lights streaks up the concrete walls. Take a seat and enjoy a break in this bustling neighborhood.

25   WARD SPRINGS PARK

Large playground and Space Needle views beckon at this slopeside park

Location: 4th Ave. N. and Ward St.; Queen Anne
Acreage: 0.3
Amenities: Playground, benches, rental facility

GETTING THERE
BY CAR From I-5, take the Mercer St. exit and continue on Mercer toward Seattle Center. After 0.7 mile turn right on 4th Ave. N. Continue four blocks; the park is on the left at the end of the block. Free street parking is available on 4th Ave. N. and Ward St. **BY BUS** Taylor Ave. N./Prospect St.; Aurora Ave. N. (Hwy. 99)/Prospect St.; Queen Anne Ave. N./Ward St.

Queen Anne has no shortage of parks with amazing views. But even better is a park that keeps kids entertained while adults enjoy the scenery, and you'll find this winning combination at Ward Springs Park on the south end of Queen Anne.

The park features excellent views of the Space Needle and the city skyline, which you can take in while relaxing on the park's benches or gently sloping lawn. Kids, of course, will shun the views for the play area. The park is small enough that you don't have to worry about losing sight of anyone while your eyes are distracted by the views.

In addition to a tire swing and crescent-shaped sandbox, the playground has a giant wooden structure that includes slides, monkey bars, a rope ladder, and small tree-house platform. While best for ages five and up, the lower sections are safe for toddlers and preschoolers with supervision.

The cute brick building with barn doors is a historic pump house that once supplied all the water for the Queen Anne neighborhood. Today you can rent it for parties and events. Follow the paved path as it cuts through the lawn and curves around the pump house and crosses a rock swale. The path turns into stone steps at the bottom, connecting to Fourth Avenue North.

26 BHY KRACKE PARK

Hidden park offers
picnicking with a view

Location: End of Comstock Pl. (near Bigelow Ave. N.); Queen Anne
Acreage: 1.5
Amenities: Playground, benches, drinking fountain, 0.15 mile of paved paths

GETTING THERE

BY CAR From I-5, take the Mercer St. exit and continue on Mercer toward Seattle Center for 0.6 mile. Turn right on 5th Ave. N. and continue six blocks. Turn left on Highland Dr.; after three blocks turn right on Bigelow Ave. N. Take the next right on Comstock Pl.; the park is at the end of this short residential street. There are spaces for three cars at the park; free street parking is also available on Bigelow Ave. N. Alternately, you can park at the lower section, close to the playground on 5th Ave. N. (half a block north of Highland Dr.). Free street parking is available on 5th Ave. N. **BY BUS** Taylor Ave. N./Lee St.; Aurora Ave. N. (Hwy. 99)/Galer St.

Bhy Kracke is a little-known park with outstanding views on Queen Anne's south end.

Slip down a quiet dead-end street in Queen Anne and you'll discover one of the best hidden parks in Seattle. With views of Lake Union, the Cascade Mountains, and downtown Seattle, this hillside park is a great place to take out-of-town visitors as an alternative to nearby Kerry Park. Bhy Kracke Park is particularly beautiful in the spring, when several varieties of trees and shrubs, including rhododendrons, azaleas, and magnolias, are in bloom.

Begin your visit with a picnic on one of the four benches or the curved cement retaining wall to enjoy lunch with a view. Then follow the paved path down into the lower section of the park. As you descend along the winding path, you'll catch glimpses of parts of the park that are almost like secret rooms hidden behind trees and hedges. Small patches of lawn, practically out of sight from the path, make for even more private picnic spots. The path ends at a playground with a small climbing structure. A picnic table sheltered under a gazebo sits within sight of the play area.

Wondering how to pronounce the park's unusual name? It comes from Werner H. "Bhy" Kracke (pronounced "crackee"). Bhy—who loved the expression "by cracky!"—was an enthusiastic gardener who lived on the upper part of the site from the 1930s to 1960s and wanted it turned into a park. He died before seeing his dream realized, but his original vision for the park is similar to what you see today.

27 TROLLEY HILL AND MACLEAN PARKS

Park twosome offers greenspace hike to Lake Union views

Location: Trolley Hill Park: 1800 5th Ave. N. (near Taylor Ave. N.); MacLean Park: 1922 Taylor Ave. N. (one block east of 5th Ave. N.); Queen Anne
Acreage: 1.9
Amenities: Natural play area, benches, picnic tables, 0.3 mile of unpaved trails, P-Patch

GETTING THERE

BY CAR From I-5, take the Mercer St. exit and continue on Mercer toward Seattle Center for 0.6 mile. Turn right on Taylor Ave. N. and continue 0.8 mile as road curves and becomes 5th Ave. N. Park will be immediately on the right. Free street parking is available on 5th Ave. N. **BY BUS** Taylor Ave. N./Blaine St.; Aurora Ave. N. (Hwy. 99)/Galer St.

Connected by a trail in a restored greenbelt, this duo showcases views from the eastern edge of the Queen Anne neighborhood. Begin at Trolley Hill Park, where you'll enter between two stone pillars topped with elegant wood carvings. A tree-lined gravel path leads into the center of the park, where a circular planter surrounded by benches encourages neighborhood socializing. Kids will easily spot the play area—a boulder and stump set atop wood chips is a natural place for jumping and scrambling. Three picnic tables are situated within view of a P-Patch. Nearby you'll find placards explaining the origin of the park's name, which comes from the streetcar line that used to extend up 5th Avenue North.

To reach MacLean Park by the wooded trail, look for stairs at the eastern end of Trolley Hill Park. The trail is short but also steep and narrow in places, so it's best for experienced hikers. Descend into a forest of maples, ferns, and young evergreens. The path winds downhill into the greenbelt and then crests a small hill and curves to the north. You'll arrive at MacLean Park by way of an old driveway, which leads uphill to the park entrance. Here you'll see benches, signs noting points of interest, and—best of all— views of Lake Union beyond. The MacLean family owned a large plot of land in this area in the early 1900s when east Queen Anne was so rural that farm animals roamed the hillside freely.

Trolley Hill Park is steps away from where streetcars once traveled up 5th Avenue North.

If you're not up for the hike but would like to experience MacLean Park, drive north on 5th Avenue North for two blocks. Turn right on Newton Street and park along Taylor Avenue North immediately in front of the park. The viewpoint is wheelchair accessible.

28   THOMAS C. WALES PARK

Former quarry exhibits rock art

Location: 2401 6th Ave. N.; Queen Anne
Acreage: 1.3
Amenities: Benches, 0.2 mile of unpaved trails

GETTING THERE

BY CAR From I-5, take the Mercer St. exit and continue on Mercer for 0.4 mile. Turn right on Dexter Ave. N. and continue for 1.2 miles to the intersection of Dexter Ave. N. and 6th Ave. N. Park for free on Dexter Ave. N. and carefully cross Dexter to the park. **BY BUS** Dexter Ave. N./6th Ave. N.; Aurora Ave. N. (Hwy. 99)/Halladay St.; Aurora Ave. N./Lynn St.

What do you do with a former gravel pit? Turn it into a park and use the gravel to make art! Five enormous rings by artist Adam Kuby loom overhead as you enter Thomas C. Wales Park, which resembles a science fiction movie set. Thousands of stones encased in wire create walls and benches.

The park, completed in 2011, is thoughtfully planted around a central low area that makes up a tiny urban wetland, where a mix of native shrubs and small trees draws wildlife. Kuby constructed the rings with birds and bats in mind—nearly one hundred containers and open slots were intentionally set in the rings to encourage nesting.

Circle the park's gravel paths around the lower section and then wander the narrow trail up the hillside to check out the rings from above.

In sharp contrast to the spot's peaceful ambiance, the park is named to honor a former assistant US attorney who lived on Queen Anne and was killed in 2001.

29 MAYFAIR PARK

Corner playground provides fun beneath the trees

Location: 2600 2nd Ave. N.; Queen Anne
Acreage: 1
Amenities: Playground, benches, picnic table

GETTING THERE

BY CAR From Aurora Ave. N. (Hwy. 99) southbound, turn right on Raye St. and go straight onto Queen Anne Dr. After 0.3 mile, turn right on Warren Ave. N. and take the next right on Raye St. The park is straight ahead at the corner of Raye St.

A long metal slide takes advantage of Mayfair Park's steep hillside.

and 2nd Ave. N. From Aurora Ave. northbound, turn right on Halladay St. Turn left immediately on 6th Ave. N. and follow as it curves around and becomes Queen Anne Dr., then follow the preceding directions. Free street parking is available on Raye St. and on 2nd Ave. N. **BY BUS** W. Raye St./Queen Anne Ave. N.; Queen Anne Dr./2nd Ave. N.; 3rd Ave. W./W. Raye St.

Tucked into the edge of a ravine at the end of a quiet residential street in the northeast corner of Queen Anne hides Mayfair Park. A chorus of birds nesting overhead might be the only noises you hear at this rarely busy park. A short paved path arcs up and around a little hill, where you'll find benches and a picnic table. The park is almost entirely shaded by trees, including large oaks, so it's a nice place for a picnic on a hot day.

The park has three features to keep kids busy. First, a small tree-house climbing structure reachable by rope and ladder is a fun perch for spying on wildlife. Second, a wooden playground has metal slides, a tunnel slide, and a wooden arch climber. Finally, peek out over the edge of the play area to find a steep metal slide to whisk you down the hillside. Large rocks next to the slide are another fun place for kids to clamber.

A set of stairs on the eastern edge of the park provides pedestrian access down to Mayfair Avenue North.

EXTEND YOUR VISIT

Two more great parks are within easy walking distance. Head four blocks west on Raye Street to reach **David Rodgers Park** and **Queen Anne Bowl Playfield**, a pair of parks sitting next to one another. You'll find a play area in the upper David Rodgers Park and short wooded trails leading down to Queen Anne Bowl Playfield, which has a running track and soccer fields.

30   WEST EWING MINI PARK

Tiny canalside park provides resting spot for bikers and runners

Location: 244 W. Ewing St.; Queen Anne
Acreage: 0.3
Amenities: Benches, picnic tables, short paved and unpaved paths

GETTING THERE

BY CAR From I-5, take the Mercer St. exit and continue for three blocks. Turn right on Westlake Ave. N.; at the T intersection turn right on 9th Ave. N., which becomes Westlake Ave. N. again. Continue for 1.4 miles, and after passing under the Aurora bridge, the road becomes Nickerson St. After 0.7 mile, turn right on 3rd Ave. W., and after one block turn right on W. Ewing St. Free two-hour parking is available in the small lot immediately in front of the park. **BY BUS** W. Nickerson St./3rd Ave. W.; 3rd Ave. W./W. Dravus St. **BY BIKE** The South Ship Canal Trail runs through the park.

On the south side of the Fremont Cut, with runners striding by and bikers zooming along the adjacent South Ship Canal Trail, is the quiet West Ewing Mini Park. Situated just behind Seattle Pacific University, the waterfront park is a popular spot for a rest break for students between classes.

A paved path invites you to meander toward the waterfront, where you can look across at marine and industrial activity on the ship canal. The dock is where crew teams from the university launch for practice sessions on the channel.

A small lawn has room for kids to play and is also a pleasant picnic spot. The concrete area with benches offers more privacy for lunch or an outdoor study session.

EXTEND YOUR VISIT

Looking for a longer walk? Set off east along the **South Ship Canal Trail** for an excursion on a tree-lined path, where several benches are positioned for rests with views of the water. For a 1-mile roundtrip walk, turn around at the Fremont Bridge. Or connect to the **Cheshiahud Lake Union Loop** to add more miles to your journey.

31   SOUNDVIEW TERRACE

Hidden hillside playground looks toward Elliott Bay

Location: 2500 11th Ave. W. (near W. Wheeler St.); Queen Anne
Acreage: 0.3
Amenities: Playground, benches, picnic tables

GETTING THERE

BY CAR From downtown Seattle, take Elliott Ave. W. northbound and continue as Elliott becomes 15th Ave. W. After 0.7 mile, take a very sharp right on Gilman Dr. W. Continue up the hill and take a slight right on 11th Ave. W. Take the next left on W. Howe St., then turn left immediately on 10th Ave. W. Go two blocks; turn left on W. McGraw St. After one block, turn right on 11th Ave. W. After one block the park is straight ahead. Free street parking is available on the upper (northbound) side of 11th Ave. W. **BY BUS** 10th Ave. W./W. Halladay St.; 15th Ave. W./W. Wheeler St.

A wheelchair-accessible wooden play structure at Soundview Terrace is hidden from the street above.

It doesn't look easy to build a beautifully landscaped wheelchair- and stroller-accessible park on a steep hillside between two one-way streets. Kudos to the geniuses behind Soundview Terrace, which makes the best of challenging geography on the western edge of Queen Anne.

If approaching from the top, you would almost miss the park if not for its colorful sign. Take the steep central staircase down or enter through a flat stone path on the south side. The long, narrow park is framed with shrubs and trees.

A fantastic play area—known as Rachel's Playground—takes advantage of the steep incline and offers slides, climbing walls, and a fire pole. The structure has a long wooden boardwalk with stairs at opposite ends that make a great route for games of tag. Rachel Pearson, who frequently played at the park, was six years old when she died in an airline crash in 2000. Dedicated friends and neighbors had the park renamed to honor her and the five other Queen Anne children who were lost in the crash, and they championed the renovation of the park.

The path continues past the playground to a pair of picnic tables, including one with a built-in checkerboard. A little farther along, the path turns into lawn and leads up to a small stone patio embedded with the directions of the compass. A stone bench here offers the best of the park's amazing views, with vistas of Elliott Bay, Interbay, Magnolia, and the Olympic Mountains. By wheelchair or stroller, this spot (and another set of benches nearby, also with views) is accessible from the upper side of 11th Avenue West.

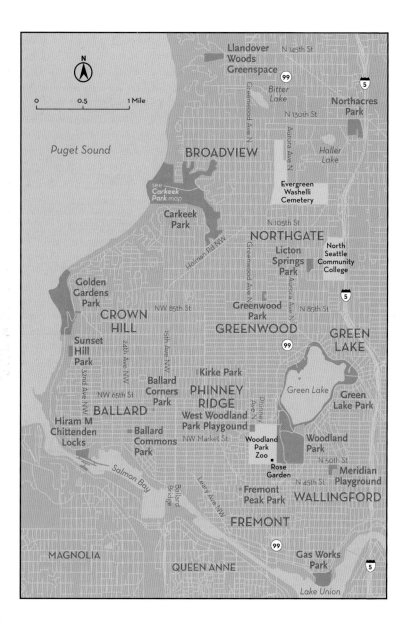

Northwest Seattle

32   CARKEEK PARK

Scenic beach and preserved forest offer picnics, hiking, and play

Location: 950 NW Carkeek Park Rd. (near NW 116th St.); Broadview
Acreage: 220
Amenities: Playground, restrooms, 6 miles of unpaved trails, reservable shelters, indoor rental facility, barbecue grills, picnic tables, benches

GETTING THERE

BY CAR From Aurora Ave. N. (Hwy. 99), exit at N. 105th St. and go west 0.5 mile. Take a slight left on Holman Rd. NW and continue 0.3 mile; turn right on 3rd Ave. NW. After 0.4 mile turn left on NW 110th St.; follow road through the S curves as it becomes NW Carkeek Park Rd. After 0.6 mile, turn left into the park entrance.

Free parking is available in several parking lots inside the park. To reach the Environmental Learning Center (closed at time of publication due to lack of funding) and its garden and trails, turn right immediately into the first lot. To access the salmon breeding stream and orchard, park in the lot alongside the road approximately halfway into the park. For the beach, playground, and picnic areas, continue straight on the one-way road into the parking lot near the large field. A small parking area near the model airplane field is accessed by passing through the beach parking lot and continuing back around; before the next open picnic area turn right on a small side road and follow to the lot.

BY BUS 3rd Ave. NW/NW 110th St.; Holman Rd. NW/7th Ave. NW; NW 105th St./14th Ave. NW; Greenwood Ave. N./Holman Rd. N.; NW 100th Pl./ 7th Ave. NW.

Children peer through the mouth of a giant salmon, gauging the slope before launching themselves through its body, emerging seconds later down the hillside. The salmon slide at Carkeek Park has become even more iconic than the real fish that were reintroduced into Pipers Creek in the 1970s and have been returning home to spawn every year for decades. A tour of this fantastic urban forest and shoreline, which was historically known as Pipers Canyon, gives you the opportunity to witness the life cycle of our region's favorite fish.

Begin your visit at the main parking lot by the beach, which is the park's central location and has restrooms and good wheelchair accessibility. Children's play equipment is spread around this area of the park and includes a traditional play structure, swings, and a nature-inspired play area that features caves for exploring and the popular salmon slide.

Carkeek Park is ideal for picnics and barbecues and can handle large groups with ease. Near the playground, and with views of the Puget Sound, you'll find two reservable covered shelters and numerous picnic tables and barbecue grills. The stone shelter on the hill behind the playground was built by the Civilian Conservation Corps and the National Park Service in the 1930s.

Cross over the train tracks on the pedestrian overpass for a dramatic approach to the beach. If you are lucky (or patient), a train will come barreling along while you are standing over the tracks—a huge thrill that elicits whoops of joy from observers of all ages.

The beach is expansive and is a fantastic place to explore sea life at low tide. Pipers Creek pours out onto the shore of Puget Sound, creating intertidal streams where sharp-eyed visitors can spot gulls, loons, and sandpipers looking for a meal.

To fully explore the park, lace up your hiking boots and take advantage of the park's 6 miles of trails. The quiet, forested paths make it a popular place

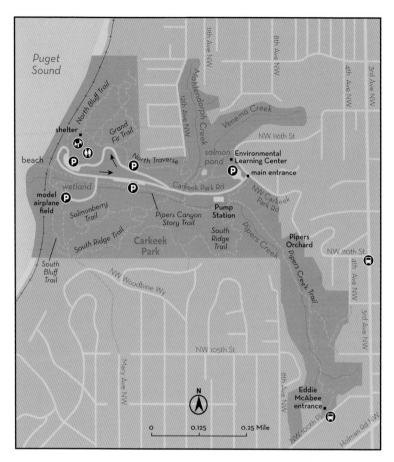

for dog walkers and trail runners. Many different trails branch off from the park's main walking thoroughfare, a flat trail that runs along the road. This is where you'll find the Pipers Canyon Story Trail, a self-guided program that helps kids (and adults) understand the ecology of this complex ecosystem. From here, take the Salmon to Sound Trail to see where elementary school groups release thousands of salmon fry they hatch in their classrooms each spring. Pipers Creek, previously polluted and damaged by logging, is one of

Salmon have a role in play and in real life at Carkeek Park, on the shores of Puget Sound.

the biggest streams in the city and has one of the largest salmon runs. Make a return visit in the fall to look for chum and coho making their way back upstream to spawn.

On the other side of the park's road look for signs for the South Ridge Trail for a hike that rises up above the canyon with views into the ravine below. Weasels, chipmunks, and many species of birds and butterflies enjoy these woods, and this peaceful end of the park is a good place to spot wildlife. Connect to several trails leading toward the Puget Sound or circle back on the Hillside Trail.

As you walk, consider that the parks department board in the 1920s strongly opposed the city's acquisition of this land on the grounds that it was not needed as a park. It is because the city council overruled the board that you are standing in the shade of mature firs, bigleaf maples, alders, and cedars. Morgan Carkeek, a builder and prominent businessman, and his wife, Emily, donated a portion of the funds to purchase the land, and Carkeek Park opened in 1929.

Pipers Creek and Pipers Canyon get their names from Andrew Piper, a former city councilman, and his wife, Minna, who built a farmhouse near the stream and planted an incredible orchard in the late 1800s. To see the one-hundred-year-old orchard, take the Pipers Creek Trail that begins behind the park's only blight, a sewage pumping station. Follow the trail to reach a sloped hillside that holds an impressive variety of apple trees, many of which are no longer available anywhere else, as well as other fruit and nut trees. Minna was skilled at grafting fruit trees, and the family sold their fruit at the market in Seattle. The Pipers later sold their land to the Carkeeks, and the land became overgrown. The fifty or so remaining trees lay undiscovered until the 1980s and are now tenderly cared for by the city and volunteers.

On your way out of the park, stop at the Environmental Learning Center. Behind the building you'll find a demonstration garden that encourages native planting, rain catchment, and wildlife-friendly gardening.

33   LLANDOVER WOODS GREENSPACE

Quiet loop trail grants forest solace

Location: 14499 3rd Ave. NW (at the dead end of NW 145th St.); Broadview
Acreage: 9.1
Amenities: 0.6 mile of unpaved trails

GETTING THERE
BY CAR From Aurora Ave. N. (Hwy. 99), exit at N. 145th St. and drive west 0.7 mile. At the intersection with 3rd Ave. NW and Boundary Ln., continue straight into a gravel driveway. Free parking is available in a small unpaved lot.
BY BUS 3rd Ave. NW/NW 145th St.; Greenwood Ave. N./N. 145th St.; Aurora Ave. N./N. 145th St.

One of the least traveled hiking spots in Seattle, this greenspace is perfect for a quiet walk in the forest. Descend from the parking lot into Llandover Woods' forested core along a gravel path that turns into a gently meandering dirt trail. You'll travel through tunnels of salmonberry bushes, with mossy logs and ferns clinging to the edges of the path. Logs turned into benches provide spots for resting or a lunch break.

Turn left at the fork to take the loop trail through a canopy of young maples. Take the wooden steps down and follow as the trail circles around and meets again with the central path. Turn left here to see the trail out to its end at a residential street—Sherwood Road Northwest—on the far western edge of the park. Or turn right to return the way you came, leading back to the parking lot. These short trails make the park an ideal hiking spot for families with young kids.

Although much of it was logged, probably around the turn of the last century, the park was spared from development. It's rarely busy, and noise from car traffic is almost nonexistent, which means Llandover Woods is a very good place for bird-watching. Look and listen for owls, hawks, chickadees, woodpeckers, and song sparrows. If you are very keen-eyed, you may be able to spot mountain beavers and coyotes. An information panel near the park's entrance shows some of the wildlife you might be lucky to spy.

34 NORTHACRES PARK

Wooded park delights kids and dogs

Location: N. 128th St. and 1st Ave. NE; Northgate
Acreage: 20.7
Amenities: Playground, seasonal spray park, off-leash dog park, baseball fields, half basketball court, restrooms, 1 mile of paved and unpaved trails, picnic tables, barbecue grills

GETTING THERE

BY CAR From Aurora Ave. N. (Hwy. 99), exit at N. 130th St. and drive east 0.7 mile. Turn right on 1st Ave. NE; the park is immediately on your left. Free parking is available in two lots; for the playground and picnic area, park in the lot off 1st Ave. NE; for the dog park and ball fields, turn left on NE 125th St., then turn left on 3rd Ave. NE and the circular lot is straight ahead at the end of the block.
BY BUS Meridian Ave. N./N. 128th St.

The sounds of kids playing and dogs barking drown out the background buzz of traffic on I-5 adjacent to this wooded North Seattle park. A great playground separated into two areas by age group is the first draw for kids. Big kids will find a large structure with a tall slide and challenging climbing equipment. Little tots can play on a smaller version with mini monkey bars and a tiny command center. The large play area, padded with wood chips, also has two swing sets and several spring rider toys. A curved concrete seating area makes for a perfect spot for parents and grandparents.

Follow the paved paths through the playground and past the restrooms to discover a round court. A basketball hoop shares this space with a labyrinth painted into the concrete for kids to explore. In the summer this becomes a spray park.

Interested in a picnic in the shade of tall evergreen trees? To the south of the playground, obscured by a grassy hill, you'll find tables and barbecues set a bit apart from one another to provide just the right amount of privacy for a family gathering or birthday party.

A heavily forested off-leash area is popular year-round at Northacres Park near I-5.

Take one of the dirt and gravel trails into the woods—a central loop allows you to reach the rest of the park's amenities, including two baseball fields, more restrooms, and a fabulous off-leash dog park on the eastern side. Let your dog run free in a fully fenced maze of narrow forested trails. On a surface of dirt and wood chips, dogs dart down the paths checking out logs and rocks while their owners enjoy a stroll in the woods.

EXTEND YOUR VISIT

A great hiking loop sits on the opposite side of I-5, a 0.2-mile walk away. The 2.2-mile **Jackson Park Perimeter Trail** is an unpaved path around an eighteen-hole golf course (a fence protects you from stray golf balls). To reach it, exit at the northern end of the park and walk east on Northeast 130th Street. After you cross over I-5, turn left on 5th Avenue Northeast and continue two blocks north until you see the southwest corner of the golf course and the trail.

35 LICTON SPRINGS PARK

Former mineral springs offers peek into geologic history

Location: 9536 Ashworth Ave. N.; Northgate
Acreage: 7.6
Amenities: Playground, 0.5 mile of paved and unpaved trails, benches, picnic tables, restrooms

GETTING THERE
BY CAR From Aurora Ave. N. (Hwy. 99), exit at N. 97th St. and drive east 0.2 mile. Turn right on Ashworth Ave. N.; the park is immediately on your left. Free street parking is available on Ashworth Ave. N. **BY BUS** Aurora Ave. N./N. 95th St.; College Wy. N./N. 97th St.

Before any development, this area squeezed between I-5 and Aurora Avenue was abundant with natural mineral springs. Duwamish Native Americans gave the springs the name "Licton," the Lushootseed word for the muddy red waters they treasured.

White settlers also saw the springs' appeal. David and Louisa Denny built a cabin here in 1870—the first house built north of downtown. A spa with thermal baths opened in 1935, and people traveled for miles to bathe in the water, which was also bottled and sold across the country.

A portion of the springs is still flowing at the park, and it's a pleasant stroll to walk the short dirt trails that cross over the streams and small ponds. Listen for the sound of frogs that have been recently reintroduced. Continue your walk by connecting with the paved paths that follow the park's perimeter, where you'll pass long stretches of lawn dotted with tall trees.

The west side of the park has a play area surrounded by benches and picnic tables. Around the playground, which features a large climbing structure, are colorful mosaics and stone tiles that describe how to play popular children's games similar to hopscotch in places like Aruba, Nigeria, and Great Britain.

EXTEND YOUR VISIT

One of the city's only disc golf courses is 0.6 mile north at **Mineral Springs Park**. Walk north on Densmore Avenue North and turn right on North 97th Street. Continue two blocks and turn left on College Way North, which becomes Meridian Avenue North. After three long blocks turn left on North 105th Street. The park will be on your right after one block. Even if you're not into hurling flying discs at a metal pole, take the gravel trail that bisects the park to admire the mysterious domes rising out of the grass by artist Stacy Levy.

36 GREENWOOD PARK

Cozy neighborhood park plays on area's past

Location: 602 N. 87th St.; Greenwood
Acreage: 2.2
Amenities: Restroom, playground, P-Patch, full basketball/multisport court, 0.3 mile of paved paths, picnic tables, benches

GETTING THERE

BY CAR From Aurora Ave. N. (Hwy. 99), exit at N. 90th St. and drive west two blocks. Turn left on Fremont Ave. N.; the park is immediately on your right. Free street parking is available on Fremont Ave. N. and on Evanston Ave. N.
BY BUS Greenwood Ave. N./N. 87th St.; N. 85th St./Fremont Ave. N.; Aurora Ave. N./N. 90th St.

More than one hundred years ago, electric trolleys stopped near here on the Seattle–Everett Interurban Railway. In a playful nod to this neighborhood history, the park includes an artistic bench shelter designed to resemble a station stop and lines in the concrete indicating the direction of the original tracks. Quotes from people who remember the trolley days are inscribed in squares in the ground.

The curving paths circle the park's perimeter. Stop in the southwest corner to read more about the history of this park. Signs divulge details about

A shelter with a pair of benches gives a nod to history at Greenwood Park.

the two Japanese families who were consecutive owners of greenhouses on the site of Greenwood Park. Both families were interned in the 1940s during World War II, and their dedication to their small farm (the Nishimuras until 1958 and the Otanis from 1958 to 1999) preserved this area as open space, allowing for it to eventually become a park.

Before any greenhouses or trains, Greenwood Park was a marshy woodland with large fir and cedar trees. A lot of effort has been made by the city and volunteers to reintroduce native plants and ecologically sensitive materials, which you'll see as you make your circuit of the park.

An innovative sports court occupies the southeast corner, with a paved surface that can be used for basketball, soccer, and field hockey. A large lawn makes up the center of the park and is popular for Frisbee and picnicking. Kids can amuse themselves in a sandbox with a digging toy, and on a couple of spring rider toys, swings, and two play structures—one challenging climbing structure and a second tamer one with bridges and a spiral slide.

A wide paved path cuts through the park, providing an accessible walkway from Evanston Avenue North to Fremont Avenue North. A handful of picnic tables sit along this tree-lined path, which also leads to an elevated P-Patch in the northeast side of the park.

EXTEND YOUR VISIT

Just half a mile away is **Sandel Playground**, with a play area, paved walking path, large playfield, basketball court, and seasonal wading pool. Drive or bike (or walk with caution as some sections have no sidewalk) north on Fremont Avenue North and turn left on North 90th Street. Continue six blocks and the park will appear on your right.

37 GREEN LAKE PARK

Seattle's Central Park hooks exercisers of every variety

Location: 7201 East Green Lake Dr. N.; Green Lake
Acreage: 324
Amenities: Two seasonally guarded swimming beaches, community center, indoor swimming pool, seasonal wading pool, playground, tennis courts, nine-hole pitch and putt golf course, 2.8 miles of paved paths, fishing piers, hand-carry boat launch, boat rentals, full basketball courts, baseball/softball fields, soccer fields, crew races amphitheater, restrooms, barbecue grills, benches, picnic tables

GETTING THERE

BY CAR From I-5 heading southbound, exit at NE 80th St. and go west; turn left on 1st Ave. NE. Go two blocks; veer left on Woodlawn Ave. NE. Turn right on Latona Ave. NE and continue straight into the park's parking lot. From I-5 heading northbound, exit at Ravenna Blvd./NE 65th St.; turn left on NE Ravenna Blvd. Continue 0.5 mile (passing under I-5) and then turn right on East Green Lake Dr. N. Continue four blocks; turn left on Latona Ave. NE into the park's parking lot.

Free parking is available in several parking lots around the lake and on residential side streets. For the indoor swimming pool, community center, playground, tennis courts, boat rentals, and sandy swimming beach, park in this lot on the east side of the park. For the golf course, crew races amphitheater, and connections to amenities at lower Woodland Park, park in the lot off West Green Lake Wy. N. at the south end. For more tennis courts, a hand-carry boat launch, and a swimming beach with lawn, park in the lot off West Green Lake Dr. N. near Stone Ave. N. in the northwest corner. To reach the children's wading pool, park along the street off East Green Lake Dr. N. near Wallingford Ave. N. on the north side.

Green Lake Park's scenic 2.8-mile paved loop is one of the most foot- and bike-trafficked spots in the city.

BY BUS East Green Lake Dr. N./4th Ave. NE; Woodlawn Ave. NE/Latona Ave. NE; Aurora Ave. N. (Hwy. 99)/N. 76th St.

Rollerbladers whizzing by, runners training in shirts advertising past races, children biking, parents with cups of coffee pushing strollers, fishermen dropping in their lines, tennis players batting the ball back and forth, crew teams slicing through the water, teens challenging each other to games of pickup basketball, and toddlers digging happily in the sand. It feels as if everyone in the city converges on Green Lake Park on the weekend to engage in nearly every outdoor activity imaginable.

Most people come to take advantage of the park's nearly 3-mile paved path that circles the scenic tree-lined lake. A run or stroll around the lake is a great way to see the diverse uses of this incredible urban asset.

Begin near the community center, which has an indoor swimming pool. This area of the park has a vast array of amenities, including basketball and tennis courts. Kids will want to hold off on the walk in order to explore the large playground that features separate climbing structures for younger and older kids, swings, interactive toys, and a huge sandpit with a digger and sand-engulfed canoe. Tables and barbecues sit near the play area for family-friendly picnics.

Take the paved, accessible path toward the water, where you'll discover one of two swimming beaches that are guarded in the summer. This one has a sandy beach and swimming platform with two diving boards.

Turn left to make a clockwise loop around the lake, the direction recommended for walkers and runners. Notice that there are two lanes marked on the path, one for those on foot and the other for users on wheels; be sure to stay in the appropriate lane. The path is paved for the entire loop but has dirt and gravel shoulders in places—a welcome alternative for many runners' knees.

Although it's easy to be distracted by great people-watching at Green Lake Park, take note of the flora and fauna along your route. Geologists believe the lake was formed fifty thousand years ago from the Cordilleran Ice Sheet during the Vashon glaciation. The lake got its name due to the green tint of the water from algae blooms, which unfortunately still plague this relatively shallow body of water (thirty feet at its deepest). Along the shoreline look for turtles sunning themselves on partially submerged logs. In addition to ducks and geese, several other species of birds frequent the park, including osprey, cormorants, herons, and bald eagles. In several spots you'll come across wooden piers where anglers try for trout, bass, carp, and catfish—fish are relatively plentiful and some species are stocked.

This tranquil body of water has not always looked the way you see it today. It has been dredged several times, beginning more than one hundred years ago, to help maintain its depth. The Olmsted Brothers firm drew up a plan for Green Lake Park, which included the suggestion to lower the level of the lake. In 1911 it was lowered by seven feet, creating more parkland around the water's edge. It's hard to imagine with today's mild winters, but Green Lake was a popular destination for dogsledding and ice-skating around the turn of the last century on years when it sufficiently iced over to be safe for winter recreation.

As you continue on your circuit, at 0.9 mile you'll pass the pitch and putt golf course on your left. A little farther ahead stop to read about the history of the Green Lake Aqua Theater, which hosted thousands of singers, actors, dancers, divers, and musicians (including Led Zeppelin and the Grateful Dead) for waterfront shows in the mid-twentieth century. The theater included two dramatic forty-foot diving platforms around a large outdoor pool, with seating for more than five thousand to enjoy a show and views of the lake in the background. Climb the steps of the remaining piece of the Aqua Theater for views down to the Green Lake Small Craft Center nearby that is a major hub for Seattle rowing clubs and hosts many exciting races.

At 1.7 miles you'll get a close-up view of the manmade Duck Island just offshore, which is a wildlife sanctuary and off-limits to humans. On land you'll also spot more tennis courts and a second swimming beach. This beach is set on a grass lawn next to the Seattle Public Theater, with two swimming platforms, one with diving boards.

This area of Green Lake features some of the most beautiful trees in the park, including flowering cherry trees, crabapples, and larches.

A little farther, at about 2.2 miles, the wading pool appears—one of the largest and most popular water features in the city—which is in operation during summer months. As you finish your loop, you'll pass a seasonal boat-rental kiosk where small sailboats, stand-up paddleboards, canoes, paddleboats, and kayaks are available for hourly rental.

Despite the park's heavy use, it's easy to find quiet spots around the lake to lay out a picnic blanket and lunch in the sunshine away from the bustle of eager exercisers.

38 MERIDIAN PLAYGROUND

Fabulous playground and grand orchard recount site's past

Location: N. 50th St. and Meridian Ave. N.; Wallingford
Acreage: 6.5
Amenities: Playground, restrooms, reservable shelter, half basketball courts, P-Patch, benches, picnic tables, barbecue grills

GETTING THERE

BY CAR From I-5, exit at NE 50th St. and drive west for 0.5 mile. Turn left on Meridian Ave. N. The park is immediately on your left. Free street parking is available on Meridian Ave. N. and adjacent residential streets. **BY BUS** Meridian Ave. N./N. 49th St.; N. 45th St./Wallingford Ave. N.

Mostly hidden from the busy street by majestic chestnut trees, Meridian Playground feels like a secret park where visitors can step back in time. Approach through the archway at the northwest corner and follow the curving ramp inlaid with stones to enter the park.

The brick Good Shepherd Center, on the National Register of Historic Places, provides a picturesque backdrop for the park's expansive lawn dotted with old trees, including the remaining specimens of a century-old orchard. Once housing an orphanage, a Catholic girls school, and a commercial laundry, the Good Shepherd Center is now home to a number of nonprofits, a private school, and artist lofts. The center's backyard was turned into a public park in the 1970s.

A large playground is the center of activity on warm days, when families flock to the park to play and picnic. The play area is partially enclosed with low stone walls and fencing, and at each opening little sculptures depicting characters from popular children's books welcome kids of all ages for climbing, jumping, and sliding. The playground has several play structures, stand-alone slides, swings, spring rider toys, and two sandboxes. A Dr. Seuss maze is painted into the concrete in bright colors. Old-fashioned curved benches give parents and caregivers plenty of places to sit and observe. A bronze statue of a dog from the *Good Dog, Carl* books also keeps track of the action.

Bring along lunch or dinner for a barbecue in the orchard, where you'll find picnic tables and grills among the trees (the apples are free for picking). Near the playground are restrooms and two back-to-back basketball hoops set at different heights. If it rains on your picnic, seek out the gazebo and large shelter that's reservable for events at the south end of the park. This is also where you'll see the entrance to a P-Patch managed by the gardening nonprofit Seattle Tilth.

Wander behind the playground toward the Good Shepherd Center to find a formal garden surrounded by hedges where it's easy to imagine how the setting looked decades ago.

EXTEND YOUR VISIT

Another fabulous playground is 0.5 mile and an easy walk away. Head south on Meridian Avenue North for four blocks; turn right on 43rd Avenue North and continue two blocks. You'll arrive at **Wallingford Playfield**, where you'll find a large climbing structure, a seasonal wading pool, tennis courts, playfields, and an unpaved walking trail.

39   GAS WORKS PARK

***Past gas plant provides
city's most unusual picnic
backdrop***

Location: 2101 N. Northlake Wy.; Wallingford
Acreage: 19.1
Amenities: Playground, reservable shelter, picnic
tables, barbecue grills, 1.2 miles of paved paths,
restrooms

GETTING THERE

BY CAR From I-5, exit at NE 45th St. and drive west 0.6 mile. Turn left on
Wallingford Ave. N. and continue 0.9 mile. Turn left on N. 34th St.; at the next
block turn right on Burke Ave. N., then turn immediately left on N. Northlake
Wy. Turn right to enter the parking lot, where parking up to four hours is free.
BY BUS Wallingford Ave. N./N. 35th St. **BY BIKE** The Burke-Gilman Trail passes
by the park.

One of Seattle's most unique public spaces, Gas Works Park is creative city planning at its best. The park sits on the site of a former gas plant, which operated for
fifty years, until it became obsolete. The city purchased the site and transformed it
into a park, which opened in 1975. The award-winning design by landscape architect Richard Haag incorporates industrial remnants of the gas plant, including
enormous rust-colored towers. Although some citizens and public officials were
upset that pieces of the plant remain at the park, others find it a compelling way to
preserve industrial history and introduce recreation into one place.

Due to its hilly and windy conditions, Gas Works Park is one of the best
places in the city to fly kites, and on a breezy day you can see colorful kites high
in the sky above the park. Paved paths cross through the park and climb a tall
artificial hill with sweeping views of downtown Seattle, the Space Needle, and
Lake Union. Look at your feet to see a sundial by artist Charles Greening—by
positioning your body correctly you will cast a shadow indicating the time of day.

With its fantastic views and industrial backdrop, the park is a popular spot
to film movies, pose for wedding photos, do amateur photography, and picnic at sunset. The two-story plaza near the water sometimes hosts salsa and
swing dancing on warm summer evenings. From here you can spot houseboats,

seaplanes, and kayaks on the water. While the shoreline is attractive, no swimming, wading, or launching of boats is permitted here due to potential water contamination in the lake sediment immediately offshore.

Many other signs of the gas plant pop out as you explore the park. Concrete train trestles near the entrance mark where trains dumped coal at the end of their route and are now popular for climbing. What was once a boiler house is now a large covered picnic area with tables and barbecue grills. Near the play area, which has several net-style climbing attractions, is the former pump house, where you can still see the original pipes.

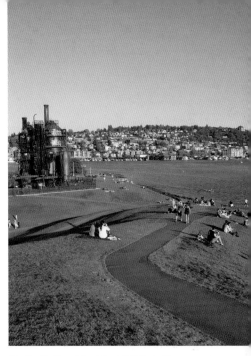

On the National Register of Historic Places, Gas Works Park overlooking Lake Union has won prestigious awards for its design.

The park hosts the city's annual Fourth of July fireworks display as well as many other community events throughout the year.

40 WOODLAND PARK

Leafy urban greenspace boasts hiking, dog park, and private picnic spots

Location: 1000 N. 50th St.; Green Lake/Phinney Ridge
Acreage: 90.9
Amenities: Playground, off-leash dog park, skate park, 1.75 miles of unpaved trails, BMX dirt jumps, tennis courts, track, softball/baseball fields, soccer fields, horseshoe pits, lawn bowling, bocce ball courts, croquet green, reservable shelters, restrooms, picnic tables, benches

Mounds of dirt create jumps for daring BMX bikers in lower Woodland Park.

GETTING THERE

BY CAR From Aurora Ave. N. (Hwy. 99) northbound, exit at N. 50th St.; drive two blocks east on N. 50th St. Turn left into the parking lot. From Aurora Ave. N. southbound, exit at N. 46th St.; drive west two blocks and turn right on Fremont Ave. N. After four blocks turn right on N. 50th St.; drive four blocks east and turn left into the parking lot.

Free parking is available in several lots in the park. To access the southern picnic areas, trails, and the Woodland Park Rose Garden, park in the lot off N. 50th St. To reach lower Woodland Park's ball fields, skate park, and BMX jumps, park in the long, narrow lot at the eastern end of the park off Green Lake Wy. N. (near N. 55th St.). To access the tennis courts, dog park, lawn bowling, horseshoe pits, trails, and central picnic areas, take West Green Lake Wy. N. and then turn west onto a park road. Follow signs to several central parking lots, including one directly in front of the off-leash area. For the playground, park along Phinney Ave. N. near N. 59th St.

BY BUS N. 46th St./Aurora Ave. N.; N. 45th St./Stone Wy. N.; Phinney Ave. N./ N. 59th St.

Meander along lovely trails under a green canopy and ponder the stroke of luck that preserved these ninety acres that serve as the intersection of the Phinney Ridge, Fremont, Green Lake, and Wallingford neighborhoods.

We can thank Guy Phinney, who developed a large estate here in 1889 and then left much of the area forested, giving Woodland Park its name. He envisioned trails, picnic areas, and a small zoo. We can also credit city officials who—despite an outcry because it wasn't close enough to downtown Seattle—purchased the park in 1900 for a steep $100,000.

Today Woodland Park is sliced in half by Aurora Avenue, but footbridges and paths allow this urban park to serve as a bridge to the Woodland Park Zoo, the Woodland Park Rose Garden, and Green Lake Park.

The park's hiking trails include both forested sections and open, rolling meadows. Tucked into the woods is a busy off-leash dog area with several gated entrances offering access into an acre of play space, which includes a tall hill with stairs for dogs to scamper up and down.

Picnic areas are scattered across a wide swath of the park along the edge of the forest and open lawn. In addition to several reservable shelters, you'll find picnic tables and barbecues hidden among the trees.

Seattleites have taken a liking to whimsical games from an earlier era, and Woodland Park is one of the only places in the city to engage in lawn bowling, bocce, horseshoes, and croquet. Don't expect a casual backyard scene—run by a private club with open times for the public, these games often draw serious competitors and have regular tournaments.

Lower Woodland Park feels like an extension of the bustling activity at Green Lake Park, which is just a few steps away across West Green Lake Way North. Many youth and adult games of baseball, softball, soccer, and tennis are played at this large outdoor complex. For those traveling on wheels, check out the seventeen-thousand-square-foot skate park designed by skate legend Wally Hollyday that features a flow bowl area, a clover combination bowl, and many street elements. Next door, a large network of dirt jumps attracts BMX bikers.

EXTEND YOUR VISIT

The park has a great playground, but it's geographically separate from the rest of the park and, therefore, is not easy to find. You'll either need to drive around to the northwest corner of the zoo or set off on foot via a hidden footpath.

A HISTORIC GARDEN IN BLOOM

While you're in the neighborhood, don't miss the chance to visit the 2.5-acre **Woodland Park Rose Garden**, which is located near the Woodland Park Zoo's southeast corner and reachable via the southernmost pedestrian footbridge that crosses Aurora Avenue from Woodland Park. With input from the Olmsted Brothers, this formal garden opened in 1924 and features two hundred varieties of roses, as well as fountains, a reflecting pool, and sculptures. It is a popular wedding site during spring and summer months when the roses are at their peak. A children's sensory garden is at the eastern edge, giving kids a place to smell and touch the flora.

From the park's wide central trail that runs adjacent to Aurora Avenue, cross over the highway using the northernmost footbridge. A narrow trail skirts the edge of the zoo (and offers a behind-the-scenes peek); turn right to follow it down the eastern and then northern sides of the zoo property. Cross the north parking lot and you'll soon see the **West Woodland Park Playground**. Kids will love the tree-house-style climbing structures plus a huge climbing net, swings, and a sandbox.

41   FREMONT PEAK PARK

Residential lots become view park with community pride

Location: 4357 Palatine Ave. N. (near N. 45th St.); Fremont
Acreage: 0.6
Amenities: Concrete seating areas, 0.1-mile unpaved trail

GETTING THERE

BY CAR From Aurora Ave. N. (Hwy. 99), exit at N. 46th St. (says Green Lake Wy. N. northbound) and drive west six blocks on N. 46th St. Turn left on Greenwood Ave. N., then take the next right on N. 45th St. and follow as it curves to the left and becomes Palatine Ave. N. The park is on your right after the first house.

Free street parking is available on Palatine Ave. N. **BY BUS** Phinney Ave. N./N. 46th St.

Follow the narrow metal ribbon as it unravels, leading you on a trip through Fremont Peak Park.

Getting this park built was a journey in itself for neighbors who saw an opportunity when the owner of three adjacent houses put them on the market. Their hard work, led by Fremont resident Jack Tomkinson, spurred a community campaign to raise money to buy the land and turn it into a park, which opened in 2007. More than one hundred volunteers weighed in on the park's design and then helped plant four thousand trees and shrubs to replace invasive species that had consumed the property. Many continue to help maintain it today. Tomkinson

In Fremont Peak Park, art unveils ties to the neighborhood's mythology.

went on to found the nonprofit organization Urban Sparks to help other neighborhoods build new parks and champion charitable and public works.

Artist Laura Haddad invokes the Greek myth of Theseus and the Minotaur with the ribbon winding along a gravel path as you pass concrete walls that resemble those of King Minos's labyrinth. Follow the trail in the shadow of tall cedars, Douglas firs, and hemlocks to reach a small clearing.

Here, as a nod to Fremont's place as the "Center of the Universe," seven orbs indicate constellations, and lines in the concrete point out the location of the sunset on the summer and winter solstices. With its position on a western-facing bluff, the park shows off views of Ballard, the locks, and the Olympic Mountains.

42 HIRAM M. CHITTENDEN LOCKS

Engineering marvel supplies up-close views of boats and salmon

Location: 3015 NW 54th St.; Ballard
Acreage: 17
Amenities: Visitors center, gardens, fish ladder, 0.6 mile of paved paths, restrooms, benches

GETTING THERE

BY CAR From Aurora Ave. N. (Hwy. 99), exit at N. 46th St. (says Green Lake Wy. N. northbound) and drive west. After six blocks the road curves downhill and becomes N. Market St. Continue on N. Market St. (it will become NW Market St.) through Ballard for 2.1 miles. Take a slight left on NW 54th St.; after five hundred feet, turn left on 30th Ave. NW, which takes you into the locks parking lot. Paid four-hour parking is available in the lot. Free street parking is available across NW 54th St. on adjacent residential streets. **BY BUS** NW 54th St./32nd Ave. NW; NW 54th St./30th Ave. NW. **BY BIKE** The Burke-Gilman Trail passes by the parking lot on the north side of the locks.

Ever wondered how the level of Lake Washington and Lake Union can be on average twenty-one feet higher than Puget Sound? The Ballard Locks, as they are more casually known, is the place to find out about this century-old engineering solution. It's also one of the most fascinating public spaces in Seattle.

Enter the park along a paved path and note the visitors center on your left if you want to dig deeper into the history and mechanics of the locks. The center is open from 10:00 AM to 6:00 PM daily May through September and from 10:00 AM to 4:00 PM Thursday through Monday the rest of the year; free tours are also offered in the summer. Head straight for the canal and cross the metal walkways to peer down at the two locks. As boats enter and leave the freshwater side, the locks open and close, filling up or letting out water to reach the appropriate water level for passage and also to prevent saltwater intrusion.

The US Army Corps of Engineers operates the locks, which were added to the National Register of Historic Places in 1978. The locks are named after Hiram Martin Chittenden, a historian, US Army major, Port of Seattle commissioner, and district engineer who helped design his namesake. He died in 1917 just months after the locks debuted. The opening of the locks allowed the fishing industry centered at Fishermen's Terminal—as well as many other marine-based businesses—to take off.

On summer weekends, the locks are an especially busy place, with captains of boats of all sizes tying up to the locks while dozens of spectators watch from above. This is also the best time of year to spot salmon returning to spawn in streams that feed into Lake Washington. Continue across the walkway to the Magnolia side of the locks. Look down

The Chittenden Locks allow leisure and commercial boat traffic to travel between Puget Sound and the freshwater lakes of Lake Union and Lake Washington.

into the water to spot the twenty-one-step fish ladder, then follow the ramp downhill and inside a small concrete building to a viewing area to get eye to eye with fish as they make their arduous journey. It's estimated that only one egg in every thousand survives to become an adult spawning salmon. Sea lions and herons are occasionally spotted fishing around the locks.

Above the fish ladder, a square plaza near the restrooms holds a sculpture of waves by artist Paul Sorey, which kids find irresistible.

On both the Ballard and Magnolia sides—the Magnolia side becomes adjacent Commodore Park—are terraced grass areas, which make lovely spots for picnicking with clear views of boat activity in and out of the locks. Free outdoor concerts are held on the lawns in the summer.

Return to the Ballard side to stroll the Carl S. English Jr. Botanical Gardens, named after the locks' first horticulturist, which feature more than five hundred species of plants, trees, and flowers from around the world. A paved path circles a large section of the park and offers peeks at the one-hundred-year-old Cavanaugh House, the private home of the district engineer of the locks.

43 BALLARD COMMONS PARK

Ballard's central hub brings together diverse neighborhood

Location: 5701 22nd Ave. NW; Ballard
Acreage: 1.4
Amenities: Seasonal spray park, skate park, benches, 0.15 mile of paved paths

GETTING THERE

BY CAR From Aurora Ave. N. (Hwy. 99), exit at N. 46th St. (says Green Lake Wy. N. northbound) and drive west. After six blocks the road curves downhill and becomes N. Market St. Continue on N. Market St. (it will become NW Market St.) into central Ballard for 1.6 miles. Turn right on 22nd Ave. NW. Go two blocks; the park will be on the left. Free street parking is available on NW 58th St., 22nd Ave. NW, and NW 57th St. **BY BUS** 24th Ave. NW/NW 57th St.; NW Market St./Ballard Ave. NW.

As Ballard has transformed from a sleepy Scandinavian fishing neighborhood into a bustling, gastronomic urban center, new parks have popped up, adding to its appeal. At the heart of Ballard's restaurants and shops is Ballard Commons Park, a central gathering area for the neighborhood that sits diagonal from the Ballard library.

Paved paths begin at the park's corners and draw you into the park for a stroll past inviting sections of lawn lined with modern lampposts and trees. The paths meet at a plaza packed with benches where in the summer concrete seashells by artist Valerie Otani turn into spray features for squealing kids.

A concrete planter works as a long bench for locals on a lunch break. Just above is a 4,500-square-foot skate bowl, where teens and young-at-heart adults drop in for tricks. The concrete bowl has shallower and deeper ends and includes a vertical "tombstone" wall.

Ballard Commons was well planned to offer accessibility to park users in wheelchairs and toting strollers. People of all ages and backgrounds, some zipping in on skateboards, swarm the park to attend popular community events and food festivals.

EXTEND YOUR VISIT

A 0.4-mile walk away is **Ballard Playground**, with a play area that includes a partially buried ship, as well as the Ballard Community Center and an indoor swimming pool. Walk west on Northwest 58th Street for one and a half blocks, then turn right on 26th Avenue Northwest. After two blocks the park is on your left.

An artistic spray park provides a delightful splash area for kids in summer at Ballard Commons Park.

44   BALLARD CORNERS PARK

Comfortable art creates outdoor living room

Location: 1702 NW 62nd St.; Ballard
Acreage: 0.25
Amenities: Playground, art, benches

GETTING THERE

BY CAR From Aurora Ave. N. (Hwy. 99), exit at N. 46th St. (says Green Lake Wy. N. northbound) and drive west. After six blocks the road curves downhill and becomes N. Market St. Continue on N. Market St. (it will become NW Market St.) toward central Ballard for 1.2 miles. Turn right on 15th Ave. NW; go 0.4 mile. Turn left on NW 62nd St. and drive one block. The park is on the right. Free street parking is available on 17th Ave. NW and NW 62nd St. **BY BUS** 15th Ave. NW/ NW 65th St.; 15th Ave. NW/NW 60th St.

The site of a former corner store is now a place for people who live in the neighborhood to play, lounge, or stroll.

For play, look to the small but challenging climbing structure set on wood chips that features a spinning toy and twisting ladder. To lounge, try out the oversized concrete couch and chair made to look like living room furniture by artist Nathan Arnold. Or enjoy a picnic on the grass under mature fruit trees.

For a stroll, take the sidewalk—constructed to feel as if it's part of the park—which draws people on walks or commuting through the neighborhood. A rock swale follows the sidewalk's curve, with ferns and other native shrubs planted around it to reflect a Northwest garden.

The entry at the northeast corner commemorates the small grocery store that sat on the north side of this lot for fifty years, one of many family-owned corner markets in Ballard in the early twentieth century. Read up on your history from a seat on one of the park's stools set next to two counters resembling those popular in the old-timey markets.

45   KIRKE PARK

Former church site becomes community picnic and play space

Location: 7028 9th Ave. NW (near NW 70th St.); Ballard
Acreage: 0.8
Amenities: Playground, picnic tables, benches, P-Patch, 0.15 mile of paved and unpaved paths

GETTING THERE

BY CAR From Aurora Ave. N. (Hwy. 99), exit at N. 80th St. and drive west 1.1 miles. Turn left on 9th Ave. NW and continue three blocks. The park will appear on your left in the next block. Free street parking is available on 9th

Ave. NW. **BY BUS** 8th Ave. NW/ NW 73rd St.

In a nod to the area's Scandinavian history and a small Christian sect that lived and worshipped on this site, Kirke Park was named after the Norwegian word for "church." Pieces of the church's foundation still stand, dividing the playground side of the park from a community P-Patch.

The playground is popular with nearby families, who park their bikes and strollers along the accessible paved path that wraps around the play area and winds through much of the park. Kids will have fun on the wooden play structure that has a plastic slide and climbing wall. A pair of saucer swings, a separate toddler slide, and a sandbox set between large rocks make up the structured play area, but a short dirt path lined with native plants along

Kirke means "church" in Norwegian, a gesture to Ballard's history and this park's origin.

the fence provides more areas to play and explore, including stumps and hollowed logs.

In the center of the park several tables partially protected from the elements make a perfect spot for a picnic. Or lay out your blanket on the flat lawn next to the play area. Many other benches are scattered throughout the park.

Follow the gravel trail into the P-Patch to examine the vegetables, herbs, and fruit being grown by members of the community.

EXTEND YOUR VISIT

A half-mile walk will lead you to another cute neighborhood spot—**6th Avenue NW Pocket Park**. To reach it, head north on 9th Avenue Northwest for one and a half blocks. Turn right on Northwest 75th Street and continue three blocks. Turn left on 6th Avenue Northwest and you'll find the park on your left after one block. The park has benches, a picnic table, a giant chessboard, and a sandbox with toys.

46 SUNSET HILL PARK

*Bluff viewpoint boasts
Puget Sound scenery*

Location: 7531 34th Ave. NW (near NW 75th St.); Ballard/Crown Hill
Acreage: 2.7
Amenities: Picnic tables, benches, 0.15 mile of paved paths

GETTING THERE

BY CAR From Aurora Ave. N. (Hwy. 99), exit at N. 80th St. and drive west for 2.5 miles. Turn left on 32nd Ave. NW; continue one block and turn right on NW 77th St. At the end of the street, turn left on 34th Ave. NW. The park is immediately on the right. Free street parking is available on 34th Ave. NW. **BY BUS** 32nd Ave. NW/NW 75th St.

Take in a sunset view of the Puget Sound from this clifftop perch at the far western edge of Ballard, just above Golden Gardens Park. You'll have your pick of nine perfectly positioned benches to gaze at Bainbridge Island, Discovery Park, and the Olympic Mountains. With few trees on this section of bluff, the park provides clear sightlines. Several hundred feet below you can spy the masts of sailboats in Shilshole Bay Marina bobbing in the harbor.

The benches sit along a paved path that extends the length of the residential block. Note the plaque set into a rock, which is dedicated to fishermen who lost their lives at sea. The park was chosen because this area was one of the first sights of home that fishermen would see as they returned to Seattle.

The park is the legacy of two Seattle families—the Moomaws and the Andersons—who donated the land for the park to the city in 1903.

47 GOLDEN GARDENS PARK

*Sandy beachfront delivers
sunset with a view*

Location: 8498 Seaview Pl. NW; Ballard
Acreage: 87.8
Amenities: Playground, off-leash dog park, fire
pits, barbecue grills, restrooms, 1.6 miles of
unpaved trails, 0.7 mile of paved paths, half
basketball court, hand-carry boat launch,
reservable shelters, rental facility

GETTING THERE

BY CAR From Aurora Ave. N. (Hwy. 99), exit at N. 85th St. and drive west
2.5 miles. Turn right at the T intersection on 32nd Ave. NW and follow as it
becomes Golden Gardens Dr. NW and curves downhill. After 0.6 mile turn right
into the parking lot to reach the off-leash dog area or continue an additional
0.4 mile as the road becomes Seaview Pl. NW until you reach a T intersection;
then turn right into the main beachfront parking lot. Free parking is available in
the off-leash parking lot, the main beach parking lot, several overflow parking
lots, and along Seaview Ave. NW just south of the park entrance. **BY BUS** 32nd
Ave. NW/NW 85th St.; Loyal Wy. NW/NW 85th St.; NW 85th St./30th Ave. NW.
BY BIKE The Burke-Gilman Trail originates just south of the park.

There's no question that the best time to visit Golden Gardens Park is on a
summer evening when—true to its name—the setting sun bathes the long
beachfront in an orange glow.

You won't find yourself alone at the golden hour at this popular park on a
warm day. Families with young children, groups of teenagers, and couples on
romantic dates seem to pack into every inch of sand, often staking out claims
to the popular fire pits hours before twilight.

During the day the shore buzzes with energy with people playing beach
volleyball, children digging in the sand, and extended families barbecuing
under the shade of tall weeping poplar trees. Amble in the sand out to the
tideline while you look across the Puget Sound at the Olympic Mountains.

Golden Gardens Park is a great spot to explore tide pools at low tide. The
park is one of several in the city where you can ask questions and learn about

Early evening is a magical time for sunset viewing at Golden Gardens Park.

marine life from Seattle Aquarium volunteer naturalists during summer low tides.

The park is also a popular spot to launch kayaks and other hand-carry vessels. For hundreds of years Native Americans used this section of coastline to set afloat their boats.

If you'd rather keep the sand out of your toes, paved paths allow you to explore the park from end to end. A good starting point is the brick bathhouse (a Seattle historic landmark), which holds restrooms and a rental facility. Nearby you'll find a half basketball court and a large playground set over wood chips that has a tall climbing net, swings, and two play structures, including one that resembles a pirate ship. Follow the paths from the play area north to discover the quieter end of the park. Take the footbridge over a restored wetland that's home to ducks and blackbirds to a viewpoint with benches.

The paved path meets the sandy beach on the south end of the bathhouse, providing access to the many benches, picnic tables, and barbecue grills that cover the park and have views of the action on the sand.

Occasional trains make their approach known with loud whistles as they whiz along the tracks that slice this park into two major sections. While dogs aren't allowed on the beach—the case for all Seattle parks—Golden Gardens has an off-leash dog area in the upper section of the park. To get there from the beach on foot, look for a tunnel decorated with mosaic tiles near the park's main entrance that will take you under the railroad tracks. Emerge on the other side, take the stairs to the left, and walk to the north end of the parking lot, where you'll see a steep trail and stairs leading up the hillside.

Golden Gardens has nearly two miles of trails that crisscross through the dense forest dominated by maple trees. Head southeast, follow the trail as it gradually leads uphill, and you're sure to hit the off-leash area. The enclosure is large, shaded, and has logs and stumps for entertainment. A small area is reserved for small and shy dogs. Owners will appreciate the little covered area for protection from rain while their pups play.

EXTEND YOUR VISIT

Walk south along the paved paths, following the shoreline of Golden Gardens Park, to reach **Eddie Vine Boat Ramp**, a busy saltwater motorized boat launch. Walk to the end of the wooden pier for more great views and the chance to spot seals and bald eagles.

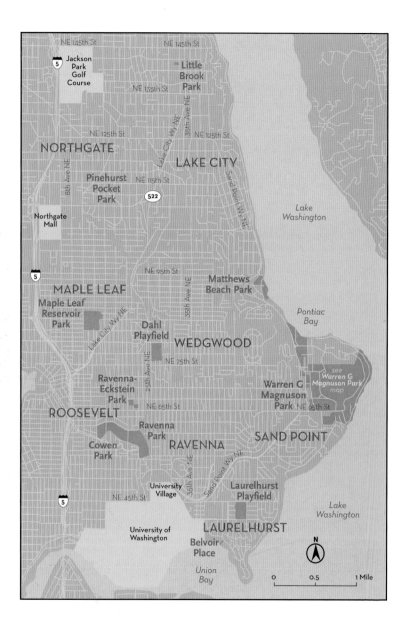

Northeast Seattle

48 WARREN G. MAGNUSON PARK

Rolling hills and wetlands combine with abundance of indoor and outdoor amenities

Location: 7400 Sand Point Wy. NE; Sand Point
Acreage: 350
Amenities: Community center, playground, off-leash dog park, seasonally guarded swimming beach, seasonal wading pool, tennis courts, half and full basketball courts, soccer fields, baseball/softball fields, cricket fields, indoor tennis center, putt-putt golf course, hand-carry boat launch, fishing pier, motorized boat launch, 4.5 miles of paved and unpaved paths, P-Patch, restrooms, barbecue grills, reservable shelters, benches, picnic tables

GETTING THERE

BY CAR From I-5, exit at NE 45th St. and drive 1.5 miles east, passing University Village. Veer slightly left to continue on Sand Point Wy. NE for 2 miles. The park will be on your right.

Free parking is available in several parking lots inside the park. To access the waterfront, wetland trails, Kite Hill, outdoor tennis courts, and fields 8–10, turn right on NE 65th St. and follow signs to your destination. To access the playground, indoor tennis center, off-leash dog area, P-Patch, community center, basketball courts, and fields 1–7 11 and 12, turn right on NE 74th St. at the main entrance and drive straight to reach the large parking lot, which will appear on your right. To access the hand-carry boat launch and fishing pier, turn into a gravel parking strip immediately off Sand Point Wy. NE 0.4 mile north of the main entrance at NE 74th St.

BY BUS Sand Point Wy. NE/NE 65th St.; Sand Point Wy. NE/NE 74th St.
BY BIKE The Burke-Gilman Trail runs adjacent to the park.

Launch a boat, take a swim, run your dog through the off-leash park, fly a kite, check out public art, windsurf, visit a butterfly garden, see what's growing in the P-Patch, climb on one of the city's best playgrounds, play basketball on a full-height or kid-friendly basketball court, or take a nature walk in restored wetlands. Magnuson Park draws people from all over the region to access this park's many fantastic amenities.

When you enter Magnuson Park's formal main entrance, it feels a little like you're sneaking onto a military base. The stodgy brick buildings are former offices, barracks, and storage sites for what was a US naval air station for more than forty years. Longtime US senator Warren G. Magnuson helped secure funding from the federal government to create the park in the 1970s. (He also played a role in preserving Pike Place Market and getting the World's Fair in 1962.) Earlier in the century this park was known as Carkeek Park, because Morgan and Emily Carkeek donated a piece of this land to be used as a park around 1900, before it became engulfed by the naval facilities.

Magnuson Park is unusual in that in addition to providing an enormous swath of recreational parkland, it is home to dozens of organizations within its grounds, including the Cascade Bicycle Club, Y programs, The Mountaineers, Seattle Musical Theatre, and the Outdoors for All Foundation, most of which are clustered near the main entrance.

At 350 acres, the park is so vast it helps to park near the amenities you're most interested in. With kids in tow, head straight for the playground, which is near the main entrance, close to the indoor Tennis Center Sand Point (which offers classes, camps, and the putt-putt golf course). You can occupy kids for hours on the twenty-thousand-square-foot playground—one of the

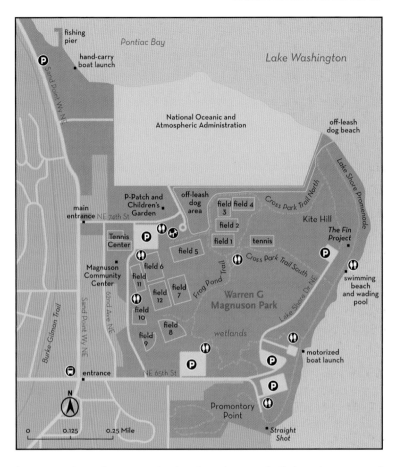

largest outdoor play spaces in the city—that was built by volunteers and donated by the Junior League. Three large play structures feature tube slides, tunnels, climbing walls, climbing nets, and suspension bridges. A clever toddler-appropriate area resembles a house with windows and tiny benches for play closer to the ground. You'll also find two swing sets, a sandbox, benches, and picnic tables under a covered shelter. Behind the playground are four basketball hoops with rims that can be raised and lowered.

The Fin Project *by John T. Young enriches the scene below Kite Hill at Magnuson Park.*

Near the playground a four-acre P-Patch and Children's Garden invites you to wander among the fruit trees, vegetable beds, and flowers—try to spot mosaic artwork tucked among the plants.

Bring your bikes as this is a great park for kid-friendly biking. Begin in the play area where yellow road lines are painted onto the rubber surface, and then set off past the soccer fields along the paved Cross Park Trail South, which takes you around a large playfield and past outdoor tennis courts to the waterfront in a little more than half a mile.

For a slower pace, consider a walk along the Frog Pond Trail, where the bird-watching is some of the best in the city. Gravel trails lead through a restored wetland among alder and cottonwood groves and across small footbridges over ponds and marshes that fill up with water seasonally. This site was originally underwater until the level of the lake was lowered in the early 1900s. It has taken extensive work by the city and volunteers to coax the land back into a more natural state after the naval station was decommissioned. Despite the challenges, many species of resident and migratory birds call Magnuson Park home, along with Pacific chorus frogs and dragonflies.

Paths continue along the waterfront, where you can explore two fascinating sculptures. Located near Kite Hill at the northeast end of the park, *The Fin Project* by John T. Young resembles a pod of orcas but is actually made from the fins of US Navy nuclear submarines. Twelve perfectly situated limestone columns set over exactly 1 kilometer make up *Straight Shot* by Perri (Lynch) Howard at the far south end of the shore where the naval airstrip used to be. Peer through one of the two holes in the first stone to look through all twelve simultaneously.

On warm summer days, the park's guarded swimming beach and wading pool fill up with kids and adults cooling off. Tables, barbecue grills, and several reservable shelters are scattered along the main section of waterfront for picnicking. Climb Kite Hill just behind the swim area for great views of Lake Washington and the Cascade Mountains. The thirty-five-foot-tall hill is free of trees, and kids are often seen running down it at full speed, trying to catch a breeze for their kites.

Magnuson Park is a favorite for boating, with both hand-carry and motorized boat launches. South of the motorized boat launch the park also has an area set aside for kiteboarders and windsurfers to launch their crafts. Fishing is possible along the shoreline and also on the pier on the far northwest side of the park on the opposite side of the National Oceanic and Atmospheric Administration (NOAA), where you'll also find the best hand-carry boat launch.

Being the only off-leash area in the city with access to the water makes Magnuson's large dog park a busy scene every day of the week. The nine-acre off-leash area has several open sections for tossing balls and running, as well as a separate fenced spot for shy and small dogs. A wide gravel path allows owners to enjoy a half-mile (one-way) walk with their pup that ends at a fenced beach area where Fido can take his own swim. The off-leash area has multiple entrances/exits so you can leash up your dog and continue a walk along the park's paths at several spots.

EXTEND YOUR VISIT

When the naval base was decommissioned, the northern section of land was set aside for NOAA. Art enthusiasts can tour the **NOAA Art Walk**, immediately north of the park, on weekdays (valid ID required) to see five pieces of outdoor art. The pipe sculpture *A Sound Garden* by Douglas Hollis was the inspiration for the name of the famous Seattle grunge band.

49 LAURELHURST PLAYFIELD

*Majestic trees rim
playground, field,
and walking trail*

Location: 4544 NE 41st St.; Laurelhurst
Acreage: 13.5
Amenities: Community center, playground, tennis courts, baseball/softball field, 0.6 mile of unpaved trails, restrooms

GETTING THERE

BY CAR From I-5, exit at NE 45th St. and drive east 1.3 miles, passing University Village. At the five-way intersection, turn right on Mary Gates Memorial Dr. NE. Follow as it curves to the left and becomes NE 41st St. Continue on NE 41st St. for 0.6 mile. The park will be on your left. Free parking is available in the small parking lot; free street parking is also available on NE 41st St. **BY BUS** NE 41st St./42nd Ave. NE.

The Laurelhurst neighborhood got its name more than one hundred years ago for being a grove of laurel. Today it's the tall maples and chestnuts that impress visitors to this community's chief park.

A tree theme plays out in the huge climbing structure that dominates the wood-chip-covered play area near the community center. Three peaked tree houses with bridges, six slides, and a rock climbing wall make for an exciting place for older kids to play. Younger kids can explore a smaller structure, as well as swings, a merry-go-round, and a sandbox. All ages will enjoy playing captain in the boat designed to resemble the flat-bottomed steam ferries that carried crops from the Squak Valley in Issaquah down the slough to Lake Washington in the late 1800s.

A wide gravel path circles the park, leading you past benches where you can sit in the shade of the enormous trees. Look for a fire pit almost hidden here among the trees, a perfect spot to roast s'mores. As you round the northern edge of the park, you'll come across baseball/softball fields with bleachers, picnic tables, and a pedestrian bridge that crosses Northeast 45th Street and leads to Laurelhurst Elementary School.

Circle back toward the beautiful brick community center, where you'll find restrooms inside. Down the hill in the park's southwest corner are tennis courts.

50   BELVOIR PLACE

Slice of waterfront welcomes
kayakers and canoers

Location: 3659 42nd Ave. NE; Laurelhurst
Acreage: 0.4
Amenities: Hand-carry boat launch, dock

GETTING THERE

BY CAR From I-5, exit at NE 45th St. and drive east 1.3 miles, passing University Village. At the five-way intersection, turn right on Mary Gates Memorial Dr. NE. Follow as it curves to the left and becomes NE 41st St. Turn right on 42nd Ave. NE; go one block and the park will be on your right, just past NE Surber Dr. Free street parking is available on 42nd Ave. NE and on NE Surber Dr. **BY BUS** 42nd Ave. NE/NE 41st St.

Only a parks department sign marks the narrow entrance to this little-known park on the shores of Lake Washington. Follow the wood-chip path into the park, dodging tree roots, and emerge onto a flat length of lawn wedged between waterfront homes.

A short dock extends into the lake, providing a spot for kayakers and canoeists to easily launch their boats. Fishing is also possible, but the lake is rather shallow at this spot. Although tempting, swimming from the dock is not permitted.

Instead, stretch out a picnic blanket on the grass and dine with views of Lake Washington, the 520 bridge, and Husky Stadium. The unlikely location of Belvoir Place means you can expect to have it all to yourself.

EXTEND YOUR VISIT

Walk 0.5 mile to the **University of Washington's Center for Urban Horticulture**. Go north on 42nd Avenue Northeast and turn left on Northeast Surber Drive. Follow the road as it curves; turn left on Northeast 41st Street and the center will be on your left. Explore the demonstration gardens and then take the gravel path to discover the wetlands, an excellent spot for bird-watching.

51 RAVENNA AND COWEN PARKS

*Enchanting urban creek
supplies hiking solace*

Location: Ravenna Park: 5520 Ravenna Ave. NE;
Cowen Park: 5849 15th Ave. NE; Ravenna/Roosevelt
Acreage: 49.9 (Ravenna); 8.4 (Cowen)
Amenities: 4.5 miles of unpaved trails, two
playgrounds, seasonal wading pool, tennis courts,
restrooms, baseball/softball fields, picnic tables,
reservable shelter, barbecue grills, full basketball
court

GETTING THERE

BY CAR For Ravenna Park: From I-5 northbound, exit at NE 65th St. and turn right on NE Ravenna Blvd. After 0.9 mile, where the road turns sharply right, turn left on Ravenna Ave. NE and then turn immediately right into a small, free gravel parking lot.

From I-5 southbound, take exit 171 for NE 71st St. and merge onto 6th Ave. NE. Turn left on NE 71st St. Immediately after crossing over I-5, turn right on 8th Ave. NE. After seven blocks take a slight right to cross northwest-bound NE Ravenna Blvd. Turn left on southwest-bound NE Ravenna Blvd. and follow the preceding directions to the parking lot. You can reach a larger free parking lot closer to the reservable picnic shelter by continuing on Ravenna Ave. NE as it becomes NE 58th St. After 0.1 mile turn right into the lot.

To reach Cowen Park's playground, ball fields, and basketball court, continue on NE 58th St. for two blocks and turn left on 18th Ave. NE. Turn immediately right on NE Ravenna Blvd. After 0.2 mile, turn right on 15th Ave. NE and then immediately left on NE Ravenna Blvd. After two blocks, turn right on Brooklyn Ave. NE. The main entrance to the park will be on your right. Free street parking is available on Brooklyn Ave. NE and on adjacent residential streets.

BY BUS Ravenna Ave. NE/Ravenna Pl. NE; 25th Ave. NE/NE 55th St.; University Wy. NE/NE Ravenna Blvd.

Shaped like a boomerang and spanning fifty-eight joint acres, Ravenna Park and Cowen Park merge together seamlessly, creating miles of quiet, wooded trails. Carved out of a ravine that was formed by runoff from glacial ice, the parks allow us to imagine what the area must have looked like before logging cleared out most of the trees in this part of North Seattle.

Lucky for us, this land was preserved by William and Louise Beck, who owned a large swath and named it Ravenna because they thought it resembled the Italian town known for its pine trees. It became a popular privately owned tourist and picnicking destination—admission was twenty-five cents in 1902. Charles Cowen, a British immigrant, owned forty acres to the west of the Becks' land. He donated a piece of it to the city in 1907, and the rest of Ravenna Park was purchased by Seattle in 1911.

The 1930s Cowen Park Bridge graces the sky above hiking trails.

Puzzle over this—one of the first things the city did after it took ownership of the parks was to cut down most of the old-growth trees. Today you can still look up into a canopy of giant second-growth pines, hemlocks, and cedars as you explore these parks on foot and get a taste of what must have been an amazing forest that covered much of our city.

The heart of the parks is a wide gravel trail running east–west that begins near Ravenna Park's playground and stretches to the open fields of Cowen Park. This central vein is the best way to accompany Ravenna Creek as it babbles along. Salmonberry bushes and ferns are lush in the forest's understory. Most of the parks' trails have trail markers indicating the direction to Cowen

Park and also to numerous side trails that lead to other exits from the parks to adjacent residential streets.

An interesting feature of the parks is the pair of overhead bridges that cross the central trail. Both are on the National Register of Historic Places and are Seattle historic landmarks. The Ravenna Park Bridge (also known as 20th Avenue Northeast Bridge) is a one-hundred-year-old bridge now only for pedestrians and bikes. The Cowen Park Bridge, dating to 1936 (also known as the 15th Avenue Northeast Bridge), is open to cars and features art deco lampposts.

A great section for hiking with kids is near the Ravenna Park baseball/softball fields at the park's most southeastern edge. A short trail begins beside the field and offers kids the chance to find hidden benches, little footbridges, poetry, and rock art. This is also where you can see recent efforts to daylight parts of Ravenna Creek after it was diverted underground by city engineers—again, shortly after the park was established.

Take a steep flight of stairs up from the ball field to reach Ravenna Park's fabulous playground. A large play structure challenges kids with rope bridges, nets, and slides. You'll also find a twisting climbing apparatus, a big sandbox, and swings. A large flat lawn borders the play area, offering space for games of Frisbee and soccer or picnicking, which is also possible on several nearby tables. Sharp-eyed kids will be able to spot three mosaic sea turtles resting in the grass. A tree with enormous branching roots is another fun place to play. You'll also find restrooms, tennis courts, and a seasonal wading pool (out of operation some years) in this area of Ravenna Park.

A trail on the northwest side of the playground provides the quickest access on foot to reach Ravenna Park's picnic area with barbecue grills, a reservable shelter, and more restrooms. Continue from here to Cowen Park to get to a basketball court and—just on the other side of the Cowen Park Bridge—another great playground with a large climbing structure, zip line, tall swings, merry-go-round, and sandbox. Don't miss the large sundial demonstrating the position of the solstices.

Take the stairs to the top of the building holding restrooms for a view down onto Cowen Park's open fields, which are popular for picnicking and sunbathing.

52   RAVENNA-ECKSTEIN PARK

*Community center park
abounds with activities
for all ages*

Location: 6535 Ravenna Ave. NE; Ravenna
Acreage: 3.1
Amenities: Playground, community center,
0.2 mile of paved paths, restrooms, full basketball
court, tennis court, tennis/wall ball/racquetball
backboard, P-Patch

GETTING THERE

BY CAR From I-5 northbound, exit at NE 65th St. At the intersection take a
slight left on 8th Ave. NE and continue three blocks. Turn right on NE 65th St.;
after 0.8 mile, turn left on Ravenna Ave. NE. After half a block turn left into a
small parking lot.

From I-5 southbound, take exit 171 and continue on 6th Ave. NE. Follow to
the left as it becomes NE 71st St. and crosses over the freeway. Turn immediately right on 8th Ave. NE and continue for five blocks. Turn left on NE 65th St.
and follow the preceding directions to the parking lot. Free parking is available
in the lot, in an additional small lot off 21st Ave. NE, and on Ravenna Ave. NE.

BY BUS NE 65th St./21st Ave. NE; NE 65th St./Ravenna Ave. NE.

Two play areas at this park offer up plenty of amusement for kids from toddler
to teenager. First, challenge your tweens and teens to an ascent on the twisted
metal climbing wall that looks like a piece of art. Younger kids will be occupied
with swings, a tire swing, and spinning toys here.

For more options, take the paved path toward the community center. Along
the walkway are markers that demonstrate previously held world records for
the pole vault, long jump, and triple jump—each now broken, but impressive
nonetheless.

A second play area close to the community center—where you can use the
restrooms during operating hours—has a large wooden structure packed with
slides, rings, and rope ladders. A smaller version for toddlers and preschoolers resembles a miniature fort.

A full basketball court and tennis court close by provide more opportunities to be active. The exterior wall of the community center functions as a

backboard for tennis, racquetball, or wall ball—a rare feature in Seattle parks. Ravenna-Eckstein Park is also a great place for young kids on bikes. A short paved path loops the flat lawn within eyesight of picnic tables and benches. At the far north end, you can examine a sweet little community P-Patch.

EXTEND YOUR VISIT

Get some more playground time in at **Froula Playground**, a 0.7-mile walk away. Exit the park at its north end and turn left to head west six blocks on Northeast 68th Street. At Roosevelt High School, turn right on 15th Avenue Northeast and continue three blocks. Turn left on Northeast 70th Street and turn immediately right on 14th Avenue Northeast. At the end of the block find the path and follow it to the left to reach another playground with a play structure, swings, sandbox, and merry-go-round, as well as a tennis court and picnic tables.

53 DAHL PLAYFIELD

Skateboarders, athletes, and waders delight in Wedgwood greenspace

Location: 7700 25th Ave. NE (near NE 80th St.); Wedgwood
Acreage: 14.5
Amenities: Playground, baseball/softball fields, soccer fields, skate park, seasonal wading pool, restrooms, half basketball court, benches, picnic tables

GETTING THERE

BY CAR From either direction of Lake City Wy. NE, turn east on NE 82nd St. and drive 0.4 mile. Turn right on Ravenna Ave. NE, which becomes 25th Ave. NE; after two blocks the park will appear on the left. Free parking is available in a lot off 25th Ave. NE and along 25th Ave. NE. **BY BUS** 25th Ave. NE/ NE 80th St.

Originally a peat bog affectionately called "Ravenna Swamp" until the 1950s, Dahl Playfield was renamed in honor of Waldo J. Dahl, who served several terms on the Board of Park Commissioners between the 1930s and 1960s.

Athletes young and old come to Dahl Playfield for games on the park's baseball, softball, and soccer fields that fill out the north end of the park. A narrow gravel path connects it to the south end, which is packed with other facilities that draw kids, teens, and adults to this fourteen-acre park.

A wooden tree-fort play structure has a curving slide and ropes and bars that beg to be climbed, while a teeny ground-level fort is perfect for toddlers. A swing set, merry-go-round, and a spinning ring provide plenty of dizzying fun. In the summer, a wading pool fills up with kids splashing and wading while parents, nannies, and grandparents watch from

Boulder Wash *serves as art and a natural play space for kids at this fourteen-acre park.*

benches nearby. The area around the play area and restrooms is paved, and is popular for kids on bikes and scooters.

Across from the play area you'll find John Hoge's *Boulder Wash*, a scattering of large granite stones, some of which are cracked in half and polished.

A four-thousand-square-foot skate park near the middle of Dahl Playfield was completed in 2009 and features a bank, a quarter pipe, ledges, rails, and a set of long stairs. A few steps away from the skate park you'll find a half basketball court and picnic tables.

EXTEND YOUR VISIT

While you're in the neighborhood, don't miss the chance to see one of the biggest glacial erratics in the state. Walk to **Wedgwood Rock**, 0.4 mile away

P-Patches offer city dwellers a chance to grow their own vegetables in community settings.

WHERE DID P-PATCH GET ITS NAME?

It may come as a surprise to many people that "P-Patch" does not refer to a pea-patch, but instead is a term native to Seattle. The *P* comes from Picardo, which is the name of the original Seattle P-Patch. A relic of Seattle's farming past, **Picardo (Rainie) P-Patch**, a block north of Dahl Playfield, was named for Ernesto Picardo and his brothers—Rainie was a nickname for one of the brothers. This family of Italian farmers settled in Seattle and farmed a twenty-acre area in what is now Wedgwood. Part of this land became Seattle's first community garden in the 1970s.

Today Seattle has more than eighty-five neighborhood P-Patches where residents can rent a small plot of land to plant an organic garden. The program is so popular that there are often years-long waiting lists to get a plot. Many say Picardo P-Patch has some of the city's best soil.

by heading south on 25th Avenue Northeast. Turn left on Northeast 75th Street; continue three blocks uphill and turn right on 28th Avenue Northeast. After one block, the erratic is on your left at the intersection with Northeast 72nd Street. This nineteen-foot-tall rock was carried to its location on an ice sheet more than fifteen thousand years ago. Warning: although at one time it was used by members of The Mountaineers for climbing practice, today it is against the law to climb it.

54 MAPLE LEAF RESERVOIR PARK

Creative playground and accessible loop path transform old reservoir

Location: 1020 NE 82nd St.; Maple Leaf
Acreage: 25
Amenities: Playground, 0.5-mile paved walking loop, restrooms, baseball/softball fields, soccer field, picnic tables, reservable shelter, full basketball court, pickleball courts, benches

GETTING THERE
BY CAR From I-5 southbound, exit at NE 80th St.; turn left on NE 80th St. and drive 0.5 mile. Turn left on Roosevelt Wy. NE. After three blocks, the park will be on your right.

From I-5 northbound, exit at Lake City Wy. (State Route 522). Drive 0.5 mile on Lake City Wy. NE. Turn left on 15th Ave. NE; after one block turn left on NE 82nd St. After 0.2 mile, turn right on Roosevelt Wy. NE. The park will be on your right. Free street parking is available on Roosevelt Wy. NE and NE 82nd St.

BY BUS Roosevelt Wy. NE/NE 85th St.; 15th Ave. NE/NE 85th St.; 5th Ave. NE/NE 85th St.

A giant water tower dominates the landscape in the Maple Leaf neighborhood as if directing traffic to its fantastic community park. For decades this area also held a massive reservoir that was off-limits to the public. Thanks to a major project by Seattle Public Utilities in recent years to cover the reservoir—along with several others in the city—this neighborhood now has a big park packed with amenities.

The park is divided into upper and lower sections. Begin at the main entrance to the upper section where a flat path creates good access into the park and a picnic shelter with tables welcomes you. Joggers and dog walkers regularly frequent the paved walking path in the upper section of the park, which features views of downtown Seattle on a clear day. The nearly half-mile loop lends the feeling of strolling in a meadow, with a large natural-grass field taking up most of the park. Short gravel trails veer into the grassy center, tempting you to wander off your circular route. It's hard to imagine you're walking on top of a sixty-million-gallon reservoir.

Look for *Confluent Boulders*, an art installation by Patrick Marold in the southeast end of the loop path. The rocks come from the Cedar River and Tolt River watersheds, both of which feed into the Maple Leaf Reservoir, and dark gray stripes on the path symbolize these sources.

On the opposite side of the loop path, a sports court holds a full basketball court, two pickleball courts, and a short hitting wall for pickleball practice.

Take one of the two staircases down to the lower section of the park—or follow the sidewalk along Roosevelt Way Northeast for an accessible route—where kids will be eager to start playing. Two play structures for younger kids, one shaped like a tree house and one more free-form, command attention in the large play area set on wood chips. As kids start to explore the area further, they'll find rock structures for bouldering, a rock cave, hillside slides, colorful hoops, and a zip line. Nearby, a large sand play area and a butterfly garden are anchored by a black iron pergola. Kids can ride their bikes on a paved path set in a figure eight around the play area. Look for butterfly art hidden around this part of the park.

This area of Maple Leaf Reservoir Park is great for picnicking, with a second covered shelter, tables, and a flat lawn. The park's only restrooms are located near the playground. A path from here leads to the park's two ball fields.

EXTEND YOUR VISIT

Rainbow Point, a little-known viewpoint, is just 0.7 mile away. Walk south from the park along Roosevelt Way Northeast for three blocks. Turn right on Northeast 75th Street and take the next left on 9th Avenue Northeast, which turns into Northeast Banner Place just as this tiny park appears on your left. Two benches provide a perch for views of downtown Seattle and Green Lake in the distance.

55 PINEHURST POCKET PARK

Hidden corner park
provides quiet picnic spot

Location: 11700 19th Ave. NE; Northgate
Acreage: 0.2
Amenities: Concrete riding toy, picnic tables, 0.1 mile of paved paths

GETTING THERE

BY CAR From I-5, exit at NE Northgate Wy. and drive east for 0.5 mile. Turn left on Roosevelt Wy. NE and veer right as it becomes Pinehurst Wy. NE; after 0.5 mile turn right on NE 117th St. After three blocks the park will be on your left at the corner of 19th Ave. NE and NE 117th St. Free street parking is available on both streets. **BY BUS** 15th Ave. NE/NE 115th St.; 15th Ave. NE/NE 120th St.

Tiny Pinehurst Pocket Park offers surprises behind its thick hedge of cistus that buzzes with bees when in bloom in the spring. Enter through one of two entrances at opposite corners of the park, each marked with a pair of basalt columns by artist Sara Mall Johani.

Dense trees and flowering shrubs encircle this cozy North Seattle park.

Follow the flat loop path, partially shaded by two mature fir trees, to discover two other pieces of Johani's work. Kids will want to climb atop the small tractor intended to mimic a local resident's steam tractor that was a common sight in the neighborhood in the 1960s. A faded round patio is imprinted with children's games to encourage play.

Pinehurst Pocket Park was previously the garden for an adjacent house and became a park in 2007. Read the information placards to learn more about the people and landscape of this corner of Seattle when it was heavily forested. Then pull out your picnic basket and have lunch on one of the two tables while you enjoy this quiet sanctuary.

EXTEND YOUR VISIT

Bike or drive 0.4 mile to clamber on the play equipment at **Pinehurst Playground**. (Walking is possible, but this area lacks sidewalks.) Go north on 19th Avenue Northeast for one block. Turn left on Northeast 120th Street and continue four blocks. Turn right on 14th Avenue Northeast. The park will be immediately on your left. The play area, accessible through a paved ramp, includes a challenging climbing structure for older kids, a midsized climber with tunnels and slides, and a swing set. You'll also find a ball field, picnic tables, and barbecue grills.

56   LITTLE BROOK PARK

Tot to tween playground and picnic tables mark quaint neighborhood spot

Location: 14043 32nd Ave. NE; Lake City
Acreage: 0.9
Amenities: Playground, 0.1 mile of paved and unpaved paths, restrooms, picnic tables, benches

GETTING THERE

BY CAR From Lake City Wy. NE (SR 522), turn west on NE 143rd St. and drive one block. Turn left on 32nd Ave. NE. The park will be on your right halfway down the block. Limited free street parking is available on 32nd Ave. NE. **BY BUS** 30th Ave. NE/NE 143rd St.; NE 145th St./30th Ave. NE; Lake City Wy. NE/NE 145th St.

Three play structures, well designed to entertain kids of all ages, will keep young visitors to this Lake City–area park occupied for quite a while. Parents and caregivers are guaranteed to have some leisure time to enjoy the park's shaded picnic area within easy reach of the play area.

Older kids will have the run of a large playground with several platforms connected by bridges and featuring three slides, a rope ladder, and monkey bars. For toddlers and preschoolers there is a small structure with dueling slides, a tunnel, and a spinning tic-tac-toe game. Even the littlest tots can explore a mini structure with handles to help support early walkers. All three structures have little roofs to protect from the sun's rays on a hot sunny day—or unexpected raindrops on others. Behind the large structure you'll also find a swing set with three baby swings and one ADA swing seat.

A short paved path surrounds the play area—perfect for kids on bikes. It meets a gravel trail that brings you to the small trickling stream at the western edge of the park. This tributary of Thornton Creek gives Little Brook Park its name.

57   MATTHEWS BEACH PARK

Lakefront park is favored destination for swimming and picnicking

Location: 5100 NE 93rd St.; Lake City
Acreage: 22
Amenities: Seasonally guarded swimming beach, playground, half basketball court, restrooms, 0.3 mile of paved and unpaved paths, barbecue grills, picnic tables, benches

GETTING THERE

BY CAR From Lake City Wy. NE (SR 522), turn east on NE 95th St. and drive for 1.3 miles. At the T intersection, turn right on Sand Point Wy. NE; take the next left on NE 93rd St. Turn left into the free parking lot. **BY BUS** Sand Point Wy. NE/NE 93rd St. **BY BIKE** The Burke-Gilman Trail runs adjacent to the park.

THE CITY'S GREAT URBAN PATHWAY

The most popular paved biking trail in Seattle, the **Burke-Gilman Trail**, was first a railway line built by Thomas Burke and Daniel Gilman in 1885. After the railroad was abandoned, Seattle residents fought to have it preserved as a public right-of-way, and it was opened as a trail in the 1970s. The 19.8-mile trail begins near Golden Gardens Park in Ballard and follows the ship canal and eastern shore of Lake Washington to Blyth Park in Bothell, where it connects to the 10-mile Sammamish River Trail. Many bicyclists use it as the primary route for their daily commute, but it's also a popular spot for weekend recreation. Bike, walk, run, scooter, or skate along the Burke-Gilman Trail for lake views and the opportunity to access many parks that sit near it.

Take advantage of Matthews Beach Park's several barbecue grills for dinner with a view of Lake Washington.

Matthews Beach Park is one of the few swimming beaches on Lake Washington in North Seattle, so it's regularly packed with swimmers, waders, and sunbathers on summer weekends. And its location just off the Burke-Gilman Trail makes it temping for bikers and joggers to detour to the park for a dip in the lake on a sunny day.

The park's flat lawn is accessible from the parking lot by a paved path and provides a large picnic and sunbathing area with views of the water and the Eastside. Swimmers can venture out to a platform with diving boards, while kids dig in a small stretch of sandy beachfront. And families can barbecue dinner on one of several grills scattered throughout the park along with picnic tables.

A playground lies just uphill from the beach and is dominated by a large climbing structure with a tall tube slide, tunnel, climbing wall, and rope ladders. A tot-sized climber has tunnels and short slides. With a merry-go-round, swings, small zip line, sandbox, spring rider toys, and slack-lining challenge, kids will be plenty busy. But don't let them miss the bridge that leads to a wooden fort with lake views. Teens will find a half basketball court appealing.

A great spot for picnicking with more privacy is above the play area, where tables and a barbecue grill are placed under mature evergreen trees. A paved path leads to the Burke-Gilman Trail from this corner of the park.

Despite its popularity in the summer, perhaps the park's busiest day is January 1, when hundreds of people participate in the annual Polar Bear Plunge into the lake's chilly waters.

On calmer off-season days bird-watching is popular, as is strolling the park's short dirt trails that cross Thornton Creek as it empties into the lake at the south end of the park.

People have been bird-watching, swimming, and sunbathing on this piece of waterfront for more than one hundred years, since John G. Matthews, a lawyer, logging investor, and homesteader, allowed neighbors to use his beach before it became a park.

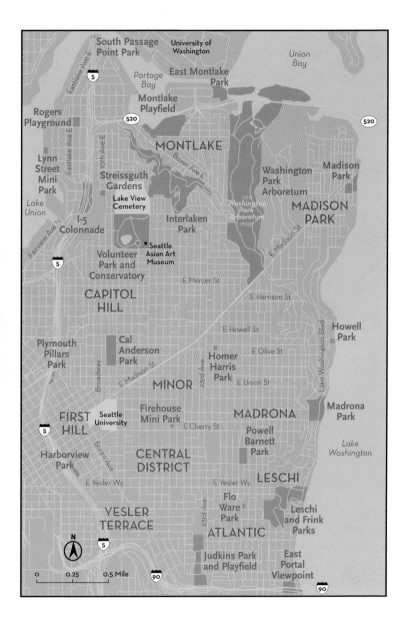

South Passage
Point Park

University of
Washington

Union
Bay

Eastlake Ave E

5

Portage
Bay

East Montlake
Park

Rogers
Playground

Montlake
Playfield

520

520

Eastlake Ave E

10th Ave E

MONTLAKE

Lynn
Street
Mini
Park

Boyer Ave E

Washington
Park
Arboretum

Madison
Park

Lake
Union

Fairview Ave N

Streissguth
Gardens

see
Washington
Park
Arboretum
map

MADISON
PARK

Lake View
Cemetery

I-5
Colonnade

5

Interlaken
Park

Volunteer
Park and
Conservatory

Seattle
Asian Art
Museum

E Madison St

E Mercer St

CAPITOL
HILL

E Harrison St

Plymouth
Pillars
Park

Cal
Anderson
Park

E Howell St

Howell
Park

Broadway

E Madison St

Homer
Harris
Park

E Olive St

Lake Washington Blvd

23rd Ave

E Union St

MINOR

Madrona
Park

FIRST
HILL

Seattle
University

Firehouse
Mini Park

E Cherry St

MADRONA

5

Boren Ave

CENTRAL
DISTRICT

Powell
Barnett
Park

Lake
Washington

Harborview
Park

LESCHI

E Yesler Wy

E Yesler Wy

YESLER
TERRACE

Flo
Ware
Park

Leschi
and Frink
Parks

23rd Ave

ATLANTIC

N

5

Judkins Park
and Playfield

East
Portal
Viewpoint

0   0.25   0.5 Mile

90

90

Capitol Hill & the Central District

58   WASHINGTON PARK ARBORETUM

Superb and diverse gardens invite exploring and walking

Location: 2300 Arboretum Dr. E.; Montlake
Acreage: 230
Amenities: Visitors center, hand-carry boat launches, two playgrounds, 6-plus miles of unpaved trails, 1.2-mile paved multiuse path, baseball/softball fields, soccer/flag football/lacrosse field, batting cages, restrooms, benches

GETTING THERE

BY CAR From downtown Seattle, take I-5 northbound, then follow State Route 520 eastbound, and exit at Montlake Blvd. Go straight through the light to take E. Lake Washington Blvd.; follow as road curves to the right and becomes Lake Washington Blvd. E. After 0.4 mile turn left on E. Foster Island Rd.; turn right on Arboretum Dr. E. Free parking is available in a lot in front of the Graham Visitors Center. To reach the Japanese Garden, large playground, and ball fields, park in the lot off Lake Washington Blvd. E. at

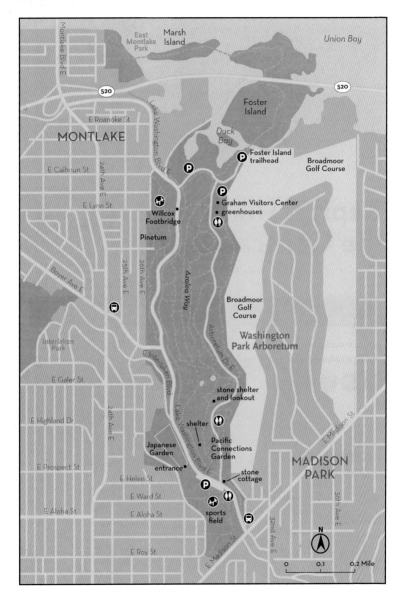

the south end of the park. **BY BUS** E. Madison St./Lake Washington Blvd. E.; 24th Ave. E./Boyer Ave. E.

With twenty thousand trees, shrubs, and vines, this park holds one of the most varied and precious collections of plant species on the West Coast. The Arboretum contains plants native to the Northwest as well as ones quintessential in the landscapes of several other countries around the globe. More than 130 plants found in the park are endangered, making this collaboration between the City of Seattle and University of Washington an important horticultural collection.

This long, slender park stretches nearly a mile and a half from Union Bay at its north end to East Madison Street at its south. The Puget Mill Company, the previous landowners, logged the area for its biggest trees, but much of the native underbrush and smaller trees were left undisturbed. Seeing that the land had tremendous potential value as a park, the city acquired it through a swap with the logging company in 1900. A few years later the Olmsteds began to lay out Lake Washington Boulevard, cutting through the park lengthwise, which led to their influence in the rest of the park's design.

Trapping, shooting, and archery were all proposed, and later abandoned, as recreational pursuits for the park. It wasn't until the University of Washington suggested a partnership with the city in 1924 that it became a botanical garden.

LEAFY LAKESIDE THOROUGHFARE

In the 1890s Seattle engineer R. H. Thomson (whom we can also thank for the Lake Washington Ship Canal, the Chittenden Locks, the Cedar River watershed, paved streets, sidewalks, and our sewer system) and his assistant George Cotterill designed a bicycle route that hugged the shoreline of Lake Washington. Later widened to hold carriages and finally paved for cars, **Lake Washington Boulevard** was then transformed by the Olmsteds into a 116-acre open space that cuts through some of our city's most scenic parks, including the Washington Park Arboretum and Madrona, Leschi, Frink, Colman, and Genesee parks. Today walkers, runners, and bikers take advantage of the 9-mile route from Montlake Boulevard to Seward Park that boasts views of the lake, Mount Rainier, and the Cascade Mountains.

The Japanese Garden at the Arboretum was constructed with help from local Japanese-American gardeners.

Today the Arboretum is still used for research by students and faculty at the university, and the park draws many types of visitors to its year-round gardens, although spring and fall are the most spectacular seasons for colorful displays of flowers and leaves.

Avid gardeners find an unmatched array of flora gracefully laid out into smaller gardens, each featuring a particular species, such as rhododendrons, Japanese maples, pines, camellias, birches, viburnums, and much more. Stop in at the Graham Visitors Center for maps detailing the best trees and plants on display for the month as well as information about plant sales, guided walks, and classes.

The Japanese Garden, built in 1959 on the west side of Lake Washington Boulevard East, is open seasonally (charges a small entrance fee; hours vary) and is renowned for its design, with stone lanterns and bridges set among carefully tended plants and trees, including many azaleas, camellias, Japanese maples, and flowering cherries.

Urban hikers will delight in the miles of quiet unpaved trails. Begin on Azalea Way, a wide gravel path lit up with color in the spring, and then climb up the eastern hillside to follow the ridge to the park's highest point. Look for the stone shelter built in 1938 with great views of the foliage in the park below. Another structure dating to the same era is the stone cottage at the south end of the park, which was intended to be housing for the park's gatekeeper. For a bike-, stroller-, and wheelchair-friendly option, check out the new 1.2-mile paved path scheduled to be completed in late 2017.

Photographers will want to pull out their tripods to capture the landscape, and especially popular spots are around the park's placid ponds. Shutter-happy parents also flock here in the fall to position their children among the piles of vibrantly colored leaves carpeting the park. If you have kids along, don't miss the chance to take the graceful Willcox Footbridge, built in 1912, across Lake Washington Boulevard East, where you'll find a small playground with slides and a mini climbing wall on the west side of the park. Nearby are secluded sections of lawn that are nice for picnics or games of Frisbee. You'll find a larger playground near the ball fields in the farthest-south end of the park.

EXTEND YOUR VISIT

Turn your visit into a longer excursion with excellent opportunities for bird-watching by tacking on a noteworthy 2-mile roundtrip walk through the wetlands to visit Foster Island and Marsh Island and connect to **East Montlake Park**. Pick up the trail just north of the visitors center off Foster Island Road and follow signs toward Foster Island.

59 MADISON PARK

Sunbathing and water play characterize posh neighborhood's marquee park

Location: 4201 E. Madison St.; Madison Park
Acreage: 8.3
Amenities: Seasonally guarded swimming beach, seasonal bathhouse, indoor rental facility, playground, tennis courts, restrooms, benches, picnic tables

GETTING THERE

BY CAR From downtown/First Hill, take Madison St. east for 3.1 miles. At the intersection with 42nd Ave. E. the park will appear on the right. Free street parking is available on E. Madison St., 42nd Ave. E., E. Blaine St., and 43rd Ave. E. **BY BUS** 43rd Ave. E./E. Blaine St.

All roads in this quaint neighborhood seem to converge on its signature park. With a fantastic playground and wide Lake Washington shoreline, Madison Park welcomes throngs of kids, teens, and adults on hot summer days.

The park is divided into two sections by 43rd Avenue East, with the beach to the east and two tennis courts and the playground to the west. The play area is packed with diversions, from swings and a zip line to several climbing structures, including one designed for toddlers and challenging equipment for older kids. Large stones shaped like animals are fun for kids to clamber on. Groupings of benches and picnic tables surround the playground next to an expansive lawn.

Summer weather draws people from all over the city to swim and play in the sand at this Lake Washington beachfront park.

Cross the street to reach the sandy shore, which was the most popular beach in the city in the late 1800s. A cable car once whisked people (every two minutes on the weekend) from downtown to the park's waterfront to spend the day enjoying amusement rides, drinking in beer halls, listening to music from a floating bandstand, and even gambling.

The pursuits are more limited these days, but the beach remains immensely popular. Serious swimmers enjoy the broad swimming lane, approximately five hundred feet long. An island platform offshore with two diving boards entices teenagers. On the north side twenty- and thirtysomethings take advantage of a gently sloping hillside to maximize catching rays. Families flock to the beach's south end for the sandy area that draws kids for hours of digging pleasure.

EXTEND YOUR VISIT

If you're looking for a quieter sunbathing spot, walk two blocks north along 43rd Avenue East to **Madison Park North Beach**. Here you'll have benches, a swing set, and a wide stretch of waterfront lawn to yourself to enjoy views of the lake.

60 HOWELL PARK

Secluded Lake Washington beachfront is escape from bustle

Location: 1740 Howell Pl. near E. Howell St. and Lake Washington Blvd. (325 feet south of Viretta Park); Madrona
Acreage: 0.9
Amenities: Unguarded beach, 0.1 mile of unpaved trails

GETTING THERE

BY CAR From downtown/First Hill, take Madison St. east for 2.1 miles. Turn right on Lake Washington Blvd. E. After 0.9 mile, the park's nearest intersection at E. Howell St. will appear on the left. Limited free street parking is available on Lake Washington Blvd. E. Walk one hundred feet east to reach park entrance.
BY BUS Madrona Dr./E. Olive St.

One of our city's best hidden beaches, this park delivers privacy and solitude on all but the busiest summer days. Howell Park is very difficult to find if you're not onto its secret location off busy Lake Washington Boulevard near several other better-known parks. At the entrance to the park you'll spot the start of a narrow dirt trail. Follow this steep path as it winds down among trees and shrubs and opens onto a wide, gently sloping lawn. Look out to views of Bellevue and the Cascade Mountains and watch busy boat traffic pass by.

Swimming and picnicking are the main activities here. Enter the lake—at your own risk as there are no lifeguards—for a swim from the rocky shoreline, where you'll also see miniature well-tended gardens worth examining. Lay out your blanket in the sunshine or seek shade under the large cedar trees. Because of the park's secluded nature, it's not uncommon to see people swimming or sunbathing nude here.

As you leave, seek out a second trail that meanders up to an even more hidden entrance and exit for the park slightly farther south. The park and nearby street get their names from Captain Jefferson D. Howell, best known for being the brother-in-law of Jefferson Davis, president of the Confederate States. Howell and his ship, as well as more than 250 crew and passengers, were lost at sea in 1875 off Cape Flattery.

EXTEND YOUR VISIT

If a sandy beach with companionship is more your style, walk 0.2 mile north along Lake Washington Boulevard East to **Denny Blaine Park**, where you'll find a slightly larger beach with similar lake and mountain views. Along the way you'll also

Little-known Howell Park basks in a pink glow before a midday summer thunderstorm.

pass **Viretta Park** on your left, a popular spot for vigils for Kurt Cobain, who lived in a mansion nearby.

61 HOMER HARRIS PARK

Playful sculptures and Seattle history on display at neighborhood picnic spot

Location: 2401 E. Howell St.; Central District
Acreage: 0.5
Amenities: Sculptural play area, barbecue grills, picnic tables, benches, chessboards

GETTING THERE

BY CAR From downtown/First Hill, take Madison St. east for 1.4 miles. Turn right on 23rd Ave.; after one block turn left on E. Olive St. Turn immediately left on 24th Ave. The park will be halfway down the block on the right. Free street parking is available on 24th Ave. and on E. Howell St. **BY BUS** 23rd Ave./E. Pine St.; E. Madison St./23rd Ave.

Intricate sculptures add a decorative and playful touch to this park, perched on a hillside overlooking the Madison Valley. Mischievous creatures line the paved walking path as you enter the park at the northwest corner. Nearby, an area softened by wood chips encourages kids to climb on other mystical animals.

Locals use the park for picnics and barbecues—there's a grill, metal tables, and plenty of grass to spread out on. The park's circular patio is a nice place to linger and look east toward views of the Cascade Mountains.

Read the decorative leaves lining a curving pathway at the south end of the park to get acquainted with Dr. Homer Harris and learn more about the history of Seattle and the many contributions of its black residents, several of whom also have parks named in their honor in the Central District. It's interesting to learn that 45,000 African Americans moved to the Northwest between 1940 and 1950 to work in various industries, and the population of blacks in the city increased dramatically.

Harris was a Seattle dermatologist and local football legend who died in 2007. Stimson Bullitt, who died in 2009, gave the city $1.3 million to honor Homer with this park. Appropriately, the park sits on land once owned by William Grose, one of Seattle's first black pioneers, who paid $1,000 in gold to Henry Yesler for twelve acres that included this plot.

EXTEND YOUR VISIT

Walk 0.2 mile down the hill to **Plum Tree Park**. Take East Howell Street two blocks east, continue down the staircase, and turn right on 26th Avenue to reach the park's entry—marked by a plum tree—and follow the paved path, which is lined with lavender and other flowering shrubs. You'll find a small tree-house-inspired playground and views of the valley.

62   MADRONA PARK

*Restored forest, creek
trails, and swimming
beach echo the past*

Location: 853 Lake Washington Blvd. (bordered
by E. Spring St., 38th Ave.); Madrona
Acreage: 31.2
Amenities: Seasonally guarded swimming beach,
bathhouse, 0.8 mile of unpaved trails, restrooms,
barbecue grills, picnic tables, benches, reservable
shelter

GETTING THERE

BY CAR From Pioneer Square, drive east on Yesler Wy. through the Central
District. Turn left on 32nd Ave.; follow road for 0.5 mile as it becomes Lake Dell
Ave. and then E. Alder St. Turn left on Lake Washington Blvd. After 0.4 mile
turn right into the free parking lot. **BY BUS** Madrona Park/Lake Washington
Blvd.; 34th Ave./E. Marion St.

Stand at the shoreline of this unassuming park and imagine that more than
120 years ago you would have been looking at a hotel, dance pavilion, boat
dock, and refreshment stand. You would have probably arrived by trolley
through the Madrona ravine for a day of recreation by the lake.

Today people arrive by car, bus, bike, or on foot along Lake Washington
Boulevard to while away some hours swimming and picnicking in a more
simple setting. An accessible paved path curls around the large sand area on
Madrona Park's south shore where kids love to dig and play among the rocks
and logs that look like a dry streambed.

The beach stretches along the length of the park, with a segment set aside
in the summer for swimming. Kids splash in the shallow waters, serious swimmers do laps, and the thrill seekers leap from the two island platforms. A
handsome brick building makes up the backdrop and houses a dance company as well as a seasonal bathhouse. Bellevue's skyline and the Cascade
Mountains shine to the east.

This is a popular place for picnicking, with several groupings of tables and
barbecue grills in the middle of the park, where trees provide shade and areas

of lawn extend for games. Stroll to the north end near the water and look for the narrow entrance to a short trail leading through a restored creek bed.

Just under a mile of trails hide in the hillside above the waterfront on the other side of Lake Washington Boulevard. You'll find two entrances to the network of trails from the boulevard—one at the north end of the park and the other near the dance studio. Both feature trickles of water from Madrona Creek and a canopy of bigleaf maples. These woods were choked with invasive species for decades before neighbors began a large restoration effort in the 1990s, which involved planting native trees and shrubs and building new paths. Many species of birds, including the occasional bald eagle, now call the woods home.

EXTEND YOUR VISIT

Convince your kids to continue to climb up the hill with the bribe of a great playground waiting at the top. Exit the top of the park's main trail at East Marion Street and 38th Avenue and follow the trails, sidewalks, and staircases along East Marion Street uphill for four blocks. At 34th Avenue, **Madrona Playground** will appear on your right. It features a large play area with wooden climbing structures, a sandbox, and swings, as well as tennis courts, picnic tables, and a grass field.

63   POWELL BARNETT PARK

Bonanza of play at gathering spot for toddlers to teens

Location: 352 Martin Luther King Jr. Wy.; Central District/Leschi
Acreage: 4.4
Amenities: Playground, adult fitness equipment, seasonal wading pool, full and half basketball courts, restrooms, 0.4 mile of paved paths, picnic tables, barbecue grills, benches

GETTING THERE

BY CAR From Pioneer Square, drive east on Yesler Wy. through the Central District. Turn left on Martin Luther King Jr. Wy. and continue two blocks. The park will be on your right. Free street parking is available on Martin Luther King Jr. Wy. **BY BUS**

Martin Luther King Jr. Wy./E. Alder St.; E. Yesler Wy./28th Ave. S.

Kids pack into the biggest and most exhilarating playground in Seattle's Central District to zip down steep slides, tackle tough climbing walls, and summit sky-high climbing nets.

The park's huge playground features dozens of ways to entertain children, including a large and challenging climbing structure, a net climbing dome, spring rider toys, and swings. Several small climbing toys, including a colorful fire truck, are designed for kids under five.

A wading pool behind the park's castle-shaped restrooms gets plenty of use on warm summer days. Teens and adults take advantage of a basketball court that includes a full court, a half

Several different climbing structures offer kids of all ages challenging fun at this fantastic Central District park.

court, and a short-height hoop. The park is a nice picnic spot for people who live nearby, with several cozy areas that have tables and barbecue grills.

The park's flat paved paths are accommodating to wheelchairs and also make a pleasant loop for neighborhood dog walkers and joggers. Other exercise options are the fitness stations set around the play area to encourage parents and caregivers to get their heart rates up—something kids have no trouble doing here.

Powell Barnett was a musician, star athlete, and community leader who helped found the Seattle Urban League and fought for racial integration. His granddaughter helped secure funding to make significant improvements to the park, which were completed in 2006.

EXTEND YOUR VISIT

For a peaceful escape from playground stimulation, walk 0.3 mile to **Nora's Woods**. From the northwest corner of the park, head north on Martin Luther King Jr. Way for one block. Turn right on East Cherry Street and go one and a half blocks, then turn left on 29th Avenue. At the end of the block on the right you'll find a wooded corner lot with short trails leading to quiet sitting areas.

64   LESCHI AND FRINK PARKS

Network of hillside trails attracts hikers

Location: Leschi Park: 201 Lakeside Ave. S.; Frink Park: 398 Lake Washington Blvd. S.; Leschi
Acreage: 18.5 (Leschi), 17.2 (Frink)
Amenities: Restrooms, swings, tennis court, 1.3 miles of unpaved trails, boat moorage, dock, hand-carry boat launch

GETTING THERE

BY CAR From Pioneer Square, drive east on Yesler Wy. through the Central District. Turn left on 32nd Ave.; follow road for 0.5 mile as it becomes Lake Dell Ave. and then E. Alder St. Turn right on Lake Washington Blvd., and continue straight as road becomes Lakeside Ave. S. After three hundred feet turn left into the small parking lot. Free parking is available in the lot and on Lakeside Ave. S. **BY BUS** Lakeside Ave. S./E. Yesler Wy.; Lakeside Ave. S./S. Leschi Pl.; 31st Ave. S./S. King St.; S. Jackson St./30th Ave. S.

Resting along the shores of Lake Washington, this area was first a seasonal settlement for the Duwamish tribe and received regular visits from the Nisqually tribe's leader, Chief Leschi. Clashes over land rights led to the Battle of Seattle downtown in 1856, which killed two white settlers. Leschi was held responsible for the killings and was executed two years later. (He was exonerated in 2004.)

Within a few decades the site had undergone a dramatic transformation, becoming a recreation destination with a dance pavilion, casino, and zoo, attracting people from throughout the region. A cable car ascended the steep hillside through what is now Leschi and Frink parks.

With dares from their friends, kids courageously dive from the pier at Leschi Park.

Today the parks are stripped back to their more natural states, although hints of their past remain, including bridges that supported the cable cars. Begin your exploration at the lower end of Leschi Park where a rolling hillside displays manicured flower beds and stately trees, including a giant sequoia planted by former parks superintendent Jacob Umlauff.

The trails connecting Leschi Park to Frink Park are disjointed, and it's helpful to consult the trail map found online (a couple are also posted in kiosks at corners of the parks). For the most straightforward route, turn right at the restrooms and pass the tennis court and grass field. Pick up the trail on the right side of the old cable car bridge, where you will soon cross Lake Washington Boulevard South. The wooded trails weave up the hillside into Frink Park, crossing the Olmsted-designed boulevard at several locations.

The land for Frink Park was donated to the city in 1907 by John M. Frink, a former state senator. The paths were created in 1909 for the Alaska-Yukon-Pacific Exposition. The highlight of a hike here is the small waterfall that spills down a rocky creek bed and under the decorative bridge. The remains of a caretaker cottage, now nearly hidden among the trees and brush, is another destination worth a stop.

After you return to lower Leschi Park, you can check out a swing set tucked up a short trail near the restrooms or cross the street to find three benches with water views. Today the Leschi dock is used for launching kayaks and fishing. A century ago it was the launching point for steam ferries—including one bearing the name *Leschi*—that crossed Lake Washington to the Eastside.

EXTEND YOUR VISIT

A spectacular viewpoint at **Leschi-Lake Dell Natural Area** is a steep 0.5-mile walk away. Head north on Lakeside Avenue South for three blocks and turn left on East Terrace Street. Continue two and a half blocks and at the dead end, take the stairs up the hill, where you'll see the park immediately on your left. Follow the wood-chip trail to a spot where wide views of Lake Washington, the Bellevue skyline, and the Cascade Mountains will make up for burning lungs.

65 FLO WARE PARK

Tribute to beloved community member means play

Location: 2800 S. Jackson St.; Central District/ Atlantic
Acreage: 0.5
Amenities: Playground, half basketball court, picnic tables, chessboards, barbecue grill, benches

GETTING THERE

BY CAR From Pioneer Square, drive east on S. Jackson St. for 1.1 miles. The park will appear on your left at 28th Ave. S. Free street parking is available on 28th Ave. S. and on S. Jackson St. **BY BUS** S. Jackson St./28th Ave. S.; Martin Luther King Wy. S./S. Jackson St.

Florasina Ware—a community activist for youth and education—holds court at the entrance to the park that bears her name on a cozy corner in the Central District. Ware's photo tops a colorful mosaic entryway created by local kids with quotes imploring visitors to build community.

More wise words are underfoot as you walk the park's concrete pathways, which are friendly to strollers and wheelchair users.

Ware passed away in 1981, but there's no doubt that the former foster parent to twenty children would have enjoyed seeing kids at play on the park's two climbing structures. Several slides, climbing walls, and a twisting ladder are designed to occupy older kids. A swing set that includes a baby swing and accessible swing sits nearby.

A round plaza in the center of the park holds three metal benches, two picnic tables (inlaid with chessboards), and a barbecue grill. At the north end, a paved area with a half basketball court, four square, and hopscotch offers more reasons to stay. A flat, partially shaded lawn is a welcome spot for all ages to play or picnic.

66   EAST PORTAL VIEWPOINT

Vantage point shows off bridge, water, and mountain views

Location: 1400 Lake Washington Blvd. S. (bordered by S. Irving St., Lakeside Ave. S.); Leschi
Acreage: 7
Amenities: Benches, connections to trails

GETTING THERE

BY CAR From Pioneer Square, drive east on S. Jackson St. for 1.4 miles. Turn right on 31st Ave. S.; after two blocks turn left on S. Lane St. Take the next right on 32nd Ave. S. and then take the next left on S. Dearborn St. After two blocks turn right on Lake Washington Blvd. S. and continue 0.4 mile. The park will be on your left. Free street parking is available on Lake Washington Blvd. S. **BY BUS** 31st Ave. S./S. Irving St.; Lakeside Ave. S./S. Day St. **BY BIKE** The I-90 Trail runs through the lower section of the park.

Look out over the roar of traffic on Interstate 90 and marvel at the engineering wonder of floating concrete bridges. What you are seeing are really two separate bridges. The Lacey V. Murrow Memorial Bridge was completed in 1940—it was the largest floating structure in the world at the time (and then was surpassed in length by the 520 bridge to the north)—and was rebuilt after it sank in 1990. Today it carries eastbound traffic.

The Homer M. Hadley Memorial Bridge was built in 1989 and brings cars westbound. Hadley, an engineer and the mastermind behind the Murrow Bridge, convinced Lacey V. Murrow, the head of the state's highway department, that a floating bridge was the best way to overcome Lake Washington's depths.

But lift your eyes from the whiz of cars and trucks long enough to enjoy the views of nature as well. Lake Washington, the Cascade Mountains, and Mount Rainier are on display from this eastern perch of our city.

Start at the park's upper section, where stately columns give

Watch bike and car traffic zoom below or take in views of Lake Washington and the Cascade Mountains from this viewpoint.

the viewpoint a formal flair. Enjoy lunch or a snack on the long, curved concrete bench set among tidy hedges. A plaque boasts of the engineering accomplishments of the Murrow Bridge, a National Historic Civil Engineering Landmark.

Walk down the steep sidewalk along South Irving Street to reach a paved path leading to the lower viewpoint. You're closer to the action from this plaza lined with a metal railing and a solitary bench.

EXTEND YOUR VISIT

The park sits along the **I-90 Trail**, which offers great bike connections west through the Mount Baker Tunnel or east over the I-90 bridge. On foot, you can also descend the stairs near South Irving Street to reach **Day Street Boat Ramp** for more views of the bridge and waterfront access.

67 JUDKINS PARK AND PLAYFIELD

Walking path, skate park, playground, and spray park pull in kids and adults

Location: 2150 S. Norman St.; Central District/Atlantic
Acreage: 18.5
Amenities: Playground, seasonal spray park, skate park, football field, baseball/softball fields, soccer field, 1.1 miles of paved paths, street hockey/bike polo court, full basketball court, restrooms, barbecue grills, reservable shelter, picnic tables, benches

GETTING THERE

BY CAR From Pioneer Square, drive east on S. Jackson St. for 1 mile and turn right on 23rd Ave. S. After five blocks turn right on S. Norman St. The park will appear straight ahead at the end of the block. Free parking is available in two lots off 22nd Ave. S. (one at S. Norman St. and one at S. Judkins St.). **BY BUS** 23rd Ave. S./S. Norman St.; 24th Ave. S./S. Norman St. **BY BIKE** The I-90 Trail runs through the south end of the park.

Laid out as a six-block corridor packed with amenities, this park appeals to users of all ages, offering dozens of opportunities for play. The park gets its name from Norman Judkins, a Seattle realtor in the late 1800s, who named two nearby streets after himself.

The park's paved paths are a well-trafficked walking, biking, and running route that is used as a connection between other parks and trails for commuting and exercise. In the park's northern section, the lighted walkway makes two loops—around the baseball/softball/football fields and around the soccer field.

You'll find a playground in the middle of the park with two structures featuring a spiral slide, suspension bridge, and tunnel, as well as swings and spring rider toys. Benches, restrooms, and a covered shelter with picnic tables are placed nearby.

Venture lower and you'll see the seasonal spray park, where columns spray water onto shrieking kids during summer months. Parents can prep for dinner and keep an eye on the action from a shaded picnic area that has tables and barbecue grills.

Skateboarders of all ages and abilities take advantage of Judkins Park's ten-thousand-square-foot skate park.

Continuing south, cross South Judkins Street to reach a ten-thousand-square-foot skate park. The skate park's circular layout allows you to hit banks, quarter pipes, a vertical wall, hips, and a three-quarter bowl as you make your way around the circuit. This is one of the city's most varied skate parks, making it appealing for both beginners and experienced riders. Also nearby is a converted tennis court now set up for street hockey, bike polo, and other games growing in popularity.

EXTEND YOUR VISIT

Walk the **Central Park Trail** to reach two other great neighborhood parks. From the northwest corner of the park, follow the sidewalk that connects to 20th Place South and passes Washington Middle School on the right. Carefully cross South Jackson Street. **Dr. Blanche Lavizzo Park** comes up immediately on your left. This fully fenced play area is one of the best in the city for kids under five. Continue north on the paved pedestrian trail, where colorful signs overhead point you in the direction of neighborhood destinations. Turn left on South Washington Street and walk one more block west to **Pratt Park**, which features a playground, seasonal spray park, covered basketball court, and restrooms.

68 FIREHOUSE MINI PARK

Imaginative playground evokes historic station

Location: 712 18th Ave. (near E. Cherry St.); Central District/Minor
Acreage: 0.3
Amenities: Playground, benches, picnic tables, drinking fountain

GETTING THERE

BY CAR From Pioneer Square, take Yesler Wy. east for 0.7 mile. Turn left on 18th Ave. After 0.5 mile the park will be on the right. Free street parking is available on 18th Ave. **BY BUS** E. Jefferson St./18th Ave.

Situated next to a former fire station, Firehouse Mini Park plays off this theme, giving kids climbing toys where they can role-play their own fire rescues. Vibrant red-and-yellow metal play equipment resembles a fire truck (complete with a steering wheel) and a fire station (yes, there's a fire pole!). You'll also find swings, a spring rider toy that looks like the dog from the Clifford series, and a merry-go-round.

A paved path creates a semicircle around the play area where young kids can ride bikes while parents watch the fun from wooden benches.

The park is filled with lofty hybrid plane trees that shade nearly the entire space, transporting you away from busy East Cherry Street just 150 feet away. Two picnic tables and a flat lawn deliver tranquil spots to picnic or read a book.

The brick fire station, on the National Register of Historic Places and now housing a human services organization, makes a gorgeous backdrop for this park. Built around 1909, its arched openings were designed for the horse-drawn equipment of that age.

EXTEND YOUR VISIT

Another shaded playground is 0.5 mile away. Walk to **Spruce Street Mini Park** by heading south on 18th Avenue for one and a half blocks. Turn left on East Jefferson Street and continue three blocks. Turn right on 21st Avenue and the park will be on your left after three blocks. This corner park offers a large grass lawn, short paved paths, and a large play area. Look for another Clifford dog and play on his multicolored house.

69 HARBORVIEW PARK

Art and views hide behind busy hospital

Location: Jefferson St. and 8th Ave. (west of Harborview Medical Center); First Hill/Yesler Terrace
Acreage: 0.8
Amenities: Benches, art

GETTING THERE

BY CAR From downtown Seattle, take James St. east up to First Hill. Turn right on 9th Ave., immediately right on Jefferson St., and immediately left on 8th Ave. The park will be on your right. Paid parking is available on Terry Ave. as well as in the parking garage on 8th Ave. between Alder St. and Jefferson St.
BY BUS Jefferson St./9th Ave.

Patients seeking solace will find a stunning view of downtown Seattle and Elliott Bay from peaceful Harborview Park.

Partially blocked by a concrete wall near the emergency room entrance, the park is easy to miss if you aren't an employee or frequent visitor to Harborview Medical Center. Take the steps or ramp down to discover the park's two tiers of lawn and benches, where nurses, doctors, and hospital staff enjoy some sun on their lunch breaks. Nicely tended flower beds with lavender, black-eyed Susan, and roses make for a cheerful respite from the hospital.

The park has several pieces of art worth examining, including a large colorful mural—overseen by artist Kristen T. Ramirez with contributions from Harborview patients—brightening a concrete ramp to the lowest section. You'll also find a couple dozen mixed-media works lining the park's western edge. Created by Seattle youth, this artwork is interactive—peep through the holes on each for a special view. To see several spectacular pieces by T. Ellen Sollod, including a whimsical seating area, follow the sidewalk south toward the parking garage and the hospital's helipad.

70 PLYMOUTH PILLARS PARK

Concrete crossroads serve city dogs and their owners

Location: 1050 Pike St.; Capitol Hill/Downtown
Acreage: 0.6
Amenities: Off-leash dog park, benches, drinking fountain

GETTING THERE

BY CAR From downtown Seattle, drive northeast on Pike St. Less than one block after crossing I-5 the park will be on your left. The entrance to the off-leash dog park is on Boren Ave. between Pine St. and Pike St. Paid street parking is available on sections of Pike St. and on Pine St. **BY BUS** Boren Ave./Pike St.; Convention Place Station.

Four giant limestone columns mimic the skyscrapers in the distance from this park at a busy intersection on the edge of downtown. Take the wide stairs down to a paved patio to examine the pillars, which originally marked the entrance to the old Plymouth Congregational Church at 6th Avenue and University Street before the building was demolished and rebuilt following an earthquake in 1965. Along the steps flowers and vines tumble out of concrete urns. The park has held summer concerts, invigorating this area that bridges the downtown and Capitol Hill neighborhoods.

Puzzling over the location of the dog park? Cross the street and walk half a block northwest on Boren Avenue, where you'll find a sidewalk leading to the fenced off-leash dog area. A second entrance sits on the opposite side of the enclosure, accessible from Pine Street.

Inside the gates, dogs can exercise by running back and forth in the long, narrow play space. The nearly one-fifth-acre space is simple, with a gravel surface, large rocks for climbing, and a small raised platform. One large tree provides some shade in the corner. Owners can rest on the bench or seating along the ledge, and lighting makes the park usable in the evenings. A drinking fountain with three spigots quenches thirst for people and dogs.

The dog park is parallel to a pedestrian walkway that crosses from Boren Avenue to Pine Street, creating a handy connection for commuters and people living nearby. More benches and colorfully planted pots along this path overlook the off-leash area.

71   CAL ANDERSON PARK

Neighborhood hub buzzes around the clock

Location: 1635 11th Ave.; Capitol Hill
Acreage: 11
Amenities: Playground, soccer field, baseball/ softball field, tennis court, full basketball court, ping-pong table, bike polo court, seasonal wading pool, fountain, 1 mile of paved and unpaved paths, reservable shelter house, restrooms, benches, picnic tables

GETTING THERE

BY CAR From downtown Seattle, take Pike St. east toward Capitol Hill; street will become E. Pike St. After 0.4 mile turn left on 11th Ave. Continue one block and the park will be on your left. Paid street parking is available on 11th Ave. **BY BUS** E. Pine St./11th Ave.; Broadway/E. Pine St.; Broadway/E. Denny St. **BY STREETCAR** First Hill line to Broadway/E. Pine St. or Broadway/ E. Howell St. **BY LIGHT RAIL** Capitol Hill Station, one block north of the park.

Of the more than eighty parks and boulevards that the Olmsted Brothers firm contributed to, Cal Anderson has the distinction of being the first park in Seattle that got the famous designers' touch. The Olmsteds envisioned the park for passive enjoyment and even urged the city not to build a baseball field because they believed boys and young men would be encouraged to curse and loaf about.

A city historic landmark, Cal Anderson Park dates back to 1901 when it was originally called Lincoln Park after the Lincoln Reservoir, now concealed, that sat just to the north of the smaller original park. In 2003 the park was named

Cal Anderson Park balances art, recreation, and green space in a dense urban neighborhood.

to honor the state's first openly gay legislator (and a decorated Vietnam War veteran). Today it reflects the energy and diversity of its neighborhood—one of the densest in the city.

Cal Anderson Park pulses with activity all hours of the day. Mornings bring children to the playground's two climbing structures to whiz down slides, hang from monkey bars, and summit climbing walls while parents, grandparents, and nannies rest on benches nearby. Joggers and dog walkers loop the park's flat paths.

In the middle of the day the park attracts Seattle Central Community College students and people working nearby to its benches and lawn for a lunch break. By afternoon soccer and baseball players are warming up for games on the Bobby Morris Playfield, named in honor of a former King County auditor and popular coach. Retirees play chess on oversized boards or practice tai chi. In the evening, the park continues to pull in people for late-night picnics or action-packed games of bike polo.

But the first thing you'll notice on a visit to Cal Anderson Park is the mesmerizing water feature—a cone-shaped fountain designed by Douglas Hollis that spills water into a stream, which then bubbles over square stones before entering a quiet reflecting pool. Along the park's central gravel trail dozens of wooden benches sit back-to-back, providing perches for views of the fountain or the large lawn where picnicking and sunbathing are popular.

Paved and gravel paths travel through the park, creating circuits that are ideal for an easy stroll and lead to the south end, where you'll pass the seasonal wading pool before finding the turf ball fields, a tennis court, full basketball court, and bike polo court.

EXTEND YOUR VISIT

Another innovative use of space is **Summit Slope Park**, 0.5 mile away. From the north end of the park, walk north on 10th Avenue East one block; turn left on East John Street, and continue four blocks (street will become East Olive Way). Turn right on East John Street and the park will be on your right at the end of the street. This quarter of an acre packs in a P-Patch, picnic area with barbecue grill, flat lawn, oversized picnic table, and skateboarding bench.

72   VOLUNTEER PARK AND CONSERVATORY

Renowned hilltop park boasts gardens, art, and Olmsted mark

Location: 1247 15th Ave. E.; Capitol Hill
Acreage: 48.3
Amenities: Historic water tower, conservatory, gardens, Seattle Asian Art Museum, playground, seasonal wading pool, tennis courts, tennis backboard, restrooms, 2 miles of paved and unpaved trails, picnic tables, benches

GETTING THERE

BY CAR From downtown Seattle, drive east on Olive Wy. toward Capitol Hill. Follow as it curves and becomes E. John St. Turn left on 12th Ave. E.; after 0.5 mile turn right on E. Aloha St. After three blocks turn left on 15th Ave. E. The entrance to the park, at E. Highland Dr., will appear on your left after three blocks. Free parking is available inside the park along sections of E. Highland Dr. and Volunteer Park Rd. **BY BUS** 15th Ave. E./E. Highland Dr.; 10th Ave. E./ E. Prospect St.

Originally called City Park but renamed to honor the volunteers involved in the Spanish-American War, this was one of Seattle's first three major public spaces

and dates to 1876 when the city paid only $2,000 for forty acres of land on Capitol Hill.

It was first used as a cemetery before the land was divided and graves were moved to the north side in what is now Lake View Cemetery, leaving the south end for recreation. The Olmsted Brothers had significant involvement with the park in the early 1900s, creating plans for many of the park's signature features, including the conservatory, and many people consider this their exemplary Seattle park.

The best way to get your bearings at Volunteer Park—and learn more about the Olmsteds—is to climb the

Black Sun *by renowned artist Isamu Noguchi perches near the edge of the reservoir at Volunteer Park.*

106 spiraling stairs to the observation platform atop the historic water tower, built just after the turn of the last century. Circle the space and peer out the windows for views of the park seventy-five feet below, as well as panoramic vistas of the city and mountains beyond. Make a second circuit to take in the fascinating signs detailing the history of Seattle's parks system and the role of the Olmsteds in shaping our city.

The rest of Volunteer Park is also set up for strolling in circles. Loop the reservoir, which has many treasures hidden nearby, including small ponds and an impressive monument dedicated to Thomas Burke, former chief justice of the state supreme court and influential early citizen of Seattle. *Black Sun* on the eastern side just across the street from the Seattle Asian Art Museum is hard to miss. Created by the world-famous artist Isamu Noguchi, this granite sculpture looks out over the still water of the reservoir and frames a view of the Space Needle through its dark doughnut shape.

Meander past the statue of William Henry Seward (former US secretary of state) to the Volunteer Park Conservatory where an exquisite collection of rare plants is on display in an elegant building made up of more than three thousand individual panes of glass (charges a small entrance fee; open Tuesday through Sunday from 10:00 AM to 4:00 PM). Completed in 1912, it houses thousands of varieties of unusual plants and flowers, including hundreds of types of orchids. A fun fact: the US Fish and Wildlife Service gives the conservatory plants that are seized from people trying to illegally import them. They can never be sold but can be traded to other botanical gardens.

Perhaps an even more impressive collection of plant life is outside the conservatory. From here, make a large counterclockwise trip around the perimeter of the park to take in the magnificent assembly of mature trees. More than 175 varieties hold court here, including 20 or so that are believed to be the largest of their kind in the state. If you are adept at identifying trees, look for the seventy-plus-foot-tall English hawthorn that is the tallest known hawthorn of this species in the world. Another horticulture highlight is the dahlia garden, on the north side of the Seattle Asian Art Museum. Planted annually, this gorgeous display shows off our city's official flower.

Your loop will end in the northeast corner of the park—the most visited area for families with young kids. The city's first wading pool was built here in 1910 and is still popular on warm summer days. The playground has three play structures, including a big one for older kids with four curving slides, bridges, a climbing wall, and a short zip line. Swings, a sandbox, a mini slide built into the stairs, and musical instruments attract younger children. Parents rest on benches or pull out lunches on the picnic tables set around the play area. Kids can still climb and explore Chas Smith's 1962 bone-shaped sculpture that has seen generations of play at Volunteer Park.

EXTEND YOUR VISIT

Just down the street you'll find more symbols of Seattle's rich history at **Louisa Boren Park**. Walk north 0.2 mile on 15th Avenue East and the park will pop up on your right. Both original settlers, Louisa Boren and David Denny married in 1853. Their wedding is believed to have been the first for non-natives in the city. The park named in her honor has views of Lake Washington and the North Cascades, benches, and a geometric steel sculpture by Lee Kelly.

73 INTERLAKEN PARK

Green canopied ravine awaits runners, bikers, and hikers

Location: 19th Ave. E. and Interlaken Dr. E. (near E. Crescent Dr.); Capitol Hill/Montlake
Acreage: 51.7
Amenities: 1 mile of unpaved trails, 1.5 miles of paved paths and roads

GETTING THERE

BY CAR From downtown/First Hill, take Madison St. east 1.2 miles. Turn left on 19th Ave. and continue 1.1 miles. The park will be straight ahead. Free street parking is available on E. Galer St. **BY BUS** 19th Ave. E./E. Galer St.; 24th Ave. E./ Boyer Ave. E.; Grandview Pl. E./E. Galer St.

Many runners know Interlaken Park as the hilly—and dreaded—22nd mile of the Seattle Marathon. Road bikers frequent the park's curving lane for scenic rides under an umbrella of trees. And hikers in the know enjoy this park's quiet trails among second-growth forest.

Interlaken Park has a long history of providing leisure opportunities for Seattle residents, beginning as a buggy path that connected Capitol Hill to Lake Washington in the 1890s. This was also one of the city's first popular bike routes—picture the old-fashioned bikes with a giant front wheel, which came before the more practical and comfortable modern style we see today. The change in bicycle styles helped kick off the bike craze in Seattle. About one-fifth of all residents around the turn of the last century owned a bike. The Olmsteds recognized the recreational value of this ravine and encouraged the city to preserve the much-coveted land surrounding the boulevard in the early 1900s.

A pleasant tour by bike can be made by starting at the corner of 21st Avenue East and East Interlaken Boulevard and cycling west through the park along the paved bike-and-pedestrian-only path. After 0.4 mile the path will join the road; continue straight to stay on the boulevard as it rounds the sharp curve. Note the fork here and veer right to stay on East Interlaken Boulevard. After another 0.6 mile you'll emerge on Delmar Drive East close to the 520 bridge.

Turn around here and return the way you came, this time veering right at the fork to take Interlaken Drive East, which skirts the southern end of the park.

If you're exploring on foot, enter the park on the corner of Interlaken Drive East and East Crescent Drive and descend the wooden steps into the dense foliage. Hike here in the fall and you'll see spectacular color changes in this mostly deciduous forest thick with ferns. Follow the trail to the left to reach a small clearing where the trails converge and a polished stone with a leaf design is a convenient resting spot. The trail bends to the left again and follows the curvature of the boulevard, which is visible below. At the trail's western end you'll meet the boulevard, which you can use to return to the intersection of the trails, or turn around and find your way back through the maples and cedars.

Even if you're not the exercise-loving type—or have limited mobility—you can still enjoy this park by taking a scenic drive along this beautiful and historic boulevard.

74   STREISSGUTH GARDENS

Hillside garden surprises with year-round blooms

Location: Broadway E. and E. Blaine St. (near 10th Ave. E.); Capitol Hill
Acreage: 1.2
Amenities: Bench, 0.4 mile of unpaved trails

GETTING THERE

BY CAR From I-5 northbound, exit at Lakeview Blvd. and turn left on Lakeview Blvd. E. After 0.1 mile turn slightly right on Harvard Ave. E.; continue for one long block and turn right on E. Boston St. Turn immediately right on Broadway E. After three blocks the park will be on your left.

From I-5 southbound, exit at Boylston Ave./Roanoke St. and merge onto Boylston Ave. E. Take a slight left on Lakeview Blvd. E. Turn immediately left on Harvard Ave. E. and follow the preceding directions. Free street parking is available on Broadway E.

BY BUS 10th Ave. E./E. Howe St.; 10th Ave. E./E. Newton St.

A visit to these lovely gardens is even sweeter when you learn about their origin. Sitting adjacent to the St. Mark's Greenbelt, this north Capitol Hill park began as the private yard of Ann and Dan Streissguth. Fifty years ago they lived as singles on two neighboring pieces of land and each started their own gardens. Over the years they began helping each other plant and prune, then fell in love, got married, and slowly began to merge and grow their gardens.

The Streissguths, together with son Ben, planted new trees and shrubs, cleared away weeds, and built small trails to encourage visitors to explore. In 1996 they deeded the land to the city but still maintain it with the assistance of many neighborhood volunteers.

Now an impressive public park, Streissguth Gardens was originally the private yard of amateur gardeners Ann and Dan Streissguth.

The gardens make up five lots on the south side of the one-hundred-year-old East Blaine Street stairs, which is a popular training spot for runners and hikers. Pick a trail and crisscross the hillside as you discover an impressive variety of trees, plants, flowers, and even fruits and vegetables. Gardeners will enjoy getting ideas for their own backyards as they wander among the sixty-eight trees and nearly three hundred shrubs.

The gardens were carefully designed to be worth a visit in every season. In spring, blooming azaleas and rhododendrons turn the hillside into a colorful scene. Kids will delight in finding hiding places among the thick vegetation in the summer and hunting down ripe wild strawberries that spill out over stone steps. Autumn brings out a wide array of changing foliage on the trees and shrubs. Dan Streissguth says his favorite season is late winter, when he watches the garden for signs of the first blooms of hundreds of crocuses that transform the garden's slope into a silvery purple.

75   I-5 COLONNADE

Previously unused space thrills urban mountain bikers

Location: 1701 Lakeview Blvd. E. (under I-5); Capitol Hill/Eastlake
Acreage: 7.5
Amenities: Mountain bike skills park, off-leash dog park, 0.2 mile of paved paths, benches, picnic tables

GETTING THERE

BY CAR From I-5 northbound, exit at Lakeview Blvd. and turn left on Lakeview Blvd. E. The park will be immediately on your left.

From I-5 southbound, exit at Boylston Ave./Roanoke St. and merge onto Boylston Ave. E. Take a slight left on Lakeview Blvd. E. The park will appear on your right. Free street parking is available on Lakeview Blvd. E. For more convenient parking for the off-leash dog area, you can park on Franklin Ave. E. on the west side of I-5 in the Eastlake neighborhood.

BY BUS Eastlake Ave. E./E. Garfield St.; Eastlake Ave. E./E. Newton St.

There's no way to miss the sounds of traffic barreling overhead on I-5, but the legions of mountain bikers testing their limits at this clever park don't mind as they cross wooden bridges and dodge concrete pillars that hold up the freeway above. The park gets its name from these mighty columns. This unusual park, which opened in 2005, provides urban recreation in an area previously chained off and marked "No Trespassing" for decades.

For a look at the variety of amenities tucked under the freeway, walk the path that bisects the north end of the park. This paved walking and biking trail provides a convenient route for commuters and exercisers, linking Capitol Hill and Eastlake. From the path, turn south to cross a segment of the East Howe Street stairs—a favorite exercise route and the longest staircase in the city. You can take the stairs down to get to a small picnic area where you'll find benches and tables. Or continue on the paved path to reach an unexpected art installation. Blue lights cast a mysterious glow and water trickles down on several tightly planted trees in *Seventh Climate* by John Roloff.

Signs will point you to the north entrance to the off-leash dog area (a second entrance is at the south end just off Franklin Avenue East). On first glance the dog park looks deceivingly small, but it is laid out like a series of connected square rooms, totaling 1.2 acres. With excellent protection from rain in bad weather and a variety of doggie distractions, including stairs, gravel paths, and open play areas, the park draws dog owners from surrounding neighborhoods and other parts of the city.

If you are on foot, stay off the dirt mountain biking trails and stick to the paved path. But several spots provide views of the high-speed action as bikers take on a huge variety of terrain over two acres in this skills park. One of the first in the country, it was built in partnership with the Evergreen Mountain Bike Alliance. Novices can start on the interpretive trail, where helpful signs explain how to master each of the course's challenges. More-skilled riders take on the switchback loop, jump lines, and bridges. A pump track is popular with all ages and abilities.

76   LYNN STREET MINI PARK

Waterfront pocket gives close-up of Lake Union

Location: 2291 Fairview Ave. E.; Eastlake
Acreage: 0.1
Amenities: Bench, picnic tables, hand-carry boat launch

GETTING THERE
BY CAR From downtown Seattle, head north on Westlake Ave.; pass Mercer St. and turn right on Valley St. After three blocks, turn left on Fairview Ave. N. and continue 1.1 miles (road will become Eastlake Ave. E.). Turn left on E. Lynn St.; drive three blocks and the park will be straight ahead. Four parking spots are available in front of the park. Additional street parking is available on Fairview Ave. E. **BY BUS** Eastlake Ave. E./E. Lynn St.

Tiny waterfront parks hide at the spots where many streets in the Eastlake neighborhood meet Lake Union. A colorful mosaic sign—an artistic interpretation of the standard parks department marker—helps catch your eye at Lynn Street Mini Park, welcoming you in for views of the busy lake.

Take the flat, wheelchair-accessible path to a small lookout area where you'll spot more artwork, this time in the form of a brightly tiled couch. Two picnic tables nearby on gravel provide spots for lunch in the sun. This is a good perch for glimpsing the lifestyle of lucky houseboat dwellers.

Dozens of waterfront street ends in Seattle are publicly accessible small parks, like Lynn Street Mini Park in Eastlake.

Wooden stairs lead down to the shore, and more hand-drawn tiles of four-legged aquatic creatures and other water scenes line the steps, which double as benches. The small sandy beach is a good place to launch a kayak for a tour of the lake.

Read the back of the park sign to learn more about how this tiny neighborhood park came to be.

EXTEND YOUR VISIT

Two other great street-end parks are a short walk in either direction. Head south on Fairview Avenue East 0.2 mile to reach **Terry Pettus Park**, where you'll find benches, a picnic table, and a wooden dock with views of the Space Needle. Or head north on Fairview Avenue East 0.2 mile to reach the **East Louisa Street End** (also called Eastlake Boulodrome), which holds a *pétanque* court and a small beach.

77 ROGERS PLAYGROUND

One of the city's first playgrounds is still a center for play

Location: 2516 Eastlake Ave. E.; Eastlake
Acreage: 1.9
Amenities: Playground, tennis courts, baseball/softball field, soccer field, restrooms, benches, picnic table

GETTING THERE
BY CAR From downtown Seattle, head north on Westlake Ave.; pass Mercer St. and turn right on Valley St. After three blocks, turn left on Fairview Ave. N. Continue 1.3 miles (road will become Eastlake Ave. E.); the park will be on your right. Free street parking is available on Eastlake Ave. E. and adjacent streets.
BY BUS Eastlake Ave. E./E. Louisa St.

Neighborhood children have been drawn to this park since 1909, when one of the city's earliest playgrounds was built here. Named after Governor John R.

Rogers, who served the state from 1897 to 1901, Rogers Playground has a long history as an anchor of the Eastlake neighborhood. Kids walked from all directions to play on the park's swings, teeter-totters, rings, chin-up bars, and slides, while fitness instructors supervised their play.

These days kids will find modern climbing structures featuring twisting ladders, spiral slides, suspension bridges, a fire pole, and a miniature airplane. Parents can supervise from benches in the well-shaded play area,

Kids have been amusing themselves at Rogers Playground in Eastlake for more than a century.

which also includes a sandbox and swings. At the south end of the park you'll find a large field set up for baseball, softball, and soccer.

The park's paved paths and a winding entrance ramp from East Louisa Street make for good wheelchair and stroller accessibility to reach the playground, as well as the nearby restrooms and tennis courts. Along the concrete walkways, purple, orange, and aqua leaf tiles demonstrate the number of people who have showed their dedication to this park.

EXTEND YOUR VISIT

Another park dating back one hundred years is a 0.2-mile walk away. Reach **Roanoke Park** by heading east on East Roanoke Street up the hill and along the sidewalk that crosses I-5. Turn left at 10th Avenue East into the park, where you'll find a playground and half basketball court. Don't miss one of Seattle's heritage trees—a white elm on the park's western edge.

78   SOUTH PASSAGE POINT PARK

Scenic promontory hides beneath freeway

Location: Fairview Ave. E. and Fuhrman Ave. E. (under I-5); Eastlake
Acreage: 0.9
Amenities: Hand-carry boat launch, picnic tables, portable restroom

GETTING THERE

BY CAR From downtown Seattle, head north on Westlake Ave.; pass Mercer St. and turn right on Valley St. After three blocks, turn left on Fairview Ave. N. Continue 1.3 miles (road will become Eastlake Ave. E.). Turn left on E. Allison St.; turn immediately right on Fairview Ave. E. The park will be on your left at the sharp curve. Limited free street parking is available on Fairview Ave. E. and Fuhrman Ave. E. **BY BUS** Eastlake Ave. E./Harvard Ave. E.

An unlikely spot for an idyllic outdoor meal, this sweet picnic park sits directly under I-5's Ship Canal Bridge. Enormous concrete columns at the water's edge remind visitors that the double-decker bridge is looming 182 feet above the water. It was the largest of its kind in the Northwest when it opened in 1962.

Despite traffic overhead, it's peaceful along the canal. Lay out a blanket under the giant willow tree just feet from the shore and watch the action at this narrow passage between Portage Bay and Lake Union.

To the east, boats of all sizes cross back and forth under the elegant arches of the University Bridge, which was built in 1919. To the west you'll see yachts and other vessels moored along the sides of the channel and seaplanes headed for a landing near the southern end of the lake. Look for picnickers enjoying southerly views across the water at North Passage Point Park, situated under I-5 at the opposite end of the span.

Kayakers pass by South Passage Point Park looking for peeks at the enviable houseboats clinging to the shores of this waterway. You can launch your own kayak, canoe, or scull from the rocky beachfront here.

EXTEND YOUR VISIT

A 0.7-mile walk north will take you across the University Bridge to reach two other parks. After crossing the bridge, turn left on Northeast 40th Street, where you'll find **Peace Park** and a sculpture commemorating the bombing of Hiroshima during World War II. Continue to follow Northeast 40th Street, then turn left on 6th Avenue Northeast. At the shore, you'll come to **North Passage Point Park**, where tables allow for picnics with a southerly view.

79 MONTLAKE PLAYFIELD

Wetland park supplies workout for adults and kids

Location: 1618 E. Calhoun St.; Montlake
Acreage: 27
Amenities: Playground, community center, restrooms, tennis courts, 0.3 mile of unpaved trails, outdoor adult exercise equipment, running track, football field, soccer field, baseball/softball field, benches, picnic tables

GETTING THERE

BY CAR From I-5, take SR 520 eastbound and exit at Montlake Blvd. Turn right on E. Montlake Pl. E. and take an immediate right on E. Roanoke St. Veer left on W. Montlake Pl. E. (road will become 19th Ave. E.). After three blocks turn

An innovative challenge course at Montlake Playfield directs kids through a series of climbing tests to a long exhilarating slide.

right on E. Lynn St. After two blocks turn right on 16th Ave. E. After two blocks the park will be straight ahead. Free parking is available in the lot. **BY BUS** Montlake Blvd. E./E. Lake Washington Blvd.

Adults can glide, squat, and press to give their bodies some exercise while they watch kids work up a sweat climbing, scrambling, and sliding on one of the city's best playgrounds.

Taking advantage of more than two dozen acres, Montlake Playfield leaves no room for excuses when it comes to getting people of all ages active. Begin your visit near the community center (the tennis courts are also a stone's throw away), where it will be tough to tear children away from the fantastic play area with two exceptional climbing structures. One is a challenge course with high nets, rope bridges, and a long tube slide. The other resembles a spaceship and involves climbing a ladder to reach a tall platform where two more steep slides test kids' bravery. Little ones have plenty to do on a smaller structure as well as with a sandbox and miniature playhouse.

An accessible paved path goes around the play area, where you'll also find the adult exercise equipment—gliders and leg and arm press machines—as well as benches and picnic tables. Steps away is a full basketball court also painted to encourage hopscotch and four-square games. A baseball/softball field and soccer fields are spread out at the park's eastern end just to the south of a football field with a running track.

From the far northeast end of the running track you'll pick up the park's waterfront trail, restored in 2009, which twists and turns around the shoreline, allowing you to observe the wetlands that cover this end of Portage Bay. It's in this marshy area that you can best see how this park started as a peat bog many years ago. Cross over logs and watch for movement among the lily pads dotting the area where the lake meets the shore. Many species of birds, as well as bass and beavers, frequent this part of the bay. You'll emerge at the park's northwest corner where a line of poplar trees behind the community center orient you and lead you back to the center of the action.

EXTEND YOUR VISIT

Three secret waterfront public-access street ends are within a mile from here. At the far western edge of the park, look for a small trail that leads to 15th Avenue East. Then turn right on Boyer Avenue East, which you will follow, stopping at **East Edgar Street**, **East Hamlin Street**, and **East Shelby Street** to check out these tiny parks with views of Portage Bay. Alternately, take the Bill Dawson Trail (Montlake Bike Path) from the park's northeast corner for a walk under the 520 bridge, where you can connect to **West Montlake Park** and **East Montlake Park**.

80 EAST MONTLAKE PARK

Canal's shore displays boats and bridges

Location: 2802 E. Park Dr. E.; Montlake
Acreage: 7.1
Amenities: Benches, connections to trails

GETTING THERE

BY CAR From I-5, take SR 520 eastbound and exit at Montlake Blvd. Turn left on Montlake Blvd. E., cross the bridge, and take the first right on E. Hamlin St. After one block, turn left on E. Park Dr. E. The park will be immediately on your right. Free street parking is available on E. Park Dr. E. **BY BUS** Montlake Blvd. E./ E. Shelby St.; Montlake Blvd. E./SR 520; Montlake Freeway Station.

This park's wooden platform is the best place to see sailboats, yachts, and small freighters navigate the Montlake Cut, the narrow passage that connects Lake Washington to Portage Bay. Watch the Montlake Bridge, built in 1925, rise to make room for masts taller than forty-six feet.

This spot is also prime viewing for the Windermere Cup, the college crew races that take place here each year on the first weekend in May, drawing thousands of fans to both sides of the cut to cheer on their alma maters. Across the water you can see the University of Washington's Canoe House (originally a navy seaplane hangar), which served as the 1936 Olympic gold medal crew team's shell house. Today it's a great spot to rent canoes and rowboats and explore the channel yourself.

Before the first crew races—and before the canal was dug—the Duwamish people carried their canoes through the passageway between the two lakes. They named the area "Carry a Canoe."

Benches here are a serene setting for observing waterfowl or taking a rest before following trails that cross Marsh Island and Foster Island to the east to reach the Washington Park Arboretum.

Turn around to admire *Story of North Island*, a forty-foot totem pole carved in 1937 by Haida chief John Dewey Wallace in Waterfall, Alaska.

EXTEND YOUR VISIT

East Montlake Park has a twin to the west. Follow the wooden stairs to a gravel path that leads you on foot along the Lake Washington Ship Canal Waterside Trail, passing under the Montlake Bridge, to reach **West Montlake Park**, where you'll find benches, views of Portage Bay, and prominent poplar trees.

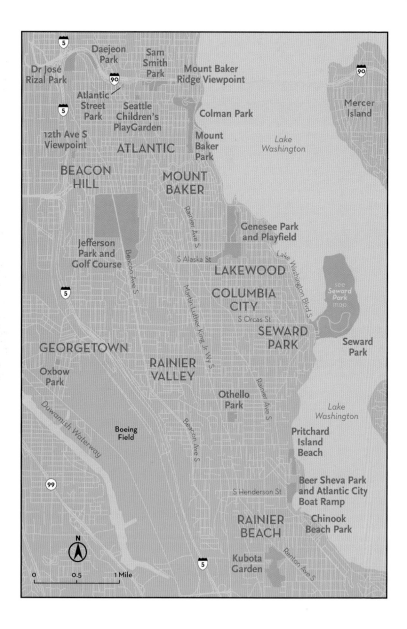

Beacon Hill & South Seattle

81   SEWARD PARK

Rare old-growth forest is hiker's nirvana

Location: 5900 Lake Washington Blvd. S.; Seward Park
Acreage: 300
Amenities: Playground, 2.4-mile paved loop path, 2.4 miles of unpaved trails, tennis courts, seasonally guarded swimming beach, bathhouse, reservable shelters, barbecue grills, Environmental Learning Center, amphitheater, art studio, restrooms, picnic tables, benches, drinking fountain

GETTING THERE

BY CAR From Martin Luther King Jr. Wy. S., turn east on S. Orcas St. and drive 1.3 miles toward Lake Washington. Turn right on Lake Washington Blvd. S. and then turn immediately left into the park. Free parking is available in several parking lots inside the park. Most amenities are easily reached by the parking lots immediately to the left and right. To access the interior of

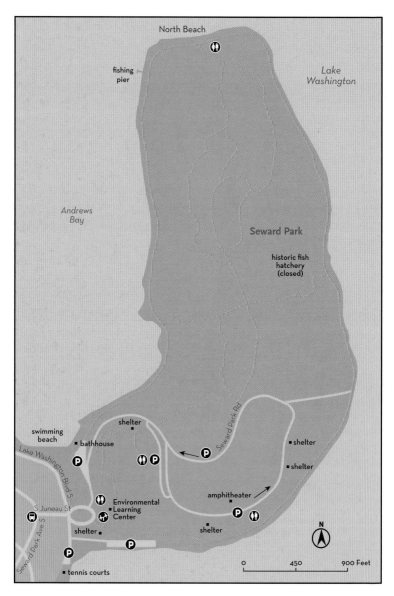

North Beach

fishing pier

Lake Washington

Andrews Bay

Seward Park

historic fish hatchery (closed)

Seward Park Rd

shelter

swimming beach

bathhouse

Lake Washington Blvd S

shelter

shelter

amphitheater

Environmental Learning Center

S Juneau St

shelter

shelter

Seward Park Ave S

shelter

tennis courts

N

0   450   900 Feet

the park, with picnic shelters, the amphitheater, and hiking trails, turn left on Seward Park Rd. and follow the road to additional lots. **BY BUS** Seward Park Ave. S./S. Juneau St.

On an airplane descending into Seattle in clear weather, you can immediately identify this park by its odd boot-like shape jutting out into Lake Washington. Purchased by the city in 1911 at the urging of the Olmsted Brothers, who designed parts of the park, Seward Park is one of Seattle's most treasured public spaces. It is thanks to the Olmsteds' influence that we are able to admire the city's only significant stand of old-growth forest, which was saved from logging by the incorporation of the park into their landscape design firm's plans for Seattle parks. It was named after US secretary of state William Seward.

The three-hundred-acre park that encompasses the Bailey Peninsula—named after William Bailey, who sold the land to the city—has one of the city's best paved, accessible paths, and this is the nicest way to start your visit. Stop off at the Environmental Learning Center, which is also a center for the National Audubon Society, for maps and a list of recent wildlife sightings. Then set off on a counterclockwise tour of the park on this flat track that begins on the south side of the playground. As you walk, imagine that up until 1916, each winter the peninsula turned into an island before the depth of Lake Washington was lowered by nine feet that year.

Pass the first pair of popular picnic shelters (the park has five), and look for Mount Rainier to the south. Soon you'll come to a small stone bridge on your left. Close to this spot a hatchery was built in 1935 to encourage sport fishing in Lake Washington. Some 250,000 trout were reared here annually. Today only pieces of the hatchery remain—and most of what's left is off-limits to visitors behind a fence.

After 1.5 miles the path opens up to a stretch of rocky beaches on the north end of the peninsula, where sporadic picnic tables make for enticing spots for lunch with views of Bellevue, downtown Seattle, and the I-90 bridge. Conveniently, you'll find restrooms here, too.

There are entrances nearby—and at several other points on the path—to reach the tangle of unpaved trails worth exploring in the park's center. This is where you'll be able to truly appreciate the park's great diversity of plants and majestic old trees, including Douglas firs, hemlocks, maples, and cedars. Keep

Seward Park's western shore provides a serene view of Andrews Bay.

your eye out for the stone markers that designate the entrances to these trails, which are also reachable from behind the Environmental Learning Center. Watch out for poison oak, which is common in the park.

As you continue your circuit, take time on the western shore to pause at the accessible fishing pier for a view of Andrews Bay and a chance to spot some of the significant bird life that frequents the park, including bald eagles. Kayaking is popular around Seward Park, and several beaches are designated as spots to launch and land hand-carry boats.

You'll end your loop at the swimming beach that bursts with kids in the summer. A small section is sandy, and the expansive lawn nearby is another idyllic picnic spot. The rest of the year, direct kids to the fantastic playground with a tree-house climbing structure that rises up the hillside. They'll also find a smaller structure intended for younger kids, a rock climbing apparatus, a sandbox, swings, and a zip line.

There's a short loop trail perfect for kids that begins behind the playground. You can also ask inside the Environmental Learning Center about programs for kids and adults, including nature walks.

Hike in or drive Seward Park Road to reach another picnic shelter and the 1953 amphitheater, once a very popular spot for concerts. A large lawn is great for games of Frisbee.

For fifty years a twenty-six-foot-tall Japanese torii (gate) made for an elegant entrance to Seward Park. Due to decay, it was removed in the 1980s, but plans are in the works to re-create this park icon.

EXTEND YOUR VISIT

Looking for something more off the beaten track? Check out **Martha Washington Park** less than a mile away. Walk south on Seward Park Avenue South, then turn left on 57th Avenue South and continue straight for two blocks. This nine-acre waterfront park has a large lawn, mature trees, and picnic tables tucked into the foliage.

82   PRITCHARD ISLAND BEACH

Former island boasts lesser-known swimming beach and trails

Location: 8400 55th Ave. S.; Rainier Beach
Acreage: 13.4
Amenities: Seasonally guarded swimming beach, bathhouse (reservable for events), restrooms (portable in winter), picnic tables, benches, 0.3 mile of unpaved trails

GETTING THERE

BY CAR From Martin Luther King Jr. Wy. S., turn east on S. Cloverdale St. and drive 0.7 mile east toward Lake Washington. Turn left on Seward Park Ave. S. and then quickly turn right on S. Grattan St. After two blocks drive straight into the parking lot, where free parking is available. **BY BUS** Rainier Ave. S./S. Rose St.; S. Henderson St./Rainier Ave. S. **BY LIGHT RAIL** Rainier Beach Station, 0.9 mile west at Martin Luther King Jr. Wy. S./S. Henderson St.

You may have noticed that you didn't cross a bridge to reach this park, so was Pritchard Island Beach misnamed? No, part of the land south of this park was actually an island until the level of the lake was lowered by nearly nine feet in 1916. Alfred J. Pritchard owned the island and had a convenient little footbridge built to reach his secluded site. Before that, this area was a Duwamish Indian village known as *Tleelh-chus* or "Little Island." In the 1930s it was developed into a park.

On the pathway near the park's bathhouse you'll see a marker indicating where the former shoreline used to be. Today the park encompasses a bay with a small section of sandy beach and several acres of wooded restored wetland.

The swimming beach is a big draw in the summer, when more popular south-end beaches fill up with people, leaving Pritchard Island Beach as an undiscovered favorite spot for locals. Kids splash in the shallow water while teenagers head for the island raft to play and sun themselves. The long sloping lawn has some shade from tall evergreens for hot days, and the views from here look out to Mercer Island and the Cascade Mountains.

Cross the lawn to the south end of the park where a kiosk marks the entrance to the wetland trail. Once an open marshland known as Dunlap Slough, this area is now dense with young alders and rich in plant and animal life. Robins, herons, flickers, starlings, and the Pacific tree frog have all been spotted.

The trail emerges on South Cloverdale Street, where you'll see the Rainier Beach Urban Farm and Wetlands, a former nursery that was converted into the city's biggest farm, operated by Seattle Tilth. From here you can either turn around or make a short loop. Continue east along the sidewalk on South Cloverdale Street and then turn left on Park Drive South, a narrow gravel road that turns into grass wedged between the park and neighboring houses. After about five hundred feet, turn left on a path into the park that reconnects to the main trail.

83 BEER SHEVA PARK AND ATLANTIC CITY BOAT RAMP

Accessible waterfront attracts flocks of boaters and picnickers

Location: Seward Park Ave. S. and S. Henderson St.; Rainier Beach
Acreage: 12.1
Amenities: Motorized boat launch, hand-carry boat launch, playground, restrooms, picnic tables, benches, barbecue grills, drinking fountain

GETTING THERE

BY CAR From Martin Luther King Jr. Wy. S., turn east on S. Henderson St. and drive 0.7 mile toward Lake Washington. The park will be straight ahead. Turn right on Seward Park Ave. S. and then immediately left into the Atlantic City Boat Ramp

From its headwaters 1 mile south, Mapes Creek empties into Lake Washington on the border of these two parks.

parking lot. Limited free parking is available for cars without trailers. Free street parking is also available on Seward Park Ave. S. **BY BUS** Seward Park Ave. S./ S. Fisher Pl.; S. Henderson St./53rd Ave. S.; S. Henderson St./Rainier Ave. S. **BY LIGHT RAIL** Rainier Beach Station, 0.7 mile west at Martin Luther King Jr. Wy. S./ S. Henderson St.

Named after our sister city in Israel, this park—together with Atlantic City Boat Ramp next door—offers a packed waterfront of amenities for this South Seattle community.

Begin near the boat launch, one of the few motorized ones in the city that provides access to Lake Washington. You can also launch kayaks and canoes here for a tour of this protected bay. From the water—or the shore—look across to Renton, Mercer Island, and the Cascade Mountains beyond the hills of the Eastside.

Mapes Creek empties into Lake Washington here, and one of the highlights of a visit to this park is seeing a recently restored section of this stream, which is helping protect Chinook salmon. Young native plants and trees embrace both sides of the creek as it emerges from an underground pipe into the sunlight and runs to the lake. John Grade's dramatic twenty-one-foot-tall sculpture, *Gyre*, is suspended in the air where Mapes Creek comes aboveground.

The stream roughly divides this large greenspace into its two respective parks, with a metal footbridge providing a connection to reach Beer Sheva Park. Cross over and you'll find an expanse of grass with amenities laid about under the many tall trees, which offer protection from sun and rain.

Kids will want to stop at the playground to slide and climb on two blue-and-green structures. A sandbox, swings, and spring rider toys will occupy little ones, and parents can take advantage of benches and an artistic metal bistro table and chair placed thoughtfully nearby. More benches as well as clusters of picnic tables paired with barbecue grills are spaced throughout the park to create a little privacy.

A flat, accessible paved path begins on the Atlantic City Boat Ramp side, continues into Beer Sheva Park, wraps around the playground, and cuts through the park to its northernmost point near South Cloverdale Street.

Chief Seattle's oldest daughter, called Princess Angeline by pioneers, is thought to have been born near this spot. This area was known as Atlantic City Park—named after New Jersey's sin city—and a boathouse and pier sat here for many years until the level of the lake was lowered in 1916, leaving the pier landlocked. A trolley line, which stopped nearby, brought people from downtown Seattle to the southern shores of Lake Washington until the 1930s. The northern section of the park was renamed in the 1970s.

EXTEND YOUR VISIT

One of the best indoor swimming pools and outdoor playgrounds in the city is 0.5 mile away at **Rainier Beach Playfield**. Walk west on South Henderson Street, and you'll find the Rainier Beach pool and community center at the corner of South Henderson Street and Rainier Avenue South. To reach the playground, turn right on Rainier Avenue South and left into the parking lot; it's in the northwest corner of the complex. Kids can be occupied for hours on the huge rope obstacle course, net climbing dome, and zip line. You'll also find ball fields and tennis courts.

84   CHINOOK BEACH PARK

Salmon and people find quiet respite on South Seattle shore

Location: Rainier Ave. S. and Ithaca Pl. S.; Rainier Beach
Acreage: 2.4
Amenities: Beachfront

GETTING THERE
BY CAR From Martin Luther King Jr. Wy. S., turn east on S. Henderson St. and drive 0.4 mile toward Lake Washington. Turn right on Rainier Ave. S. and follow for 0.7 mile as it curves. After you pass Ithaca Pl. S., the park will appear immediately on your left. Free street parking is available on Rainier Ave. S. Walk down the driveway to the right of a three-story brick apartment building to reach the park. **BY BUS** Waters Ave. S./S. Fletcher St.; Seward Park Ave. S./Rainier Ave. S.; Rainier Ave. S./54th Ave. S. **BY LIGHT RAIL** Rainier Beach Station, 1 mile west at Martin Luther King Jr. Wy. S./S. Henderson St.

Instead of this stretch of quiet rocky shore, picture what used to be here: an eroding slope, a chain-link fence, a crumbling concrete parking lot that served a former marina, and many invasive plants and weeds. Instead of a salmon- and wildlife-friendly urban beach, this was once an inhospitable and nearly forgotten piece of property. In 2004, it was transformed, and today new native shrubs and trees shade the waterfront, providing vital protection for Chinook salmon fry after they emerge a couple of miles south of here from the Cedar River on their journey to reach Puget Sound.

A placard as you enter Chinook Beach Park details the salmon life cycle and depicts how the beach used to look. You can walk along the narrow beachfront, which spans about 750 feet. Climb over rocks and logs partially submerged in the lake and find a spot to enjoy the solace. Because the park slopes down steeply to the shore and has a buffer of trees, including cedars, firs, and maples, traffic just above on Rainier Avenue South is easily forgotten.

Look straight across Lake Washington to views of the south end of Mercer Island and, to your right, north Renton. To your left you'll see the southern side of Seward Park, 2 miles away. The Cascade Mountains are on display in the distance to the east.

85   KUBOTA GARDEN

Spectacular Japanese garden enchants

Location: 9817 55th Ave. S.; Rainier Beach
Acreage: 34.2
Amenities: Portable restroom, benches, 1.5 miles of unpaved trails, covered shelters

GETTING THERE
BY CAR From Martin Luther King Jr. Wy. S., turn east on S. Henderson St. and drive 0.1 mile. Turn right on Renton Ave. S. and continue 0.9 mile; turn right on 55th Ave. S. and turn right into the parking lot, where free parking is available. **BY BUS** Renton Ave. S./55th Ave. S.; Renton Ave. S./S. Norfolk St.; Renton Ave. S./51st Ave. S.

Discover a hidden set of stairs, stumble upon a stone lantern, find a narrow bridge providing passage over a serene pond. Around nearly every bend in the path, a surprise pops up to delight visitors from young to old who take the time to linger at this remarkable garden.

Started as a private garden and nursery in 1927 by Japanese immigrant Fujitaro Kubota, the garden has been cultivated slowly for years. It's painful to remember that it was abandoned for several years while the Kubota family was interned in Idaho during World War II. Fujitaro and his sons returned to Seattle and continued their work on Kubota Garden, eventually selling it to the city in 1987. Fujitaro, who died in 1973 and never had any formal schooling in gardening, also left his mark as a landscape designer at gardens at Seattle University and the Bloedel Reserve on Bainbridge Island.

The garden is best visited with time on your hands, allowing you to stroll the quiet paths and let your curiosity lead you around each curve, where you're rewarded with waterfalls, sculptures, views, and bridges. Outside the main gate pick up a brochure, which includes a map and some historical information, provided by the Kubota Garden Foundation. The nonprofit also offers free public tours and volunteer opportunities to work in the garden.

Enter through the stunning bronze gate by Gerard Tsutakawa that sets the tone for what's to come inside the park. Paths lined by a diverse arrangement of plants and

The Heart Bridge is one of the most visited—and photographed—spots at Kubota Garden. Many other less-frequented corners of the park beckon explorers.

trees split off in several tempting directions. Stick to the main arterial if you're looking for the most wheelchair- or stroller-friendly route, but be warned that it is unpaved gravel and is sloped in places.

Highlights in the park include the traditional Japanese Garden with its spring-fed pond and tiny stone bridge, the Necklace of Ponds fed by Mapes Creek, and the park's two most photographed features—the bright red Moon and Heart bridges. For the best views of the garden, climb to the two highest points—the Terrace Overlook in the southern section of the park and the Mountainside in the western corner with its spectacular waterfall.

Fall is particularly magical at Kubota Garden as the Japanese maples burst into displays of red. Other notable flora are several species of bamboo, pine trees, and a large Norway spruce. The park's boundaries include acreage to the south that surrounds and protects Mapes Creek, which runs through the park.

86   OTHELLO PARK

Popular playground and paved trails center South Seattle neighborhood

Location: 4351 S. Othello St.; Rainier Valley
Acreage: 7.6
Amenities: Playground, restrooms, basketball/sports court, 0.5 mile of paved paths, benches, picnic tables, barbecue grills

GETTING THERE
BY CAR From Martin Luther King Jr. Wy. S., turn east on S. Othello St. and drive one block. The park will be on your right. Free street parking is available on S. Othello St. and on 45th Ave. S. **BY BUS** S. Othello St./44th Ave. S.; Martin Luther King Jr. Wy. S./S. Othello St. **BY LIGHT RAIL** Othello Station, one block west at Martin Luther King Jr. Wy. S./S. Othello St.

On a sunny day you might see a group of preschoolers sprinting across the huge lawn, leaving their teachers far behind, and dashing up the steps to the top of the cherished Othello slide. Set into the hillside, this steep metal slide shoots kids down the hill at what feels like the speed of an Olympic luger. After you've tested your nerves on the slide, check out the rest of this park's fantastic play features.

If you're looking for a big lawn for games of Frisbee or pickup soccer or to hold a large picnic, Othello Park is perfect. The park has benches, picnic tables, and barbecue grills near the play area, and the lack of dense vegetation allows you to easily keep an eye on kids. The play area includes climbing equipment, as well as swings and a zip line.

Adults can get moving on the popular paved walking path that takes advantage of the park's more than seven acres. The biggest loop, which begins nearby, is about a third of a mile and circles among the park's handful of trees. Most of the park's paths are flat and wheelchair-friendly.

EXTEND YOUR VISIT

Two more playgrounds are less than a mile away. Walk west 0.3 mile on South Othello Street to reach **John C. Little Sr. Park** (on your right), where you'll find basketball courts, a playground, a seasonal spray park, adult fitness equipment, and picnic shelters. Then continue on South Myrtle Street a few more blocks up the hill and you'll come to **Van Asselt Playground** on your right, which has bright blue climbing structures, more basketball courts, and a community center.

87 OXBOW PARK

Giant art plays on city's kitschy past

Location: 6430 Corson Ave. S.; Georgetown
Acreage: 0.8
Amenities: Playground, P-Patch, picnic tables, benches, drinking fountain

GETTING THERE

BY CAR From I-5, take exit 162 and continue on Corson Ave. S. for 0.5 mile. The park will appear on your left. Free street parking is available on Corson Ave. S. and on Carleton Ave. S. **BY BUS** Carleton Ave. S./S. Warsaw St.

There's no missing what's probably the country's biggest hat and cowboy boots, a landmark in the Georgetown neighborhood. The gigantic pair salutes visitors at this neighborhood's most interesting park. Created in 1954 by Lewis Nasmyth, the Hat 'n' Boots previously decorated a gas station on East Marginal Way, helping to make it one of the busiest places in the state to fill up the tank. (Rumor is that even Elvis dropped by in 1963 when he was in Seattle filming *It Happened at the World's Fair*.) Then I-5 opened and car traffic began to dry up, leading to the station's eventual demise. The community fought to have the giant icons saved, restored, and moved to a park to keep them in a publicly accessible spot.

The hat creates a nice shelter if rain rolls in while you're exploring this park. Follow the gravel path as it curves around a lawn to one of the few playgrounds in Georgetown. The small play structure's bright red and orange match the vibrancy of the oversized art, which kids will have a great view of while getting to work on the two slides, fire pole, steering wheel, and tiny platforms. Two X-shaped concrete

Hat 'n' Boots is an example of roadside attractions that were popular in the 1950s.

benches provide seating nearby. Continue along the path to find a small community P-Patch and picnic tables on the east side of the park.

The park's name comes from the U-shaped bend in the Duwamish River that used to surround Georgetown before a redirection in 1917 straightened it out. Georgetown is one of the oldest neighborhoods in Seattle, with settlers arriving around the same time as the more famous Alki pioneers, and it operated as an independent city until it was annexed in 1910.

EXTEND YOUR VISIT

Walk north on Corson Avenue South 0.4 mile (carefully cross South Michigan Street) to check out the neighborhood's other playground. In addition to soccer fields, basketball courts, and a tennis court, **Georgetown Playfield** has a playground with picnic tables and a shelter nearby. Visit in summer to take advantage of the seasonal spray park.

88 JEFFERSON PARK

Beacon Hill's pinnacle park draws kids, walkers, and athletes

Location: 3801 Beacon Ave. S.; Beacon Hill
Acreage: 165.9
Amenities: Community center, playground, skate park, seasonal spray park, tennis courts, full basketball court, lawn bowling green, 2.5 miles of paved trails, eighteen-hole golf course, nine-hole executive golf course/footgolf course, driving range, putting green, soccer field, three-lane track straightaway, restrooms, reservable shelters, picnic tables, benches

GETTING THERE

BY CAR From I-5, exit at Columbian Wy. and turn immediately left on S. Spokane St.; continue uphill for 0.3 mile. Turn right on Beacon Ave. S.; turn immediately right into the free parking lot. **BY BUS** Beacon Ave. S./Jefferson Community Center; 15th Ave. S./S. Spokane St.; 15th Ave. S./S. Dakota St. **BY LIGHT RAIL** Beacon Hill Station, 0.6 mile north at Beacon Ave. S./S. Lander St.

This Beacon Hill park was named in 1908 after Thomas Jefferson and was originally intended to be a cemetery. Luckily, it was instead turned into one of the most action-packed parks in the city. People young and old and many with dogs in tow frequent the park's accessible looping path system.

Follow the 0.8-mile path that circles the outer rim of the park, heading first to the western edge for views of downtown Seattle, the Space Needle, and Elliott Bay. Continue your loop and notice the young cherry trees planted in 2012 to commemorate Japan's gift of cherry trees to our country's capital more than one hundred years ago. As you walk, you'll see clusters of picnic tables and benches placed thoughtfully throughout the park if you need a rest or lunch break. The park gained more acreage in 2011 when the city completed covering the water reservoir here, creating an enormous lawn for games of soccer, ultimate Frisbee, and cricket, a game that's growing in popularity in the region.

Jefferson Park's gentle paved paths are one of the best spots in the city for young kids to bike, and it's easy to keep track of them with open sightlines.

THE INCREDIBLE EDIBLE PARK?

Hugging the western side of the hill below Jefferson Park is an experiment in public land use. On land owned by Seattle Public Utilities, the volunteer-run **Beacon Food Forest** grows fruit, berries, vegetables, and herbs that are free for picking for anyone wandering through the garden. (Be respectful and leave plenty for others.) Reach the park through a staircase or paved path on the southwest side of the outer loop walking path of Jefferson Park or by parking in a lot near South Dakota Street and 16th Avenue South. Start your visit of this national phenomenon inside the colorful tent-like shelter, where a map of the gardens tells you what's ripe and which beds are open to picking (some are private P-Patches).

C. J. Rench's bright red sculpture, designed to be skateboarded on, marks the background at Jefferson Park. The Beacon Hill park has outstanding views from its western edge.

But biking is just the start at this park, where dozens of activities can keep kids busy for an entire day. The fabulous playground includes four separate climbing structures—three for older children and one for younger kids. Two geometric structures make up a unique bouldering wall for ambitious climbers. You'll also find swings, spring rider toys, and a sunken sand area.

When the kids are ready to move on, follow the path to the top of Beacon Mountain. The lookout tower points out the elevations of nearby mountains. Play air traffic controller as you and your kids watch for planes heading in to Sea-Tac Airport.

Nearby you'll find two zip lines and the entrances to two quite steep slides. Keep an eye on children under three near the long one, which is built into the hillside at an impressive angle. In the summer the spray park that sits near the bottom of the slides is packed with preschool-aged kids enjoying the fun water features.

Skateboarders congregate at Jefferson Park's lighted skate park near the community center, which has an eleven-foot-deep bowl, one of the deepest in the region. Set up for street and transition skating, it also has smaller corner bowls, quarter pipes, a spine, stairs, handrails, and a hexagonal dish. Separate from the main fourteen-thousand-square-foot skate park, a unique skate feature is the twenty-three-foot-tall red sculpture by artist C. J. Rench at the north end of the park. Shaped like chopped-up letters of the alphabet, this skateable art is a new icon for this historic park.

If you want to keep walking, follow the path past the driving range and lawn bowling club at the south end of the park to where a paved trail, hugging the nine-hole golf course, will bring you on foot to the soccer fields at the southwest edge of the park's boundaries. To reach the one-hundred-year-old eighteen-hole course, cross Beacon Avenue South. A small dirt footpath offers a view of the fairways from the outside of the fence along the entire north and west sides of the course.

89   12TH AVE. S. VIEWPOINT

City and Sound overlook illustrates city's rhythm

Location: 2821 12th Ave. S.; Beacon Hill
Acreage: 1.1
Amenities: Benches

GETTING THERE

BY CAR From I-5, exit at Columbian Wy. and turn immediately left on S. Spokane St. Turn left at the next stoplight on 15th Ave. S. and continue 0.4 mile. Turn left on S. Forest St. After three blocks the park will be straight ahead. Free street parking is available on 12th Ave. S. **BY BUS** 15th Ave. S./S. Stevens St.; Beacon Ave. S./S. Lander St. **BY LIGHT RAIL** Beacon Hill Station, 0.3 mile east at Beacon Ave. S./S. Lander St.

Peaceful vistas of nature aren't quite what you'll find at this north Beacon Hill lookout. Instead come here to feel the pulse of our busy city and enjoy a rare western view from this neighborhood. See and hear Seattle in motion from this narrow urban park, which covers about a block and a half.

Cars and trucks rumble below on I-5 and then cross onto the West Seattle Bridge. Mammoth container ships come and go in Elliott Bay. Cargo is unloaded at the port, one of the busiest on the West Coast, and then reloaded onto trucks and trains. You can hear the whistle of the trains from here as they pass through on their tracks, carrying goods or people. Helicopters cross the horizon to land at Harborview Medical Center just 2 miles to the north. And every couple of minutes a plane flies overhead on its approach to Sea-Tac Airport.

WHERE DID BEACON HILL GET ITS NAME?

M. Harwood Young, an army veteran transplant from New England, named the hill in 1889 after Boston's historic neighborhood. He also built a street-car line that went down Seattle's Beacon Avenue to connect homes and businesses on the hill with downtown.

Have a seat on one of the park's two benches and look beyond the city to see the Olympic Mountains and Puget Sound making up a serene background to all this activity. The buildings that compose the downtown Seattle skyline gleam in the sunshine with the Space Needle framing the view. For the clearest sightlines, come in the winter when the trees in front of the park have finished dropping their leaves.

90 DR. JOSÉ RIZAL PARK

Picnic vistas and scenic off-leash dog area mark hero's park

Location: 1007 12th Ave. S.; Beacon Hill
Acreage: 9.6
Amenities: Playground, off-leash dog park, restrooms, 0.3 mile of unpaved trails, barbecue grills, picnic tables, benches, reservable shelter, amphitheater, drinking fountain

GETTING THERE

BY CAR From Pioneer Square, drive east on S. Jackson St. through the International District and turn right on 12th Ave. S. Continue 0.3 mile (you'll cross the 12th Ave. S. bridge) and the park will appear on your right. Free parking is available in the lot. **BY BUS** 12th Ave. S./S. Judkins St. **BY LIGHT RAIL** Beacon Hill Station, 1 mile south at Beacon Ave. S./S. Lander St. **BY BIKE** The I-90 Trail runs adjacent to the park's off-leash area.

A statue of Dr. José Rizal, an international hero of the Filipino community who lived in the late 1800s, looks out over the park that bears his name at the very north end of Beacon Hill. Under his handsome bust are the labels "national hero, martyr, and genius," deservedly earned for his role (and ultimate martyrdom) in fighting for political reform in the Philippines under Spanish rule. Not to mention, he was also a doctor, teacher, poet, sculptor, and playwright and spoke at least a dozen languages. A little concrete amphitheater nearby looks ready to host a lecture, perhaps on the topic of Filipinos in World War II about which a plaque nearby details key historical points.

A few yards away sit three mosaic panels composed of ceramic tile and bits of mirror and glass. Titled *East Is West*, this mural by Val Laigo is dedicated to the local Filipino

Peek through a mosaic sculpture by Val Laigo to spy the Seattle skyline at Dr. José Rizal Park.

community. Peer through the openings of this colorful piece of art to spy the downtown Seattle skyline. You can enjoy that view, which also encompasses Elliott Bay, the Olympic Mountains, and the stadiums, from the picnic area consisting of tables, barbecue grills, and a large shelter. Kids can climb and slide on a tiny play structure within sight.

A paved path extends north, connecting to the restroom and two more rugged sections of park. Here a winding unpaved trail descends the hillside, passes an apple orchard, and connects to the I-90 Trail (part of the Mountains to Sound Greenway that stretches all the way to Ellensburg in Central Washington). It's important to note that this area sometimes holds temporary encampments, which may make some visitors uncomfortable.

A second trail is reached at the northernmost point of the park, and this is also the entrance to the four-acre off-leash dog park, which isn't visible from the street and is easy to miss. Enter this fenced area through the double gates and take the wooden stairs down into an expansive space where dog owners can continue to enjoy the views from benches or on a walk along the approximately 1,000-foot gravel path lined with trees. A wheelchair-friendly entrance is available via the I-90 Trail.

EXTEND YOUR VISIT
Walk one block south on 12th Avenue South to **Katie Black's Garden**, where you can wander the quiet brick paths in this simple but sweet Japanese-inspired garden and listen to birds chirp overhead.

91 DAEJEON PARK

Beautiful pagoda in serene setting celebrates South Korean sister city

Location: 1144 Sturgus Ave. S.; Beacon Hill
Acreage: 2
Amenities: 0.3 mile of paved paths, covered pagoda

GETTING THERE
BY CAR From Pioneer Square, drive east on S. Jackson St. through the International District. Turn right on 12th Ave. S. Continue 0.3 mile (you'll cross the 12th Ave. S. bridge) and turn left on S. Charles St., which will immediately become Sturgus Ave. S. After 0.2 mile the park will appear on your left. Free street parking is available on Sturgus Ave. S. **BY BUS** S. Charles St./Golf Dr. S. **BY LIGHT RAIL** Beacon Hill Station, 1 mile south at Beacon Ave. S./S. Lander St. **BY BIKE** The I-90 Trail runs adjacent to the park.

Known for years as Taejon Park, this peaceful greenspace just south of I-90 was changed to Daejeon in 2009. Seattle and Daejeon, about 100 miles south of Seoul, established a sister city relationship in 1989. When the city switched out the Taejon sign, people thought Seattle had made a huge sister city faux pas.

It turns out the South Korean government had adopted a new Romanization style of the Korean language in recent years to better represent the sound of the language. A member of a visiting Korean delegation pointed out that we needed to update our park sign.

Orthography is quickly forgotten when you spot the magnificent Korean pagoda, erected in 1998. A sign nearby explains the complex engineering of the structure. A paved, accessible ramp leads into the pavilion, which is supported by eight cinnamon-colored columns. On a clear day, you can spot Mount Rainier through the columns to the southeast. Look up to appreciate the intricate ceiling painted with flowers and stripes. The paved patio surrounding the pagoda melds into a serene setting of carefully pruned shrubs and a gently rolling lawn interrupted only by a trio of Kousa dogwoods.

EXTEND YOUR VISIT

Daejeon Park melts into **Sturgus Park** immediately to the west. Walk or bike the **I-90 Trail** in the northwest direction to see that park's best feature—*Equality*, a sculpture by Ken Leback and Rolon Bert Garner consisting of thirty-five house-shaped pieces of granite placed in careful rows and a thirty-sixth, cast in bronze, overlooking the rest.

92   ATLANTIC STREET PARK

Colorful play space works out kids and adults

Location: 1501 21st Ave. S.; Mount Baker/Atlantic
Acreage: 0.75
Amenities: Playground, outdoor adult exercise equipment, bench, picnic table

GETTING THERE

BY CAR From Rainier Ave. S. turn east on S. Massachusetts St. and drive one block. Turn left on 21st Ave. S.; the park will be on your left at the end of the block. Free street parking is available on 21st Ave. S. and on S. Atlantic St. **BY BUS** Rainier Ave. S./S. State St.; 23rd Ave. S./S. Massachusetts St.; I-90/Rainier Ave. S. **BY BIKE** The I-90 Trail runs adjacent to the park.

One of the first to have adult fitness equipment installed, this park models a fantastic concept: take a neighborhood park, put in an appealing playground, and add exercise equipment for adults around the edges.

Kids can't resist the bright orange play structure at Atlantic Street Park, with slides, climbing walls, and ladders. Ascend the climber through tunnels to reach higher levels where you can look down on the entire park. Littler kids can explore the interactive gears and dials closer to the ground or take a ride on the baby swings. A painted mural and partial fence help keep little ones contained in the area.

For adults, there are five stations within steps of the playground that make up a mix of stretching, strengthening, and cardio, including an exercise bike. You can rotate through the equipment and do a complete circuit of lunges, stair steps, seated abdominal curls, and arm exercises.

When everyone needs a break, a picnic table provides a snack or lunch spot. The park is pleasantly shaded by deciduous trees.

93   SEATTLE CHILDREN'S PLAYGARDEN

Unusual playground elates kids of all abilities

Location: 1745 24th Ave. S.; Mount Baker/Atlantic
Acreage: 1
Amenities: Playground, full and half basketball courts, vegetable and flower garden, restrooms, drinking fountain, benches, picnic tables

GETTING THERE

BY CAR From Rainier Ave. S., turn left on S. Holgate St. and drive east two blocks. Turn left on 24th Ave. S.; then turn immediately right on S. Grand St. and immediately left on 24th Ave. S. again. The park will be on your left. Free street parking is available on 24th Ave. S. **BY BUS** 23rd Ave. S./ S. Massachusetts St.; Rainier Ave. S./S. Grand St.; Martin Luther King Jr. Wy. S./ S. Massachusetts St. **BY BIKE** Access to the I-90 Trail is one and a half blocks north of the park.

Topiary animals greet you as you step into this special playground, offering a hint at the playful surprises around every corner. Secure the gate behind you

A pickup truck is repurposed as a garden bed and a place to play at this unique South Seattle park.

and let your kids explore freely within this fully fenced park adjacent to the Colman Playground.

"Education is not the filling of a pail, but the lighting of a fire," William Butler Yeats reminds us on a square of concrete underfoot. This sentiment is echoed everywhere at the Seattle Children's PlayGarden, where kids have opportunities to discover and play in ways completely unique to this park.

A spark from speech pathologist Liz Bullard, who recognized a gap in outdoor amenities that support children with special needs, led to the development of this park beginning in 2002. Kids can pick raspberries from the garden, dig in a muddy sand area, play pirates in an accessible tree fort, hide under cedar trees, watch bees enter a hive, help feed chickens, and create music with the interactive installation by sound artist Trimpin. Narrow kid-sized trails lead to all sorts of things adults don't always identify as play objects but children immediately find use for, including barrels, stumps, fishing buoys, and ropes. A space with wood chips near the southeast corner holds more traditional play equipment, including swings, a spinning ring, and spring rider toys. A mix of curving gravel and paved paths connect the various areas.

The heart of the park is a brightly colored climbing mound where you can look out over the gardens, accessible basketball courts, and animal pens where free-range chickens, geese, ducks, and bunnies live. In a red pickup truck, kids take turns at the wheel, and strawberry plants fill the spot where the engine used to be. Nearby, a white canvas triangle overhead provides some shelter from the elements, and tables and chairs welcome everyone to picnic.

The Seattle PlayGarden operates as a nonprofit organization in partnership with the parks department. A preschool and other programs operate on the grounds and in the multipurpose room that includes a kitchen where food is prepared from things children pick in the gardens. This is a public park open to all during daylight hours, although public visits are restricted during summer camp hours (9:30 AM to 1:30 PM Monday through Thursday, late June through August).

94 SAM SMITH PARK

Green I-90 gateway offers strolling and play

Location: 1400 Martin Luther King Jr. Wy. S.; Mount Baker/Atlantic
Acreage: 23.8
Amenities: Playground, tennis courts, off-leash dog park, paved path, portable restroom, benches, drinking fountain, picnic tables

GETTING THERE
BY CAR From Pioneer Square, drive east on S. Jackson St. through the International District. Turn right on Martin Luther King Jr. Wy. S. and continue 0.6 mile. The park will appear on the left and right. Free street parking is available on many residential streets adjacent to the park. To access the playground, park on S. Atlantic St. near 29th Ave. S. To access the off-leash dog area, park on 26th Ave. S. off S. Massachusetts St. **BY BUS** Martin Luther King Jr. Wy. S./S. Irving St.; Martin Luther

King Jr. Wy. S./S. Judkins St.; 23rd Ave. S./S. Massachusetts St.
BY BIKE The I-90 Trail runs through the park.

An incredibly creative use of public space, this park shows little hint of the traffic that hurtles directly below on I-90. Often called "the lid," the park is a major passage for bike commuters, who travel through on the paved path between the Mount Baker Tunnel and connections to central and downtown Seattle.

The park is named after the first black member of the city council. Sam Smith, who died in 1995, also served five terms in the state legislature, promoted social justice, and fought discrimination in housing.

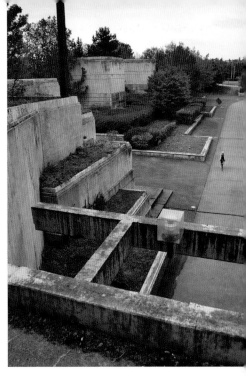

A busy bike commuter route, the I-90 Trail passes through Sam Smith Park. Highway vehicle traffic runs underneath the park.

A slower pace is good for appreciating all the amenities tucked around this park's nearly two dozen acres. Look underfoot and along the sides of the path for wise sayings and little inlaid bronze plaques by artists Keith Beckley and Dennis Evans. Veer slightly off the main path to locate the tennis courts and a new play area installed in 2016. The green, red, and blue climbing structures have slides, bridges, and innovative ladders to tempt young visitors. Kids will also find a tire swing, an eighteen-sided net climber, and a wheelchair-accessible driving station with a steering wheel. Adults have a couple of pieces of fitness equipment to keep themselves busy, and tables are placed around the play area to make picnicking a breeze.

For a bird's-eye view of the park, climb the almost hidden stairs on either side of the tunnel entrance, not far from the playground. This vantage provides a great western angle on the geometric design of the park. It's particularly attractive in fall when the park's many deciduous trees turn bright shades of orange and red.

Head back west toward Martin Luther King Jr. Way South and look to your left for Gerard Tsutakawa's sculpture *Urban Peace Circle*, which commemorates children killed by gun violence. Entombed below the bronze piece are guns acquired from a buyback program.

The off-leash dog park is separate from the rest of the park and also has a distinct name—Blue Dog Pond. Walk south on Martin Luther King Jr. Way South and turn right on South Massachusetts Street, where the off-leash area appears in the corner. A detention basin for storm water, Blue Dog Pond's 1.7-acre space is a flat bowl with hills on the sides and a scattering of trees for shade. Owners can rest on benches and appreciate the colorful art that brightens the space. Read about the water basin and some interesting history of the site on signs at the south end.

EXTEND YOUR VISIT

Jimi Hendrix Park features accessible curving paths, rain and butterfly gardens, a round plaza, and information on the life and music of the park's namesake. Continue west along the paved **I-90 Trail** and branch off south to reach the park that sits just east of the Northwest African American Museum.

95   MOUNT BAKER RIDGE VIEWPOINT

Earth and sun are at play on I-90 crest

Location: 1403 31st Ave. S.; Mount Baker
Acreage: 0.1
Amenities: Benches, drinking fountain

GETTING THERE

BY CAR From Pioneer Square, drive east on S. Jackson St. through the International District. Turn right on 31st Ave. S. and continue 0.6 mile. The park will appear on your right. Free street parking is available in front of the park. **BY BUS** 31st Ave. S./ S. Day St.

This secret viewpoint on top of I-90 looks west to the city and Olympic Mountains.

It feels as if you're standing on a platform suspended in the trees at this west-facing viewpoint. Take in the unbarred views of downtown Seattle and the Olympic Mountains, but don't look down if you're nervous about heights. Foliage peeks through the metal grates underfoot, reminding visitors that they are elevated on this ridge. In fact, 125 feet below, traffic is traveling through I-90's Mount Baker Tunnel.

Several benches provide a great place to enjoy lunch with your view. From this vantage, you can admire the 1909 Colman School, now home to the Northwest African American Museum, in the valley below, as well as the sixteen-story Pacific Tower (former Amazon.com headquarters) that marks the top of Beacon Hill. Both buildings are historic landmarks.

Curious about the seven sets of basalt stones? They are placed so that the narrow space between each pair will precisely line up at sunset with the equinoxes, solstices, and points equidistant between them. Helpful placards detail this astronomical phenomenon as well as historical information about the neighborhood.

Before you leave, check out the witty refrigerator poetry left on the two-sided magnetic board or add your own creative contribution.

EXTEND YOUR VISIT
Bradner Gardens Park is worth the short 0.3-mile walk. Head south on 31st Avenue South for two blocks and turn right on South Massachusetts Street. Walk downhill two blocks, then turn left on 29th Avenue South and the park will appear on your right. Kids will especially love the quirky art hiding around every corner of this 1.6-acre garden. Don't miss the pieces created from old gardening tools that adorn the fence near the basketball court. You'll also find restrooms (with fabulous art awaiting you inside), a small shelter, picnic tables, and benches.

96 COLMAN PARK

Elegant curving boulevard park entertains bikers and hikers

Location: Lake Washington Blvd. S. and Lakeside Ave. S.; Mount Baker
Acreage: 24.3
Amenities: Unguarded beach, 0.8 mile of unpaved trails, P-Patch, benches, lookout

GETTING THERE
BY CAR From Rainier Ave. S., turn east on S. McClellan St. and drive 0.5 mile. Turn left on Lake Park Dr. S. and follow to Lake Washington Blvd. S. Turn left, then turn immediately right into the entrance to the free parking lot. **BY BUS** 31st Ave. S./S. Massachusetts St.; Lakeside Ave. S./S. Day St.

The name Colman pops up on a ferry dock, building, school, swimming pool, and more than one park in Seattle. James Colman was a Scottish-born engineer who moved to Seattle in 1872. He built the original Colman Dock, operated Henry Yesler's mill for a time, founded a coal company that made him rich, and helped the city build its first railroad.

This park that bears his name—different from Colman Playground south of the original Colman School—was initially land owned by the city's first municipal water company. It was also an early project of the Olmsted Brothers, who designed the serpentine Lake Washington Boulevard, which journeys through the park, following the natural topography of this hillside. It's appropriate that James Colman was honored with this park—it is believed that in 1886, after working for thirty-six hours straight, he fixed a broken pump that supplied water to the city. Colman's estate later donated some of the land that makes up the park.

Begin your visit by exploring the wheelchair-accessible waterfront section of Colman Park. Here a paved path brings you to a rocky (unguarded) beach that looks south to Mount Baker Park's seasonally guarded swimming area. The two parks sit next to one another, making it difficult to tell where one ends and the other begins.

Bikers enjoy a leisurely ride as they cross one of several Olmsted-designed bridges at Colman Park.

Stroll past a gently sloped lawn to a formal overlook with graceful concrete balustrades lining the square patio. From here you can enjoy views of Lake Washington and the Bellevue skyline and watch activity on the I-90 bridge. Look southeast to try to spot Mount Rainier on a clear day.

The paved path continues on the west side of the parking lot, taking you under the first two of four historic bridges. Unpaved trails begin here—follow the main one straight uphill for 0.3 mile. You'll pass under two additional moss-covered bridges where the occasional car or bike crosses overhead. This quiet path has hidden secrets, including a pond that is home to colonies of frogs and a forested P-Patch bursting with vegetables and flowers. The trail ends with a long staircase up to 31st Avenue South.

EXTEND YOUR VISIT

For an alternate hike, after the second underpass from the waterfront, instead of taking the main trail west, turn left and follow the trail heading south for a 0.2-mile hike through more acres of peaceful forest. You'll end at the Olmsted-designed Dose Terrace steps. Take them down to reach **Mount Baker Park**.

97 MOUNT BAKER PARK

Beach and forested ravine deal out play and quiet walks

Location: 2521 Lake Park Dr. S.; Mount Baker
Acreage: 21.7
Amenities: Playground, tennis courts, 0.3 mile of paved paths, fishing pier, seasonally guarded swimming beach, bathhouse, restrooms, picnic tables, benches

GETTING THERE

BY CAR From Rainier Ave. S., turn east on S. McClellan St. and drive 0.5 mile. The upper (south) end of the park will be on your left. Free street parking is available on S. McClellan St.; park here to access the playground. To reach the beach, turn left on Lake Park Dr. S. and follow to Lake Washington Blvd. S. Turn right and then turn immediately left into the free parking lot. **BY BUS** S. McClellan St./Lake Park Dr. S.

A paved walking path traverses the length of this long, narrow park from the play area at the top down the ravine until it spills out on the shores of Lake Washington, where people young and old come in droves in summer months.

A playground with two tree-house-inspired play structures, a zip line, and swings is the focal point at the top of the park. Little bikers can make use of the flat paved path around the area. Seating created out of polished stones and mosaics adds more playful flourishes and practical resting spots for parents, nannies, and grandparents.

This is the start of the accessible path. Enjoy a peaceful walk through the trees as it descends toward the water. You'll pass tennis courts and restrooms as you trace the shape of this ravine. About halfway down the third-of-a-mile trail, veer off the path to your right, where you'll find a series of small waterfalls spilling from a tiny creek that flows through the park. A solitary bench makes a nice place for quiet reflection.

Near the end of the path you'll come across a six-ton stone lantern, a gift from a Japanese businessman more than one hundred years ago. Cross Lake Washington Boulevard

Designed by the Olmsted Brothers firm, Mount Baker Park dates to 1908. This stone lantern was added in 1911.

South here to reach the beach, which has been popular for bathing since the 1920s. Views of the I-90 bridge, Bellevue skyline, and Cascade Mountains from the sandy shore and Y-shaped fishing pier are fantastic. You'll want to linger here on a hot summer day to take advantage of the guarded swimming beach and picnic tables.

GREEN CONNECTIONS: ELEGANT OLMSTED-DESIGNED BOULEVARDS

Curving like a tail connected to Mount Baker Park, **Mount Baker Boulevard** was designed by the Olmsted Brothers firm and built around 1908. Mature trees dot the wide swath of lawn, which winds like a river between graceful homes on each side of the street. You can walk the 0.5-mile stretch along the grass (there's no sidewalk in the center of the boulevard) or admire it from the street in a car or on a bike. This elegant boulevard creates a green passage between Mount Baker Park and Rainier Avenue South, where it connects to **Cheasty Boulevard**, another Olmsted influence that is now a Seattle historic landmark. E. C. Cheasty was a member of the parks board in the early 1900s and helped bring the European-style boulevard to Seattle. This 1.3-mile road traverses uphill to reach Jefferson Park. A mountain bike park is being planned for the greenspace adjacent to the boulevard.

Cheasty Boulevard winds gracefully through wooded greenspace.

EXTEND YOUR VISIT

From the top of the park, walk northwest 0.7 mile to **Martin Luther King Jr. Memorial Park**, a powerful testament to the country's most famous civil rights leader. A thirty-foot-tall sculpture designed by Robert W. Kelly resembles a mountain, a tie to King's "I've Been to the Mountaintop" speech, which was his last. Walk west on South McClellan Street for four blocks; turn right on 30th Avenue South. After three blocks turn left on South College Street and continue to where it dead-ends at the top of the park.

98   GENESEE PARK AND PLAYFIELD

*Open meadows and paths
create green gateway*

Location: 4316 S. Genesee St.; Columbia City/
Lakewood
Acreage: 57.7
Amenities: Three playgrounds, off-leash dog park,
3 miles of paved and unpaved trails, restrooms,
reservable shelter, picnic tables, barbecue grill,
football and soccer field, benches

GETTING THERE

BY CAR From Rainier Ave. S., turn east on S. Genesee St. and continue 0.4 mile.
The park will appear on your left and right, with free parking lots on either
side near 43rd Ave. S. An additional free parking lot is located adjacent to the
Rainier Community Center at 38th Ave. S. and S. Alaska St. **BY BUS** S. Genesee
St./45th Ave. S.; Rainier Ave. S./S. Alaska St. **BY LIGHT RAIL** Columbia City
Station, 1 mile southwest at Martin Luther King Jr. Wy. S./S. Angeline St.

Sometimes city dwellers need to escape from cramped urban quarters to wide
open spaces, and this park delivers. The long green expanse stretches from
Lake Washington into the Rainier Valley and then turns like the crook of an
elbow and connects to other parks in the heart of Columbia City.

Start by exploring the park's wilder north section, where an unpaved trail
travels around a meadow that's undergoing efforts to restore it to its natural
state after decades of abuses that included the site's use as a landfill from
the 1940s to the early 1960s. Before the level of the lake was lowered in 1916,
this was a slough with diverse wildlife. A 760-foot wooden bridge nearby connected Lake Washington Boulevard to Seward Park. Today more than eighty
native plant species are being introduced to revise the ecosystem and encourage animal life to return to Genesee Park. Educational signs at points around
the park detail the species of birds, reptiles, and mammals sometimes seen
here. The sparse scattering of trees at this corner creates a sense of openness
in the landscape. At the most northern point of your loop, look across Lake
Washington Boulevard to the waterfront Stan Sayres Memorial Park, the hub
of the Seafair hydroplane races each summer.

Flat gravel paths circle wide, open space on the north end of Genesee Park.

Three playgrounds are spread across Genesee Park, with one settled next to a picnic shelter and restrooms in the north section. Older kids will like the blue-and-yellow obstacle course made up of rings, ladders, and bars.

Cross the street that gives this park its name—and originates from the Seneca Native Americans' word for "beautiful valley"—to reach an abundance of amenities. Here the trails turn into paved paths, which make the south and west parts of the park ideal for kids to bike and also wheelchair accessible. A three-acre off-leash area entertains dogs and their owners at the southeast corner. The circular space with surfaces that include gravel, sand, and grass has logs and rocks for dogs and colorful chairs and a picnic table for owners.

Immediately to the west, soccer and football fields, restrooms, and another playground make up the center of Genesee Park. A red-and-blue climbing structure features slides and a bridge, and a set of swings sits nearby.

EXTEND YOUR VISIT

Genesee Park extends across 42nd Avenue South, where you can bike or walk the paved path all the way to the Rainier Community Center. You'll pass a neighborhood community garden, a picnic shelter, and the park's third playground (two play structures with a spiral slide and ladders). Continue even farther, across 38th Avenue South from the community center, and at the north the end of the block, you'll find another fabulous playground at **Rainier Playfield** (multiple structures, a net climbing dome, picnic tables, barbecue grills, tennis and basketball courts, and ball fields). **Columbia Park**, with a short paved walking path, is farther west, across Rainier Avenue South.

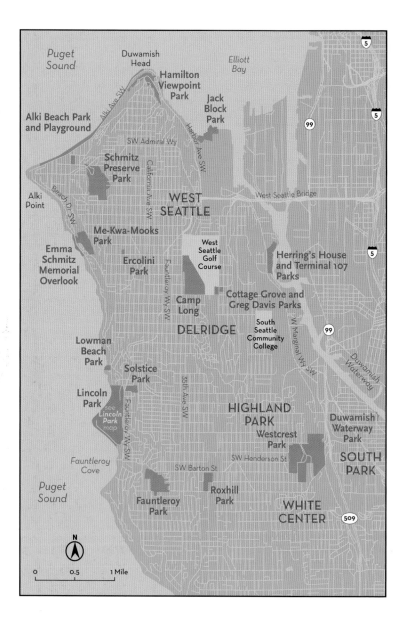

Puget
Sound

Duwamish
Head

Elliott
Bay

Hamilton
Viewpoint
Park

Jack
Block
Park

Alki Ave SW

Alki Beach Park
and Playground

SW Admiral Wy

Harbor Ave SW

Schmitz
Preserve
Park

California Ave SW

West Seattle Bridge

99

5

Alki
Point

Beach Dr SW

WEST
SEATTLE

Me-Kwa-Mooks
Park

Emma
Schmitz
Memorial
Overlook

Ercolini
Park

West
Seattle
Golf
Course

Herring's House
and Terminal 107
Parks

Fauntleroy Wy SW

Camp
Long

Cottage Grove and
Greg Davis Parks

DELRIDGE

South
Seattle
Community
College

W Marginal Wy SW

99

Duwamish
Waterway

5

Lowman
Beach
Park

Solstice
Park

Lincoln
Park

see
Lincoln
Park
map

Fauntleroy Wy SW

35th Ave SW

HIGHLAND
PARK

Westcrest
Park

Duwamish
Waterway
Park

SW Henderson St

SOUTH
PARK

Fauntleroy
Cove

SW Barton St

Puget
Sound

Fauntleroy
Park

Roxhill
Park

WHITE
CENTER

509

N

0   0.5   1 Mile

West Seattle & South Park

99 LINCOLN PARK

Oasis of nature and recreation options mark neighborhood's signature park

Location: 8011 Fauntleroy Wy. SW; West Seattle
Acreage: 135.4
Amenities: Two playgrounds, 4 miles of unpaved trails, 0.8-mile paved walking and biking paths, reservable shelters, seasonal wading pool, seasonal outdoor saltwater swimming pool, hand-carry boat launch, baseball and softball fields, soccer fields, horseshoe pits, restrooms, picnic tables, benches

GETTING THERE
BY CAR From the West Seattle Bridge, take the Fauntleroy exit and continue on Fauntleroy Wy. SW for 2.7 miles. The park will appear on your right. Free parking is available in two parking lots as well as on Fauntleroy Wy. SW during some hours (read signs carefully as towing is frequent). Limited disabled parking is available near the beach; look for the driveway at the south end of the south parking lot. The beach is accessible by hiking trails from

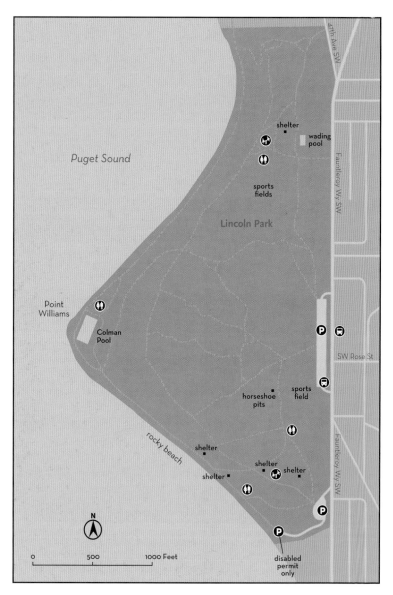

47th Ave SW

shelter

wading pool

Puget Sound

sports fields

Lincoln Park

Fauntleroy Wy SW

Point Williams

Colman Pool

P

SW Rose St

horseshoe pits

sports field

rocky beach

shelter

shelter

shelter

shelter

Fauntleroy Wy SW

P

P

disabled permit only

N

0   500   1000 Feet

either of the parking lots. For the playfields, park in the northern lot. Playgrounds are located at the north and south ends of the park. **BY BUS** Fauntleroy Wy. SW/SW Rose St.

Look at West Seattle on a map and this park is the large green bulge on the western side of the peninsula. If you've ever taken the ferry to Vashon Island, you've probably sat in your car in line and gazed longingly to the north at the expanse of beach that makes up this fantastic waterfront park.

Until the early 1930s this area was dotted with summer cottages. After briefly being known as Fauntleroy Park, it was renamed Lincoln Park after the sixteenth president when it was acquired by the city in 1922.

With both paved paths and miles of hiking trails, the park is a favorite spot for exercising year-round. Kids on bikes or scooters, dog walkers, and joggers share the busy beachfront path in all weather. In the summer, children and adults take advantage of the brief open season for Colman Pool, the city's only outdoor saltwater swimming pool.

For a sweeping tour, begin at the south parking lot and start on the paved path. You'll first come to the south playground, with swings, a sandbox, a zip line, and a wooden play structure that includes a spiral slide and bridges. Kids familiar with the park know where to find the colorfully painted metal statue of a gargoyle-like creature that doubles as a slide. This area is also one of several spots in Lincoln Park that is great for picnicking, with two reservable shelters, barbecue grills, and dozens of picnic tables here.

Follow the path as it curves downhill to the waterfront, where a long rocky beachfront greets you. Amble along the paved path and take in views of Vashon, Blake, and Bainbridge islands, and admire the Olympic Mountains, snowcapped and dazzling in winter. Pause here for a picnic (you'll find two more shelters, barbecue grills, and plenty of tables and benches) and watch ferries float back and forth across the water. Behind you, tucked into the start of the hillside, is a small stone building concealed beneath vegetation, with cylindrical skylights jutting toward the sky—this is one of the most unusual bathroom facilities in the parks system.

At the park's westernmost point—a spot known as Point Williams—you'll find Colman Pool, a heated public saltwater swimming pool where you can take a dip or swim laps with incredible views of the Puget Sound. The pool

A mile of uninterrupted Puget Sound shoreline in West Seattle's top park attracts people from all over the region.

started out in the 1920s as a swimming hole, which was fed by the tides. City officials wanted to get rid of it because the fire department had to periodically hose out all the mud and gunk. The pool is named after Laurence Colman, son of Seattle pioneer James Colman, who was active in civic life in West Seattle. The Colman family donated funds to turn it into a real swimming pool in 1941.

Point Williams is also a popular fishing spot, especially every two years in summer months when the pink salmon run just offshore. Besides a number of fish species, other wildlife frequent the park's waters, and lucky visitors have spotted orca whales, seals, and sea lions nearby. On land, look up to try to see bald eagles that often rest in the barren branches of tall trees along the waterfront. The park is dominated by bigleaf maples, red alders, cedars, firs, and madronas.

The paved path turns into gravel along the northern shoreline. At the northernmost point—as well as near the swimming pool—you can connect to steep trails leading to upper Lincoln Park. Make the climb and then join the trail that hugs the bluff, where the views continue through the trees from high above the waterfront.

At various points on your route back to the south end of the park, smaller side trails lead to other places of interest, including a second playground with new climbing equipment installed in 2016, a seasonal wading pool, more picnicking amenities, horseshoe pits, and soccer and baseball and softball fields. If you're looking for solitude, seek out one of the many quiet meadows surrounded by tall trees just off the main trail.

100 SOLSTICE PARK

Water, mountain, and sunset views draw solstice observers

Location: Fauntleroy Wy. SW and SW Webster St. (bordered by SW Fontanelle St., 44th Ave. SW); West Seattle
Acreage: 7.2
Amenities: Tennis courts, tennis backboard, 0.3 mile of unpaved paths, P-Patch, portable restroom, drinking fountain, picnic tables, benches

GETTING THERE
BY CAR From the West Seattle Bridge, take the Fauntleroy exit and continue on Fauntleroy Wy. SW for 2.4 miles. Turn left on SW Webster St., then turn immediately left into a small free parking lot. **BY BUS** Fauntleroy Wy. SW/SW Webster St.; California Ave. SW/SW Othello St.

A six-court tennis complex makes up the lower end of this park, an extension of the amenities of Lincoln Park across the street. This is a popular spot in West Seattle for casual games as well as camps and lessons. You'll find benches inside and outside the courts, as well as a picnic table.

The rest of Solstice Park is hidden on the hillside above. Track down the narrow trail near the courts and ascend the steep hill, passing through a well-tended neighborhood P-Patch as you rise up onto a knoll. The leg-burning climb will be worth it when you reach the top and turn around to take in the views of Lincoln Park's treetops, Puget Sound, and the Olympic Mountains.

This is a fun spot to celebrate the changing of the seasons. The round gravel viewing area has three large stones that point out the direction of the sunset on the summer solstice, vernal and autumnal equinoxes, and winter solstice. Three paths extending from the viewing area feel primeval as they cut through a grass mound, creating channels perfectly aligned to capture the sunset on these four days of the year. Visit at day's end on one of these special dates and you certainly won't be alone—Solstice Park is a gathering spot, particularly on the shortest and longest days of the year.

A flat lawn spreads out nearby with a picnic table and bench for lingering over the views. A small patch of forest, made up of both mature and newly planted trees, sits on the hill behind the viewing area. A trail cuts through the woods and emerges on a residential street above.

Paths climb the hillside to a secret viewing area at Solstice Park.

101 LOWMAN BEACH PARK

Tucked away waterfront spot satisfies sunset watchers

Location: 7017 Beach Dr. SW; West Seattle
Acreage: 4.1
Amenities: Tennis court, swings, hand-carry boat launch, bench

GETTING THERE

BY CAR From the West Seattle Bridge, take the Fauntleroy exit and continue on Fauntleroy Wy. SW for 2.4 miles. Turn right on 47th Ave. SW, which will become Lincoln Park Wy. SW as it curves down to the water. At the bottom of the hill turn left on Beach Dr. SW; the park will be immediately on your right.

Free street parking is available on Beach Dr. SW and on Lincoln Park Wy. SW.
BY BUS 48th Ave. SW/Beach Dr. SW; Fauntleroy Wy. SW/SW Myrtle St.

A mostly unknown beach just north of popular Lincoln Park, this little treasure
offers up Puget Sound waterfront access to those in on its secret. It is thanks
to the Yesler Logging Company, which donated this stretch of saltwater shoreline to the city more than one hundred years ago, that this is a public park.
Otherwise, surely it would have been developed as much-coveted beachfront
property. The park honors James Lowman, a former parks commissioner and
Henry Yesler's nephew.

Come at low tide for excellent beachcombing or in the evening for a sunset
view of the Olympic Mountains and Blake Island. From the water's edge you can
look south to see expansive Lincoln Park and ferries crossing to Vashon Island
and Southworth. Kayakers often launch here because of the easy carry-in access.
Lucky visitors may spot orcas or seals offshore. In addition, a tennis court and
swing set sit on the hill above the water.

A huge city works project—a newly constructed one-million-gallon underground sewage-storage tank—has transformed the county-owned property
across Beach Drive Southwest from the park. As part of the project, a new
publicly accessible space on top of the tank features a staircase surrounded
by native plants that provides a pedestrian shortcut to the waterfront. Artist
Robert Horner created walls and rock gardens from materials salvaged on-site.

102 ERCOLINI PARK

*Corner playground is West
Seattle favorite for tykes*

Location: 4542 48th Ave. SW; West Seattle
Acreage: 0.5
Amenities: Playground, 0.1 mile of paved paths,
benches, picnic tables, portable restroom

GETTING THERE
BY CAR From the West Seattle Bridge, take the Fauntleroy exit and continue
on Fauntleroy Wy. SW for 0.4 mile. Turn right on SW Alaska St.; after 0.6 mile
the park will be on your right. Free street parking is available on 48th Ave. SW.

BY BUS SW Alaska St./48th Ave. SW; SW Alaska St./44th Ave. SW; SW Alaska St./California Ave. SW.

What's now one of West Seattle's most well-loved playgrounds used to be the site of Joe and Julia Ercolini's garden. The Ercolinis were Italian immigrants who farmed on this corner lot. For several decades starting in the 1930s, people would show up at the garden and buy produce that the Ercolinis would pick for them on the spot. The land was sold to the parks department in 2005.

Today the park is a busy spot for toddlers and young kids, who dash from their parents' minivans to claim favorite toys. Local families donate used ride-on toy cars, trikes, and scooters for everyone to enjoy, so kids find something new to play with on every visit. Two climbing structures are the main fixture in the play area, which sits on a cushion of wood chips. The taller suits older kids and features a long spiral slide and monkey bars. The smaller has short dueling slides, a steering wheel, and a mini climbing wall. Kids will also find a merry-go-round, swings, and a sandbox, which is filled with construction trucks and sand toys.

A paved path wraps like a figure eight through the park, making a loop around the playground and a flat, circular lawn that's the site of soccer and Frisbee games for older kids. Parents and grandparents use the path—dodging tots on bikes—to get a little exercise while children play within sight nearby. The park's benches and tables welcome playdate picnics.

103 EMMA SCHMITZ MEMORIAL OVERLOOK AND ME-KWA-MOOKS PARK

Marine preserve shows off spectacular sunset views

Location: 4503 Beach Dr. SW; West Seattle
Acreage: 37.6
Amenities: Benches, picnic tables, barbecue grills, portable restroom, 0.5 mile of unpaved trails

GETTING THERE
BY CAR From the West Seattle Bridge, take the Fauntleroy exit and continue on Fauntleroy Wy. SW for 0.4 mile. Turn right on SW Alaska St. Continue for 0.6 mile,

Soak up outstanding sunset views of the Olympic Mountains and Puget Sound from western-facing Emma Schmitz Memorial Overlook.

then turn left on 49th Ave. SW. After two blocks turn right on SW Hudson St. Follow down the hill as it becomes SW Jacobsen Rd. At the stop sign turn right on Beach Dr. SW. The park is immediately on your left. Free street parking is available along Beach Dr. SW. **BY BUS** Beach Dr. SW/SW Snoqualmie St. (runs very infrequently); no other convenient bus service.

With a third of a mile of waterfront, Emma Schmitz Memorial Overlook has some of the best unobstructed views in Seattle. This narrow park is named in honor of the prominent Seattle citizen who donated the land for this park. Schmitz and her husband, Ferdinand, who served on the parks board, were German immigrants who came to Seattle in the 1880s and settled on property across the street. This park is sometimes mistaken for Schmitz Preserve

Park, another popular West Seattle park that was donated to the city by the Schmitz family.

The park's jaw-dropping views of the Olympic Mountains across the Puget Sound are best seen at sunset. Bring binoculars and look for orca whales, seals, sea lions, and river otters that occasionally can be spotted from the shore. Emma Schmitz Memorial Overlook has been designated a marine preserve to help protect wildlife and restrict some types of fishing.

On summer evenings, locals bring camping chairs and blankets to take advantage of the park's slender strip of flat lawn for a picnic dinner as the sun sets. Take the stairs down to the lower area of the park for a closer view of the waves crashing against the shore, especially at high tide. In addition to more than a dozen benches placed throughout the park, a long, narrow concrete berm here provides a great spot to linger. Continue farther north around the corner to find a wide set of a dozen stairs leading down to a small, rocky beach, a popular spot to sit at low tide. To head back, follow the paved path that runs the length of the park and looks out on Vashon, Blake, and Bainbridge islands.

Because the park is so narrow and sits next to a main road, you can't escape the sounds of moderate car traffic from the upper section of this park. But the views are so outstanding that you're sure to be quickly distracted.

For more picnic options, cross the street to Me-Kwa-Mooks Park (Lushootseed for "Prairie Point"), where you'll find picnic tables and a barbecue grill on a sloped hillside, also with water views. Look for entrances at the northeast and southeast ends of the park to a short trail system. If you look carefully among the trees and brush you'll find remnants of the Schmitz homestead.

EXTEND YOUR VISIT

For a flat 0.7-mile stroll (one-way), walk north on the sidewalk along Beach Drive Southwest, where you'll pass three other small waterfront parks—**Weather Watch Park**, **Andover Place**, and **Cormorant Cove**—and end at a fourth, the lovely **Charles Richey Sr. Viewpoint**. For a longer walk, continue an additional half mile on Alki Avenue Southwest to **Alki Beach Park**. Don't miss the one-hundred-year-old Alki Point Lighthouse on your way.

104 ALKI BEACH PARK AND PLAYGROUND

*Immensely popular sandy
shore marks city's start*

Location: Alki Beach Park: 1702 Alki Ave. SW
(from 64th Ave. SW to the Duwamish Head); Alki
Playground: 5817 SW Lander St.; West Seattle
Acreage: 140
Amenities: Playground, 2 miles of paved walking
and biking paths (connects to 3-plus more miles
of paths), reservable shelter, restrooms, drinking
fountain, fire pits, picnic tables, benches, barbecue
grills, hand-carry boat launch, tennis courts,
soccer field, baseball and softball field, reservable
bathhouse, art studio

GETTING THERE
BY CAR From the West Seattle Bridge, exit at Harbor Ave. SW and turn right.
Continue on Harbor Ave. SW for 3.5 miles as the road becomes Alki Ave. SW. The
park will be on your right. Free street parking is available on Alki Ave. SW. **BY BUS**
Alki Ave. SW/61st Ave. SW. **BY BIKE** The Alki Trail runs adjacent to the park.

It's fitting that the birthplace of Seattle becomes a cross section of our population on warm summer days, when people of all ages and backgrounds congregate on our city's southwestern shore.

It was on the site of Alki Beach Park that the schooner *Exact* arrived in 1851
carrying the people who would become the founders of Seattle, including the
Denny and Boren families. They were actually not the first white settlers to
make it to this remote part of the country—others had scouted the area in the
previous year. Chief Seattle and his tribe greeted the arrivals, and the settlers
named the beach after the Chinook word for "by and by." After a cold, misera-
ble winter on the exposed Puget Sound, they moved their settlement to Elliott
Bay and founded Seattle.

In 1910, Alki became an official city-owned park. Just as it is today, the
beach was a very popular weekend spot for sunning and recreation.

Anchor yourself at the centrally located bathhouse. To the south is where
you'll find prime picnicking territory, with a shelter and dozens of picnic tables,

Alki Beach Park's paved waterfront path is one of Seattle's best walks.

benches, and barbecue grills. Large groups and extended families gather here on summer evenings, and the delicious scents of dinner being grilled over a bed of charcoal waft through the air.

A seawall at this end of the park protects the paved path from high tide and makes a favorite perch for couples enjoying sunset views of the Olympic Mountains and Bainbridge Island. Curious about the model of the Statue of Liberty? A Boy Scouts project in the 1950s placed more than two hundred replicas of the famous statue in communities across the country, including Seattle.

On the north side of the bathhouse is where summer is epitomized in Seattle. Car stereos boom with music, teenagers gather at fire pits, volleyball players set up for competitions, kids wade in the frigid Puget Sound, groups of moms run with jogging strollers, dog walkers amble, families pack into six-person bikes, Rollerbladers whiz by at high speed, and tourists fill the bars, coffee shops, and restaurants that line the street opposite the beach.

California transplants can take one look at the long stretch of sand and boardwalk-style running and biking path, and they'll be cured of homesickness. On sunny afternoons, bring your patience as you search for a parking spot and then a piece of beach to lay out your blanket. It's worth strolling the flat paved path northward where you'll find poems, art, and historic tidbits set into stones underfoot.

You'll also find an extension of Alki Beach Park one block to the southeast near 59th Avenue Southwest. Referred to lovingly by neighborhood children as Whale Tail Park, this playground is protected from the sometimes windy beach. Kids can frolic in the large sandbox and on a climbing structure with two tall, bending slides, swings, and a climbable toy boat and whale tail. Nearby are a soccer field, baseball and softball field, tennis courts, and restrooms. The park connects to Alki Elementary School and Alki Community Center to the south, where you'll find basketball hoops and a second playground.

EXTEND YOUR VISIT

From the Alki Bathhouse, it's a flat 1.5-mile one-way walk or bike ride north to the **Duwamish Head**, the most northern point in West Seattle. This area is renowned as offering one of the best views of downtown Seattle across Elliott Bay. Fewer people know that this is the former site of the Luna Park amusement park that operated from 1907 to 1913, with a hand-carved carousel, roller coaster, and other rides. All that remains of Luna Park are some pilings visible at low tide.

105 SCHMITZ PRESERVE PARK

Old-growth forest hides in West Seattle neighborhood

Location: 58th Ave. SW and SW Stevens St. (near SW Admiral Wy.); West Seattle
Acreage: 53.1
Amenities: 1.7 miles of unpaved trails, benches

GETTING THERE

BY CAR From the West Seattle Bridge, exit at Harbor Ave. SW and turn right. Continue on Harbor Ave. SW for 3.5 miles as road becomes Alki Ave. SW. Turn left on 58th Ave. SW; after one block turn right on SW Lander St. and then turn immediately left on 58th Ave. SW. The entrance to the park is at the end of the block straight ahead. Free street parking is available on 58th Ave. SW. Another entrance to the park is on SW Admiral Wy. near SW Stevens St. **BY BUS** SW Admiral Wy./59th Ave. SW. **BY BIKE** The Alki Trail is 0.2 mile away along Alki Ave. SW.

Nearly 2 miles of trails at Schmitz Preserve Park provide fantastic year-round urban hiking.

With Seattle's first industry revolving around logging, Ferdinand Schmitz, a German immigrant and early Seattle pioneer who served on the parks board, was unhappy with the loss of the area's forests. In 1908, he and his wife, Emma, donated thirty acres of land that now make up more than half of this park. Thanks to his generosity, most of the park has remained untouched except for some small patches that had been logged prior to 1908. This makes Schmitz Preserve Park one of the only places in Seattle with native old-growth forest.

There are several entrances to access the nearly 2 miles of hiking trails inside Schmitz Preserve Park, but the best is from the northwest corner along the elegant Olmsted-designed Schmitz Boulevard. To enter the park, walk this wide paved path, which in the fall is blanketed in leaves from big-leaf maples. Soon you'll cross under Southwest Admiral Way, known as the Schmitz Park Bridge. Built in 1936, it is on the National Register of Historic Places and is a city landmark. Artists, both semiprofessional and graffiti-inclined, love the underside of this large concrete bridge.

As the trail becomes unpaved, it follows the path of Schmitz Preserve Creek, leading up a gentle ravine. Stick to the main central trail until you reach the middle of the park, where you'll see a bench in a small clearing with paths going in four directions. It's possible to make two small loops from this point, one if you head right and another if you head left. (Straight leads uphill to

Southwest Hinds Street, a residential street and convenient route for local residents to reach Alki Beach Park on foot.)

Standout flora include Western hemlocks, yews, maples, and Douglas firs, and you'll also see ferns, moss, salal, and salmonberry bushes in abundance. More than sixty types of native plants and trees have been noted in the park. You may also hear or see evidence of the many species of birds who live here along with raccoons, bats, and squirrels.

Small bridges and wooden walkways keep the park hikeable year-round. West Seattle neighbors work hard to keep the park in good condition and to battle against invasive species harmful to the native growth.

106 HAMILTON VIEWPOINT PARK

Northern clifftop of West Seattle displays outstanding city views

Location: 1120 California Ave. SW; West Seattle
Acreage: 16.9
Amenities: Benches, large picnicking lawn

GETTING THERE

BY CAR From the West Seattle Bridge, exit at Harbor Ave. SW and turn right. Continue for 1.4 miles and then veer left on California Wy. SW. Continue up the hill for 0.5 mile and the park will appear on your left. Free parking is available in the lot. **BY BUS** SW Atlantic St./44th Ave. SW; SW Seattle St./California Ave. SW. **BY BIKE** The Alki Trail is 0.5 mile away along Harbor Ave. SW.

People have been admiring the view from this spot since at least the 1800s, though the Duwamish Native Americans may have spent time lingering on the northern bluff of West Seattle much earlier. Then, they would have looked out at a dense forest across Elliott Bay. This spot would also have made an excellent lookout point for anyone tracking activity coming in and out of the young city's harbor. Although early settlers identified this as an ideal spot for a park, it wasn't made a reality until 1954.

Rupert L. Hamilton was the publisher of the *West Seattle Herald* in the 1920s and 1930s and helped to preserve the land that eventually became this park. Today it's a favorite spot for locals—and tourists who are in the know—to look out across the entrance to the busy port and wide-open views of the city skyline.

A trio of benches rests on the park's small paved area, where you'll find the most unobstructed views. To the left you'll see Magnolia, Interbay, and Queen Anne. The Space Needle and skyscrapers of downtown Seattle are straight across Elliott Bay, where container ships and ferries cross in and out. In the distance the Cascade Mountains frame the scene.

Many people stop by Hamilton Viewpoint for a quick look, but you can easily find reasons to delay your departure. Large sections of lawn make up the rest of the park—the one at the south end is flat and good for games of soccer or Frisbee. Another just behind the parking area is bordered by trees and shrubs and would be a nice spot to picnic with the view beyond. You can easily see why the park is popular for wedding ceremonies.

EXTEND YOUR VISIT

Walk down the curving hill 0.5 mile as California Avenue Southwest becomes California Way Southwest to **Seacrest Park**. This waterfront park, which is popular for scuba diving, has a fishing pier, restaurant, boat and bike rentals, restrooms, and beach access. It's also where the pedestrian-only King County Water Taxi docks in West Seattle on its route to downtown Seattle. Turn north and walk the Alki Trail 0.2 mile along Harbor Avenue Southwest to reach **Don Armeni Boat Ramp**, one of the few saltwater motorized boat launches in the city.

107 JACK BLOCK PARK

City views and accessible trails mark little-known jewel

Location: Harbor Ave. SW and SW Florida St.; West Seattle
Acreage: 15
Amenities: Sand play area, restrooms, 0.5 mile of paved paths, lookout tower, drinking fountain, benches, picnic tables

GETTING THERE

BY CAR From the West Seattle Bridge, exit at Harbor Ave. SW and turn right. Continue for 0.9 mile and then turn right on SW Florida St. into the park entrance. Free parking is available in two lots, one near the entrance and one 0.3 mile farther into the park. **BY BUS** Harbor Ave. SW/SW Florida St. (limited bus service). **BY BIKE** The Alki Trail runs adjacent to the park.

This fantastic Port of Seattle park squeezes out accessible public space and some of the city's best views from a jungle of port activity on all sides—and even occasionally below your feet. This rare proximity to the bustle of the port is one of the things that makes this park,

Spectacular views of the city skyline shine from an elevated viewing platform at Jack Block Park.

named after a former port commissioner, so interesting. Ignore the chain-link fencing on both sides as you drive into the park, which makes for an odd, and slightly disconcerting, entrance.

It will be tough to coax kids away from the sand play area, the first thing you see as you leave the parking area. Bring your own sand toys and dig into the enormous gravelly sandpit. Oversized buoys and bollards resting in the sand encourage climbing. Several picnic tables are positioned around the area, making it too easy for visitors to end their visit here.

The entirety of Jack Block Park is wheelchair and stroller accessible thanks to an excellent paved path that stretches from the first parking lot to the final viewpoint. It's a long haul for little legs or those pushing wheelchairs—about

0.4 mile from start to end—so a smaller second parking lot at the park's midpoint may come in handy for some people.

It's rewarding to explore the whole park, so begin near the sand area and follow the path as it zigzags through the park. Geographically appealing, the space has hills, footbridges, and enticing walkways, making you want to see what's around the next corner. In a couple of spots you will cross over access points for trucks and trains to reach the water.

At the park's halfway point, you'll come out to a rocky beach that was cleaned up and is now open to the public. From here you can see barges, tugboats, and the King County Water Taxi come and go in this bay. A large concrete patio just a bit farther holds more picnic tables and the entry point to an old wooden dock where you'll find benches and clear views of downtown Seattle.

Backtrack a bit and take the upper path to reach the park's pinnacle, a viewing platform suspended forty-five feet above the shoreline. It feels as if you're standing in an eagle's nest, looking down on the shipping crates and cranes. With so much happening at the port, you almost forget to look at the outstanding views of the skyline across the water.

This area was used as a wood treatment plant and shipbuilding facility for years, leading to its contamination with dangerous chemicals. Although it was cleaned up and turned into a park in the 1990s, it remains one of West Seattle's least-known parks.

108 CAMP LONG

Depression-era Scout camp now provides weekend escape

Location: 5200 35th Ave. SW (near SW Dawson St.); West Seattle

Acreage: 68

Amenities: Historic lodge housing the Environmental Learning Center, reservable shelters and cabins, barbecue grills, fire pits, picnic tables, benches, 1.5 miles of unpaved trails, climbing rock, challenge ropes course, restrooms

GETTING THERE

BY CAR From the West Seattle Bridge, exit at Fauntleroy Wy. SW. Turn left immediately on 35th Ave. SW and continue 0.7 mile. Turn left on SW Dawson

St. into the park's entrance. Free parking is available in the lot. The park is open Tuesday–Sunday from 10:00 AM to 6:00 PM in the summer, Tuesday–Saturday from 10:00 AM to 6:00 PM in the winter. **BY BUS** 35th Ave. SW/SW Dawson St.; SW Alaska St./35th Ave. SW.

Who knew you could go to summer camp without leaving Seattle? This eighty-year-old park was envisioned as an urban spot for Scouts to learn outdoor skills. Kids could have campfires, hike, and sleep overnight in cabins within just a few miles of their homes.

In the 1980s Camp Long was opened up to the public, and now anyone can rent a cabin for the night, roast s'mores over their own campfire, and pretend to earn a wilderness merit badge. The park is named after Judge William Long, one of the original advocates for the camp.

Stop in at the beautiful stone lodge, built as a Works Progress Administration project (and available to rent for events), and grab a trail map. Paths beginning right outside lead to clusters of little wooden cabins, several dating to the 1930s and each with its own picnic table and stone barbecue grill just outside the door. It's easy to imagine a cozy evening roasting hot dogs over the flames.

Descend to a large flat field, known as the Parade Ground, where you'll find a campfire ring and seating. A few steps away is the most interesting feature at the park: twenty-five-foot-tall Schurman Rock, the country's first manmade rock climbing structure. Clark Schurman, a guide on Mount Rainier, designed this rock, which was built in the late 1930s for generations of future mountaineers to enjoy. Famous Everest climber Jim Whittaker used to practice on the structure. The rock is available for individuals, groups, and classes. (Check in at the lodge first.)

Camp Long is fantastic for urban hiking, with several miles of relatively easy trails. From Schurman Rock, you can descend to the half-mile Middle Loop Trail or dip lower on the Lower Loop Trail for a slightly longer and hillier hike that abuts the West Seattle Golf Course. From the Lower Loop Trail it's possible to connect to the Longfellow Creek Legacy Trail adjacent to the park's southeast corner. As you hike, you'll tramp through a forest of alders, birches, maples, Douglas firs, and cedars. Curious about the platforms and rope contraptions set among the trees? This is part of a challenge ropes course available for team-building events.

As you complete your loop, several trails converge at Pollywog Pond just north of the Parade Ground. See the little island in the middle of the pond? It was built as a safe cooking spot for Scouts to avoid burning down any part of the camp.

EXTEND YOUR VISIT

Half a mile north on 35th Avenue Southwest you'll find **Rotary Viewpoint**, with peek-a-boo views of downtown Seattle and Beacon Hill through the trees. Most interesting is the eighteen-foot-tall totem pole by artist Robin Young that was stolen by brazen thieves in 2009. Luckily it was soon found, restored, and returned to the park.

109 COTTAGE GROVE AND GREG DAVIS PARKS

Pair of parks provides stopover along Longfellow Creek Legacy Trail

Location: Cottage Grove Park: 5206 26th Ave. SW; Greg Davis Park: 2600 SW Brandon St.; West Seattle/Delridge
Acreage: 3.9
Amenities: Playground, portable restroom, small shelter, picnic tables, benches, 0.1 mile of paved paths, 0.3 mile of unpaved trails

GETTING THERE

BY CAR From the West Seattle Bridge, exit on Delridge Wy. SW and continue 1.5 miles. Turn right on SW Brandon St. After two blocks the parks will appear on your right. Free street parking is available on 26th Ave. SW and on SW Brandon St. **BY BUS** Delridge Wy. SW/SW Brandon St.

Explore this pair of not-so-well-known parks and you'll get a close-up view of one of the only streams in Seattle that isn't piped mostly underground. Longfellow Creek runs for more than three miles, emptying into the Duwamish Waterway.

Begin at Greg Davis Park on the west side of 26th Avenue Southwest, which melds into a greenspace to the north called Puget Boulevard Commons. Get oriented on the map and see how the site has changed since the 1970s, when it was destined to be an expansion of the West Seattle Golf Course that sits next

A wooden bridge crosses Longfellow Creek at Greg Davis Park in West Seattle.

door. Davis was a Delridge resident who was instrumental in getting the space turned into a park before he died in 1993.

Follow the unpaved trail along the creek to see this important urban ecosystem. If you're a bird-watcher, this is a great area for spotting—and hearing—a variety of species. The park is especially nice in the fall when the trail crunches under a blanket of maple leaves.

Cross to the east side of the street to check out Cottage Grove Park, a fully accessible space with a flat paved path that stretches through the park. The Recovery Garden, made up mostly of ferns, was planted at the south end of the park in 2004 to provide a peaceful spot for individuals recovering from substance abuse as well as the friends and family who support them. A faded labyrinth on the pavement was designed to help calm and restore visitors.

Continue on the path, which takes you alongside a lawn for picnicking to a patio area. Here you'll find a small shelter, a couple of picnic tables, and a playground. Best suited for older kids, the play equipment is made up of an ambitious climbing structure with a monkey-bar zip line, ladders, and climbing walls. Younger kids can use the swings set low to the ground. A rock wall imitating natural stone is a fun spot for bouldering.

EXTEND YOUR VISIT

You can continue hiking by crossing Southwest Brandon Street. Look for the decorative silver gate to access a trail that follows the creek to the south and another that connects to **Camp Long** to the west. For an accessible alternative, walk north along 26th Avenue Southwest to reach **Delridge Playfield**, where you'll come to a playground, a thirteen-thousand-square-foot skate park, a seasonal wading pool, ball fields, tennis courts, and a community center with indoor restrooms.

110 HERRING'S HOUSE AND TERMINAL 107 PARKS

Duwamish waterfront parks offer peek at area's history

Location: Herring's House: 4570 W. Marginal Wy. SW; Terminal 107: 4700 Marginal Wy. SW; West Seattle
Acreage: 18
Amenities: 0.5 mile of paved and unpaved trails, picnic tables, benches, portable restroom, small shelter

GETTING THERE

BY CAR From the West Seattle Bridge, exit at SW Spokane St. At the light, turn right on Chelan Ave. SW and continue onto W. Marginal Wy. SW. After 0.9 mile the parks will appear on the left. Free parking is available in the parks' two parking lots. **BY BUS** No convenient bus service. **BY BIKE** The Duwamish Trail runs adjacent to the park.

The wooden frame of a replica of a Seattle fishing boat from the early 1900s looms overhead at this pair of neighboring parks on the Duwamish River. The boat, a sculpture by Donald Fels, provides a visual reminder to visitors that people have been living and fishing here for at least 1,400 years, beginning with the Duwamish people who referred to their village just north of here as *Tohl-ahl-too* ("Herring House") and later as *Hah-Ah'-poos* ("Where There Are Horse Clams"), which hints at the area's abundance of seafood. A second village, *Yee-leh-khood* ("Basket Cap"), was in the current site of Terminal 107 Park.

This land's uses have changed dramatically during the past 150 years. In the late 1800s it was built up with small homes, and squatter shacks appeared in the 1930s. The northern end of the park was the site of one of Seattle's lumber mills, Seaboard Lumber, from the 1920s to 1980s. The southern part was a brick factory for more than eighty years until 1965. This was also an area of illegal activity during Prohibition, when people would sell booze from their houseboats just offshore.

In 1999 the city, the Port of Seattle, and many other partner organizations and volunteers began to restore this area, which involved removing industrial waste, including concrete, pieces of railroad,

A replica of an early 20th-century fishing boat sits near a stand of trees close to the Duwamish River.

and former docks, before re-creating the tidelands and reintroducing native species. Today the result is a pair of wonderful waterfront parks with great wildlife viewing. Bald eagles are regularly spotted nearby. Ospreys like to nest in the foliage.

Restored intertidal habitats are slowly allowing for fish species to return, although fishing of many species is still strongly discouraged due to contamination in the Duwamish River. Take a short walk on the mix of paved and unpaved paths that wind through the parks department's Herring's House Park to the north and the Port of Seattle's Terminal 107 Park at the southern end. Metal plaques and viewfinders along the trail help you follow the story of a young salmon trying to make its way to the Puget Sound.

Take your time to explore and you'll be rewarded with views of the Duwamish River and Kellogg Island at several mostly secluded spots. Picnic tables, a small shelter, and benches are tucked among the trees and other vegetation. The park provides a quiet spot to glimpse the activity along this busy industrial riverfront. Note: the park has a reputation for some illicit activities, so take caution if visiting alone.

EXTEND YOUR VISIT

To learn more about the history of the Duwamish tribe, cross West Marginal Way Southwest and visit the **Duwamish Longhouse** (small donation requested; Monday through Saturday 10:00 AM to 5:00 PM). For a short bike ride, follow the Duwamish Trail north 0.7 mile to the port's **Terminal 105 Park**, whose waterfront setting is also worth a visit for a slightly different angle on the bustling Duwamish. For a longer 4-mile ride, continue on, crossing under the West Seattle Bridge to Harbor Avenue Southwest, a route that takes you all the way to **Alki Beach Park**.

111   DUWAMISH WATERWAY PARK

Quiet riverside renders waterfront picnic spot

Location: 7900 10th Ave. S.; South Park
Acreage: 1.5
Amenities: Picnic tables, benches, barbecue grills, hand-carry boat launch

GETTING THERE

BY CAR From East Marginal Wy. S., turn south on 16th Ave. S. and cross the South Park Bridge. Turn right at the first intersection on Dallas Ave. S. After 0.3 mile, turn right on 10th Ave. S. Free street parking is available on 10th Ave. S.
BY BUS 8th Ave. S./S. Kenyon St.; 8th Ave. S./S. Monroe St.; S. Cloverdale St./8th Ave. S.

At the end of the street in a mixed residential and industrial neighborhood sits an acre and a half of refreshing greenspace and waterfront access for the South Park community. A lively center of activity on warm summer evenings

SEATTLE'S ORIGINAL FARMLAND

One of only two original farms still remaining in the city—the other is Picardo Farm in North Seattle—Marra Farm is a major pride of the South Park community. For more than forty years the Marra family, Italian immigrants who arrived in Seattle just after the turn of the last century, farmed part of the area that is now known as **Marra-Desimone Park**. (Joe Desimone was the previous landowner, who sold the family the plot.) Marra Farm wasn't the only farm in the South Park area in the 1900s, but it's the only one that remains, thanks to being set aside as park space. Today the farm hosts important work by local nonprofit organizations to promote youth, gardening, sustainability, and food security. Visit the park (9026 4th Avenue South) and you'll find picnic tables and a short path around the gardens.

when families occupy picnic tables and bring food to grill on the park's barbecues, it is often empty and quiet here on weekdays.

Find a seat on one of the benches and delight in views of this always-active channel. This park and many others along the Duwamish River have been adopted by citizens determined to reverse the damage of one hundred years of pollution in this waterway. Despite the pollution, several species of salmon and trout call the river home. Community events celebrating the river and the cleanup's progress are held regularly on the park's flat lawn.

Duwamish Waterway Park isn't dense with vegetation—which means mostly clear water views—but salal, dogwoods, and vine maples have been planted here to boost native species and to protect and encourage wildlife. A large ponderosa pine in one corner provides shade in the summer.

A short gravel trail skims the perimeter of the park for dog walkers and those who want to stroll. The sandy beachfront is perfect for launching a kayak or canoe to see this important waterway up close.

EXTEND YOUR VISIT

Just 0.3 mile away is the **South Park Playground** and Community Center, a hub of this tight-knit community. Walk south on 10th Avenue South for three blocks. Turn right on South Thistle Street. The park will be straight ahead at the end of the block. In addition to the community center with indoor restrooms, you'll find baseball/softball and soccer fields, basketball courts, tennis courts, a playground with climbing structures and swings, and a seasonal wading pool.

112   WESTCREST PARK

Covered reservoir and wooded trails create huge playground for kids, dogs, and hikers

Location: 8th Ave. SW and SW Cloverdale St.; West Seattle/Highland Park
Acreage: 128.4
Amenities: Two playgrounds, off-leash dog park, 2.5 miles of unpaved trails, 1 mile of paved paths, restrooms, picnic tables, barbecue grills, benches, P-Patch

GETTING THERE

BY CAR From the West Seattle Bridge, exit at Delridge Wy. SW and follow for 3.5 miles. Turn left on SW Trenton St.; continue 0.6 mile and turn left on 9th Ave. SW. After one block turn right on SW Cloverdale St., then turn immediately right on 8th Ave. SW and left into the free parking lot; park here to access the main playground and paved walking path. To reach the off-leash dog park, continue east on SW Cloverdale St. After three blocks, turn right into the lot. To reach the hiking trails and P-Patch, a third parking lot is available at the south end of the park, accessed from SW Henderson St. **BY BUS** 9th Ave. SW/SW Trenton St.; SW Roxbury St./8th Ave. SW; 16th Ave. SW/SW Trenton St.

Don't expect to get in and out with a quick visit to this park if you have kids or dogs in your party. With fantastic playgrounds—both the human and canine variety—there's a lot to do.

Dog owners relish the 8.4 acres of off-leash area that stretch from north to south, creating a quarter-mile-long wooded walking path for exercise. Several open areas encourage playing fetch, and pups will find large concrete pipes to tunnel through while owners rest on benches or plastic chairs. A shelter provides protection from rain and sun. Small and shy dogs have a separate area, with good protection from the elements provided by evergreen trees.

West Seattle's only off-leash dog park is a wooded wonderland for owners and pets.

From both inside and just outside the off-leash area, you'll come across a number of entrances to the park's forested hiking trails. Illustrated signs indicate you're stepping into either the Bigleaf Maple Forest or the Douglas Fir Forest, although the trees are more varied and the two sections meld into one another. You may want to consult the map posted near the south parking lot before you venture in, since dozens of short trails intertwine, making it easy to get lost, although you're sure to eventually wind up on a main thoroughfare.

Twenty acres were added in 2015 after a giant reservoir was covered and the park expanded onto its lid. This northern section of park rests on a crest with views of Beacon Hill and the Cascade Mountains. *Flyers*, by artist David Boyer, move in the wind and look like birds imitating planes—appropriate since real ones on their way into Sea-Tac Airport are easy to spot from the park. The playground here is fantastic, with a wooden climbing structure with a spiral slide and suspension bridge, a dome net climber, and two long, exhilarating zip lines. Younger kids will find swings and a net merry-go-round. Taking advantage of its position on the top of the hill, the playground also includes two consecutive slides built into the hillside.

A paved path loops around the circumference of this part of the park, creating a flat, pleasant route for walkers and kids on bikes. Benches and tables around the play area make a nice picnic area. The path then dips down into a small valley and connects to the older section of the park. On your way, look for a viewing platform that is suspended over the brush and looks south over a natural area. Continue south to find the community P-Patch and a second picnicking area with tables and barbecue grills. A smaller play area here includes more swings, a teeter-totter, and spring rider toys.

EXTEND YOUR VISIT

If you still haven't exhausted the kids, walk two blocks west on Southwest Cloverdale Street to reach **Highland Park Playground**. In the summer, kids can cool off in the spray park or take advantage of the climbing structure and ball fields. You'll also find restrooms and tennis courts.

113   ROXHILL PARK

Climbing playground, skate park, and barbecue spot reshape ancient peat bog

Location: SW Barton St. and 29th Ave. SW; West Seattle/White Center
Acreage: 13.4
Amenities: Playground, skate park, restrooms, barbecue grills, 0.5 mile of unpaved trails, benches, picnic tables, soccer field, baseball/softball fields

GETTING THERE

BY CAR From the West Seattle Bridge, exit at Delridge Wy. SW and drive 3.6 miles. Turn right on SW Barton Pl.; after half a mile the park will be on the left. Turn left on 29th Ave. SW to access free parking in the lot. To access the ball fields, instead turn left on 30th Ave. SW, left on SW Roxbury St., then left immediately into a small parking lot adjacent to the elementary school. **BY BUS** SW Barton St./26th Ave. SW; SW Roxbury St./28th Ave. SW.

Affectionately known as Castle Park by its fans, this park at the south end of West Seattle has one of the area's best playgrounds. With miniature turrets and kid-sized arches, the large climbing structure looks like home for imaginary princes and princesses. A climbing wall and curved tube slide provide a perfect way to enter and exit the fortress. A smaller structure for toddlers nearby mimics the larger one and has dueling slides.

The playground encourages climbing with both a net climbing dome and an obstacle course of parkour-style challenges, including poles with climbing holds. Younger kids will also like the sandbox, accessible merry-go-round, and swings. Parents and grandparents will find plenty of benches surrounding the play area, some shaded by trees.

Near the playground is an area well designed for picnicking and barbecuing, with tables and seven barbecue grills. An expansive flat lawn nearby invites games of Frisbee or tag.

Tweens, teens, and even adults congregate in the skate park in the park's northwest corner. The ten-thousand-square-foot space is set up mostly for street skating, with multiple rails, ledges, and stairs. The park also offers the challenge of several banks, and skaters can rest on benches nearby.

Short unpaved trails offer a chance to explore away from the rest of this amenity-packed park. Roxhill Park marks the southern end of the Longfellow Creek Legacy Trail that follows the creek for several miles through West Seattle. This wetland area of the park is the headwaters for the creek, and gravel trails travel over small footbridges to help you keep your feet dry. This is one of the last peat bogs in the region and may have begun developing as long as ten thousand years ago. Community volunteers have planted thousands of native plants in the area in recent years to protect this important wetland.

114 FAUNTLEROY PARK

Thick forest protects
precious creek with trails

Location: 3951 SW Barton St.; West Seattle
Acreage: 32.9
Amenities: 1.5 miles of unpaved trails, bench

GETTING THERE
BY CAR From the West Seattle Bridge, exit at Fauntleroy Wy. and turn left at the first light on 35th Ave. SW; continue for 3 miles. Turn right on SW Barton St. After 0.3 mile, the park will be on the left. Free street parking is available on SW Barton St. There are multiple other entrances to the park from neighboring residential streets and from the parking lot of the Fauntleroy Church/Fauntleroy YMCA.
BY BUS California Ave. SW/SW Barton St.; SW Wildwood Pl./45th Ave. SW.

Step into this heavily wooded park for a refreshing departure from city life, but remember you are sharing it with many creatures, including coyotes, bald eagles, barred owls, and coho salmon. An incredible eighty species of birds have been noted in Fauntleroy Park in recent years.

Study the map on the kiosk before you enter to plan your route. Although several of the trails dead-end or lead out to residential streets, it's possible to make a loop that lets you explore most of the park (you will need to skirt the eastern edge of the Fauntleroy Church parking lot to complete the circuit). As you hike you'll cross small wooden footbridges where you can peek down at the stream running below. This is the headwaters for Fauntleroy Creek and a precious habitat for salmon, which were reintroduced in the 1990s.

At the south end of the park stairs will lead up to higher points on the hillside where you can get a nice view of the ravine below. The park was logged in the 1920s and 1930s, but the regrowth is dense and varied, with a canopy made up mostly of hemlocks, cedars, maples, and alders. Look more closely to find bitter cherry trees, cottonwoods, and madronas. Volunteers work regularly to rid the park of invasive plants to protect the native species.

Several natural features and historic places in this neighborhood bear the name Fauntleroy. It originated in 1857 when surveyor George Davidson named Fauntleroy Cove to honor his fiancée's last name. He also ensured that she, her sister, and two brothers would be remembered by naming three peaks in the Olympic Mountains after them: Mount Ellinor, Mount Constance, and The Brothers.

EXTEND YOUR VISIT

Follow the path of the salmon by walking to **Fauntleroy Creek Ravine**, 0.5 mile downstream. Walk west (downhill) on Southwest Barton Street and turn slightly right on Southwest Director Street. Continue several blocks to the dead end and turn left on the trail to reach the park. Look down at the creek as it nears its exit into the Puget Sound. If you're lucky,

Hiking trails traverse a heavily wooded ravine that follows Fauntleroy Creek.

you'll spot coho salmon returning to spawn. Take the stairs down and cross Fauntleroy Way Southwest to reach **Cove Park**, just north of the Fauntleroy Ferry Terminal. Here playful salmon art celebrates the coho's journey and directs you to a small public beachfront.

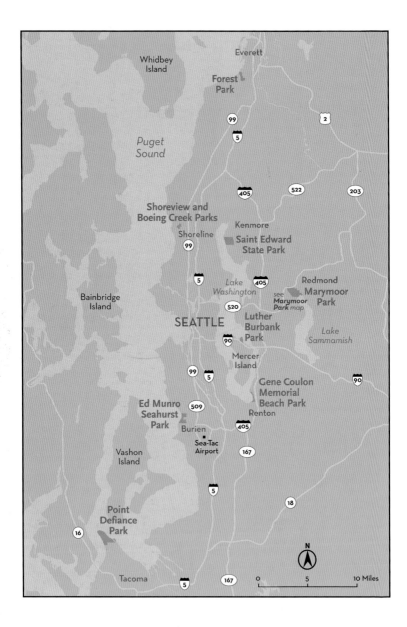

Beyond Seattle: Great Regional Parks

Playground, easy trails, and seasonal animal farm create kid-centered park

Location: 802 E. Mukilteo Blvd.; Everett
Acreage: 197
Amenities: Playground, seasonal spray park, indoor swimming pool, seasonal animal farm, 1.5 miles of unpaved trails, reservable indoor facilities, tennis courts, street hockey court, horseshoe pits, half basketball court, reservable shelters, restrooms, barbecue grills, picnic tables, benches, drinking fountains

GETTING THERE

BY CAR From I-5 northbound, take exit 192 and turn left immediately on 41st St. After 0.7 mile, the road curves slightly left and becomes E. Mukilteo Blvd. Continue 0.2 mile and turn left into the park. Veer slightly right and follow signs to a free parking lot near the swimming pool and playground. **BY BUS** E. Mukilteo Blvd./Pigeon Creek Rd.; E. Mukilteo Blvd./Forest Park.

Everett's oldest park is true to its name, with dense clusters of second-growth Douglas firs and cedars encasing its north end, where hiking is ideal for kids' short legs and attention spans. But if kids are along on your visit, you'll want to start at Forest Park's enormous playground, set in an open area in the heart of its nearly two hundred acres.

In the summer bring swimsuits to cool off at the seasonal spray park, where kids can dart among the many nozzles and sprays directing water in all directions. (An indoor swimming pool is also part of this complex as an off-season option.) The playground is nearby and covers a large area, with two traditional climbing structures boasting slides, short zip lines, bridges, and towers. Two other popular toys are an airplane and a climbable black-and-red train. You'll also find a teeter-totter, arched ladder, and two swing sets.

An unusual charm of Forest Park is the animal farm, open in summer months, where kids can pet farm animals for free and ride ponies for a small fee. It's the second-generation animal attraction after a zoo (housing monkeys, lions, bears, and elephants, among other animals) that operated here for sixty years closed in the 1970s.

Easy access to the kid-friendly trails begins near the playground, behind the picnic shelter. A quarter-mile loop is noted on a kiosk map and points out trees and shrubs that you may see on your walk. The dirt trail follows a ridge through a corridor of salal and ferns and circles back where side paths lead to more trails to the west. Cross the gully and wander along until you emerge on the edge of a large open field where the trail continues along the north side and brings you to an overflow parking area a bit west of the playground.

116 SHOREVIEW AND BOEING CREEK PARKS

Fantastic urban hiking abounds north of the city

Location: Shoreview Park: 700 NW Innis Arden Wy. (bordered by Shoreline Community College); Boeing Creek Park: 17229 3rd Ave. NW; Shoreline
Acreage: 88
Amenities: Two playgrounds, off-leash dog park, 3 miles of unpaved trails, soccer field, baseball/softball field, tennis courts, restrooms, benches, picnic tables, drinking fountain

GETTING THERE

BY CAR From I-5 northbound, take exit 175 and drive west on N. 145th St. for 1.5 miles. Turn right on Greenwood Ave. N. and then immediately veer left to continue 0.7 mile on Greenwood Ave. N. Turn left on NW Innis Arden Wy. After 0.7 mile the entrance to the park will be on your right. Free parking is available in the lot.

A second smaller parking lot is available closer to the off-leash dog park, accessible from NW Innis Arden Wy. Turn right into the Shoreline Community College parking lot and follow signs to the off-leash area on the west side of the complex.

BY BUS Shoreline Community College; N. Innis Arden Wy./Greenwood Ave. N.

There's no doubt that William Boeing, founder of the Boeing Company, left an enormous stamp on our region, but this pair of parks is a much less known mark of his legacy. In 1913, he built a mansion on this land, which he used for hunting and fishing. He eventually donated the land that makes up Shoreview Park, which is now owned by the City of Shoreline. The 1.6-mile-long creek that empties into the Puget Sound just west of the parks is also named after Boeing.

Shoreview and Boeing Creek parks work as one, with a network of hiking trails that includes several loops with varied terrain, making for excellent urban walks. Orient yourself on the map at the entrance to the primary trailhead at the north end of the main parking lot. Several loops, all under 1 mile, connect at different locations, so you can piece together a long hike or a short kid-appropriate outing.

Take the Forest Loop Trail for a more challenging, hilly climb in the dense woods. Choose the Boeing Creek Loop Trail for a tour of the creek bed, which has dry and wet sections. The Hidden Lake Loop Trail is rewarding for its peek at the small, sandy beachfront lake, a result of William Boeing's manmade dam. For the easiest access to the flat, stroller-friendly Pond Loop Trail, consider parking on Northwest 175th Street near the intersection with 6th Avenue Northwest.

Towering hemlocks, firs, and cedars govern this forest. The land making up these parks was probably selectively logged more than one hundred years ago,

Named after the airplane company founder, Boeing Creek flows through the park that also bears his name.

but many massive trees remain. Look for metal placards in the park pointing out a few of the largest species, including a two-hundred-foot-tall Douglas fir. Note: Erosion and mudslides have been an issue on several of the trails in recent years, so look for updates on trail conditions and closures of some sections. The creek has significant flow during winter and spring months, making it easy to get wet feet.

A multisport recreation center is at the heart of the park, near the main parking lot. Ball fields and tennis courts attract athletes of all ages for rec-league games. The park's two colorful playgrounds are enough to warrant a visit on their own. A large play area with two climbing structures sits in a sunken spot reachable by stairs or a long paved wheelchair-friendly path from the parking lot. The bright red, yellow, and blue climbers feature a half dozen slides—including a pair of two-story tube slides for daredevils. A second, smaller play area is located next to the upper baseball field, a great distraction for younger kids while their older siblings are playing Little League.

Dog owners can reach the off-leash dog park by taking a trail that starts at the top of the tennis courts or parking in the lot next to the off-leash area. This long space on a mix of dirt and gravel has chairs and benches for owners and stretches of open area for playing fetch. A separate section is designated for small or shy dogs.

117   SAINT EDWARD STATE PARK

One of area's biggest lakefront parks offers treats for hikers, bikers, and kids

Location: 14445 Juanita Dr. NE (near NE 145th St.); Kenmore
Acreage: 316
Amenities: Playground, 6.5 miles of unpaved hiking and mountain biking trails, restrooms, reservable picnic areas, picnic tables, barbecue grills, reservable indoor facilities, soccer field, baseball/softball field, sand volleyball court, drinking fountain, benches

GETTING THERE
BY CAR From Bothell Wy. NE/SR 522 in Kenmore, turn south on 68th Ave. NE, which becomes Juanita Dr. NE, and continue for 1.8 miles. Turn right on NE 145th St. (entrance sign will say "Bastyr University") and stay right at the fork to follow signs into the park instead of the university. Parking is available in several lots in the central area. Discover Pass required (can be purchased at park). **BY BUS** NE 153rd Pl./Juanita Dr. NE.

The grand, towering brick building of a former seminary commands attention from its spot on a grassy mound as you enter this state park. The Romanesque Revival building with its impressive bell tower was built in 1931 by the Archdiocese of Seattle to be used as a seminary named in honor of Edward the Confessor (born one thousand years ago). The buildings served as a school for boys before much of the land became a park in 1978.

What to do about the deteriorating buildings at Saint Edward (they are on the National Register of Historic Places) has been discussed for many years,

A large wooden play structure at Saint Edward State Park was designed by local kids.

with local residents and users weighing in on a variety of options, including selling the buildings for private development. Bastyr University sits like an island inside the park on fifty-one acres sold by the archdiocese.

Orient your visit near the seminary, where a paved path leads to a smaller building and gymnasium with restrooms and trail maps. A major draw at the park is the network of wooded trails beloved by hikers, trail runners, and mountain bikers, many of which were built by boys who attended school at Saint Edward. From the heart of the park, paths spread out in all directions, with varying lengths and elevation changes, making it tough for first-time visitors to plot a route. You can appreciate the trail builders' hard work on a roughly 1.5-mile loop that touches Lake Washington and begins on the North Trail—look for the trailhead across the parking lot on the north side of the gymnasium.

The trail descends toward the lake through a forest of Douglas firs, big-leaf maples, and cedars. Luminous green moss coats the trunks of these tall trees, and ferns line the often-muddy trails. Continue as your path becomes the beach trail and skirts the edge of the lake, where fallen trees are partially submerged. You'll come to a sandy beach lined with cottonwoods and alders, where views open up across the water to North Seattle. What's little known to many park users is what lies just offshore. More than 1,100 years ago a landslide prompted by an earthquake sent a cascade of trees into the depths of Lake Washington, where they remain today as a sort of underwater forest.

From the beach, follow the Seminary Trail back up the hill—or extend your hike onto the South Ridge, South Canyon, or Grotto trails, all of which have branches near this point. On the Seminary Trail you'll emerge again in the center of the park, with views of the majestic building on the hill. The open field on the west side of the building frequently hosts multigenerational picnics on its vast lawn, with tables and barbecue grills placed in the shade of the tall evergreens.

Turn right and head for the south side of the field if you want to see the Grotto, a secluded altar made of concrete and stones, built in the 1940s for the seminary and now used for weddings and quiet meditation.

On the south side of the seminary is one of the Eastside's best playgrounds. Designed by kids, the fifteen-thousand-square-foot play area is dominated by a massive wooden tree-house-style structure with bridges, tunnels, and slides that can occupy kids for a long time while parents sit on benches or tables nearby. The partially enclosed area also has a smaller structure for toddlers, ride-on toys, an airplane toy, and a sandbox. A paved path by the playground is perfect for kids to ride bikes on. Adults can mountain bike on designated trails, which connect to other bike trails in greenspaces adjacent to the park.

118 MARYMOOR PARK

Regional superpark draws visitors for recreation and events

Location: 6046 W. Lake Sammamish Pkwy. NE; Redmond
Acreage: 640
Amenities: Three playgrounds, outdoor adult exercise equipment, off-leash dog park, pet memorial garden, rock climbing pinnacle, velodrome bicycle track, community garden, historic Clise Mansion reservable for events, park office/visitors center, 2 miles of unpaved trails, 1.5 miles of paved bike paths, sports fields (soccer, baseball/softball, cricket, lacrosse, and rugby), tennis courts, radio-controlled model airplane field, reflexology path, outdoor concert venue, boat house/rowing club, hand-carry boat launch, reservable shelters, restrooms, barbecue grills, picnic tables, benches, seasonal concession stands, drinking fountains

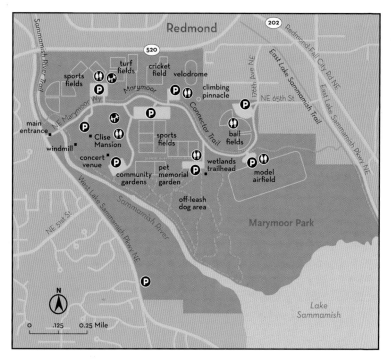

GETTING THERE

BY CAR From Seattle or Bellevue, take SR 520 eastbound and exit and turn right at West Lake Sammamish Pkwy. NE. Turn immediately left on NE Marymoor Wy. into the park. Parking is available in several lots for a small fee; read signs to find the closest one to your destination. **BY BUS** West Lake Sammamish Pkwy. NE/Leary Wy. NE. **BY BIKE** The Sammamish River Trail and Marymoor Connector Trail run through the park.

As you enter Marymoor Park, a totem pole by artist Dudley Carter reminds you that the first visitors to the shores of Lake Sammamish were Native Americans. Evidence found near the park shows a settlement existed here a stunning three thousand years ago.

The land was acquired by the Tosh family in the 1870s and then sold in 1904 to James Clise, who built a large home and developed what would become Willowmoor farm. So renowned were Clise's livestock that Henry Ford insisted that the Michigan hospital he built only serve milk from Willowmoor cows.

Marymoor Park became the first park in the county when it was purchased in 1962, and today it is one of the most popular recreation areas in the region, with more than three million visitors annually. With top amenities, it is a magnet for enthusiasts of all kinds—bikers, birders, gardeners, dog owners, climbers, model airplane pilots, and much more. Several points of interest are worth checking out on your visit.

For kids, the park's three play areas are a big draw. The best and largest is near Lot K, where you'll find two colorful climbing structures with spiral slides, bridges, ladders, and miniature climbing walls. A cute ride-on dinosaur is popular. Adult exercise equipment surrounds this playground so parents and grandparents can be active, too.

Nearby you'll find a reflexology path designed for strolling barefoot. The different sizes of stones place pressure on parts of the foot to ease a wide range of health maladies. Benches provide a quiet spot for rest or meditation around the circular path.

The forty-five-foot-tall climbing pinnacle is one of the only free public walls in the region. Extremely popular for bouldering and lead climbing, the artificial tower has dozens of routes for beginners and advanced climbers.

Next door you'll find the velodrome. Opened in 1975, this outdoor bike-racing track with steeply banked curves has hosted national and international competitions, including the Goodwill Games and regional Olympic trials. Grandstands put spectators up close to the action as bikers zoom around the oval in a blur.

Just down the road is an open area set aside for operators of radio-controlled model airplanes. The Marymoor Radio Control Club puts on classes and events for flyers. You have to be a member or a guest of one to pilot here, but a low fence makes it easy to watch the action over the airfield.

It's no surprise that dog owners swarm to the enormous off-leash dog area in the south end of the park. With forty acres of space, multiple spots with water-front access for dogs to splash in the river, and hiking paths, the Marymoor Park off-leash area is a dream for pets and their owners. Look for the entrance to the peaceful pet memorial garden inside the off-leash area. One warning: some of the dog park's entrances are not gated, and because the off-leash area is so large, it's not unusual for owners to lose sight of their pets.

With so many manmade amenities, it's easy to leave Marymoor Park without feeling you've connected with nature. But the park has three hundred acres of protected woods and wetlands that are home to many different species of birds. More than 220 species have been seen in the park. A local chapter of the Audubon Society helps maintain the bird-watching trail that begins near Lot G and meanders through meadows and woods to reach the north shore of Lake Sammamish. You can return along the same trail or continue through the off-leash dog park.

119 LUTHER BURBANK PARK

Island's biggest asset sees swimmers, boaters, and fishermen

Location: 2040 84th Ave. SE; Mercer Island
Acreage: 77
Amenities: Playground, seasonally guarded swimming beach, off-leash dog park, 1.5 miles of paved and unpaved trails, tennis courts, fishing pier, public boat dock, amphitheater, community garden, barbecue grills, picnic tables, benches, restrooms

GETTING THERE

BY CAR From Seattle go eastbound on I-90 and take exit 7A. Turn left on 77th Ave. SE, then turn immediately right on N. Mercer Wy. After 0.2 mile, turn left on 81st Ave. SE, then turn right on SE 24th St. At the T intersection, turn left on 84th Ave. SE and continue straight into the free main parking lot. To reach the swimming beach, instead turn right on 84th Ave. SE and then left into the free parking lot. **BY BUS** N. Mercer Wy./80th Ave. SE; SE 26th St./82nd Pl. SE.

Occupying a large section of Mercer Island's desirable northeast corner, Luther Burbank Park is one of several great parks on the island.

Most activities center on the waterfront, where people assemble in warm months to take advantage of more than half a mile of shoreline. Designated spots for swimming, boat mooring, fishing, and even "dog paddling" are spread across the park with a mix of paved and unpaved trails connecting points of interest.

For a full tour of this popular park, begin at the main parking lot and head north to the off-leash dog park. With several gated entrances, this 1.25-acre play space features a mix of grass and sand and is dotted with trees for shade and protection, but it's the access to the lake that draws dogs and their owners here year-round. A doggie shower just outside the gates is a thoughtful addition to the park.

Put your pet's leash on and head south along the shoreline trail that follows the wooden fence. The lake peeks through trees and shrubs, and you'll pass a public-moorage dock

Trails hug four thousand feet of shoreline with intimate Lake Washington views.

and then a fishing dock along the dirt path. Emerging at the south end of the park, you'll come to the swimming beach, where kids swarm in the summer for swimming in shallow water and sand play. A small play area has a fire engine climbing structure for toddlers. Wetlands bookend the park at its north and south ends, where more than 180 species of birds, mammals, reptiles, and amphibians have been recorded.

Head west from here where strange formations in the grass will encourage you to stop for a closer look. As part of John Hoge's earth and stone sculpture *The Source*, a series of concentric mounds were designed to draw in and return lake water. Turn north along the paved path, which splits in a loop around a large meadow great for picnicking or games. Arriving back in the amenity-packed heart of the park, you'll find one of the area's best playgrounds—an enormous space with multiple climbing structures, slides, a zip line, and a net climbing dome.

Luther Burbank Park was first home to the historic and ornate Calkins Hotel (President Benjamin Harrison stayed there). It then became a home for "delinquent youth" (most of the kids came from tough upbringings) around the turn of the last century. The school included a farm and garden plots and so was named in 1931 to honor the American botanist who developed more than eight hundred varieties of plants. It's ironic that one of his specimens, the Himalayan blackberry, now congests many parks in the region, including Luther Burbank Park.

120 GENE COULON MEMORIAL BEACH PARK

South shore of Lake Washington offers water recreation and accessible walking paths

Location: 1201 Lake Washington Blvd. N.; Renton
Acreage: 57
Amenities: Playground, outdoor adult exercise equipment, motorized boat launch, hand-carry boat launch, seasonally guarded swimming beach, fishing pier, boat dock with day moorage, 2.2 miles of paved paths, horseshoe pits, tennis courts, reservable shelters, barbecue grills, bathhouse, picnic tables, benches, restrooms, fast-food restaurants, drinking fountains

GETTING THERE

BY CAR From Interstate 405, take exit 5 and drive west on NE Park Dr. for 0.2 mile. Turn right on Lake Washington Blvd. N. Take the first left into the park. Free parking is available in several large, consecutive lots. **BY BUS** Park Ave. N./ Lake Washington Blvd. N.

Bustling with lively crowds gathering to swim, boat, and picnic in the summer, this waterfront park thins out to host anglers, bird-watchers, and walkers in quiet winter months. More than a mile of shoreline makes up this slender park clinging to the southeastern edge of Lake Washington.

Gene Coulon Park, named to honor the former Renton parks director who helped make the park a reality, is a delight to explore on foot, with flat paved

Gene Coulon's nine-hundred-foot-long dock offers excellent opportunities for fishing.

paths that span the entire shore and include a series of piers suspended over the water. Begin at the far southwest end on the tiny island reachable by a footbridge, where many varieties of birds can be spotted. Mallards, geese, gulls, bald eagles, sparrows, hawks, and many other species have been seen throughout the park.

Continue along the shoreline, where you can't miss the colorful playground. Kids' attention will be diverted to the slides, bridges, tunnels, ladders, and swings that make up this large play area (there's adult exercise equipment, too, for parents and caregivers to bide their time). Then walk out onto the dock that surrounds the sandy swimming beach. When you reach the other side of the beach, cross over the creek and pass the boat launch on your way to the next dock, which hosts a two-story pavilion, dozens of picnic tables with water views, and two casual restaurants.

Climb the stairs here for a high vantage point of the park or walk out on the nine-hundred-foot-long pier and look back at the park from a new angle. You will also have clear vistas of points around the lake, including to the west, where you can see activity at Boeing's Renton plant. Straight across the lake you'll spot South Seattle, just a couple of miles away by boat. Look north for views of the southern tip of Mercer Island. Have a seat on one of the pier's benches and watch boat traffic come in and out of the park or enjoy lunch on one of the two floating picnic docks. Docks have stood in this area for more than a century, dating back to when this area was used for coal transport by boat in the early 1900s.

Many visitors don't realize that the park continues north from here along the southeast shore for another two-thirds of a mile. This quiet stretch is a wetland area, and bikes and dogs are prohibited in order to protect plants and wildlife. Small signs help you identify trees and shrubs, including aspens, beeches, and larches along the path.

This is an excellent area of the lake to explore by canoe or kayak, with a varied shoreline and an easy launching spot on a small dock designated for hand-carry boats. A separate dock a little to the north is set aside for fishing, with anglers trying for catches of trout, perch, and bass.

121 ED MUNRO SEAHURST PARK

Picnicking paradise embraces views and saltwater shoreline

Location: 1600 SW Seahurst Park Rd.; Burien
Acreage: 182
Amenities: Playground, 2.2 miles of unpaved trails, hand-carry boat launch, Environmental Science Center, reservable shelters, restrooms, picnic tables, benches

GETTING THERE

BY CAR From State Route 509 southbound, exit at State Route 518 and keep right to turn right on S. 146th St. After 0.2 mile, turn right on Ambaum Blvd. SW, then turn immediately left on SW 144th St. After 0.2 mile, turn right on 13th Ave. SW and follow for 0.8 mile into the park (it becomes SW Seahurst Park Rd.). Free parking is available in two lots: upper (overflow) and lower (closer to the beach). **BY BUS** Ambaum Blvd. SW/SW 144th St.

Nearly a mile of quiet beachfront and views of the Olympic Mountains, Vashon Island, and the glittering Puget Sound attract picnickers and hikers to this park 12 miles south of downtown Seattle.

The park takes its name from two important players in its history. The Seahurst Land Company owned two hundred acres of forest here in the early 1900s, some of which is now part of the park. Former King County Commissioner Ed Munro saw the value of this land and encouraged the county to buy it in the 1960s so it could be preserved. It became a county park in 1975 and is now owned and maintained by the City of Burien.

More than a thousand feet of seawall built in the early 1970s were removed recently, and today Seahurst Park excels in offering visitors a balance between great amenities and a wild, natural setting. The park boasts a national award for best beach restoration.

The heart of the park is a central area off the lower parking lot, where you'll find a playground, a picnic shelter, restrooms, and the first access to the beach. The play area reflects its surroundings with a nature-inspired obstacle course with ropes and artificial rocks best suited for older kids. Younger children will appreciate the swing set—and parents won't mind stalling at the playground with such sweeping views on display.

Three large picnic shelters with tables and barbecue grills are the coveted spots for family gatherings and birthday parties, each with unobstructed views and close access to the water. You'll find them at the north, central, and southern ends of the park.

On the beach, driftwood the length of cars litters the shore, creating hours of play and fascination for kids. The chances of spying wildlife are excellent with bald eagles, herons, and many species of seabirds making stops here. Several times per month during summer low tides, volunteer naturalists from the Seattle Aquarium come to the park to help visitors spot sea life and educate about habitat protection.

Head either south or north for a short hike. The South Shoreline Trail crosses the park's largest creek and ends less than half a mile away. For a longer, steeper climb follow the North Shoreline Trail, a wide gravel path, toward the Environmental Science Center, which provides programs and events from moonlight beach walks to classes that build underwater exploration robots. Curious about the second building to the north? It's home to a marine technology program that offers high school students college credit and a head start in careers in marine science and oceanography. A fish ladder just steps away from the facility is designed for returning coho salmon, helping to rear and restock the population.

Follow the service road up to its end at the northern edge of the park and loop back through the North Nature Trail, which crosses the road in several spots. Hemlocks, alders, bigleaf maples, and cedars make up this serene forest that teems with small springs. You'll emerge on the North Shoreline Trail halfway between two picnic shelters.

122 POINT DEFIANCE PARK

*Regional star harbors
old-growth forest and
endless attractions*

Location: 5400 N. Pearl St.; Tacoma
Acreage: 760
Amenities: Playground, off-leash dog park, 14 miles of unpaved trails, 5-mile scenic drive/ bike route, tennis courts, Point Defiance Zoo and Aquarium, marina (with boat launch, fishing pier, bait shop, moorage, and gas), hand-carry boat launch, seasonal kayak rentals, seasonal visitors center, gardens, restaurants and seasonal concessions, Fort Nisqually Living History Museum, reservable shelters, barbecue grills, benches, picnic tables, restrooms, drinking fountains

GETTING THERE
BY CAR From Seattle, take I-5 south to Tacoma. Take exit 132B and merge onto State Route 16 westbound. After 3 miles take exit 3 to 6th Ave.; continue straight through the first light, crossing 6th Ave. At the next intersection turn right on N. Pearl St. Continue for 3 miles, then continue straight into the park. Free parking is available in more than a dozen locations throughout the park. Follow signs to your destination. **BY BUS** Point Defiance Ferry Terminal. **BY FERRY** Ferries depart from the Point Defiance Ferry Terminal (inside the park near the marina) to the south end of Vashon Island (Tahlequah).

Unquestionably the best urban park in the south Puget Sound—and rivaling any in Seattle—this peninsula was set aside for preservation and recreation more than 125 years ago.

With hundreds of acres of old-growth forest occupying a headland sticking out into the Sound, this area was a camp for the Salish Native Americans who hunted and fished from its shores. In 1866 the federal government set aside the land to be used for military purposes—then abandoned its plans twenty years later, allowing the City of Tacoma to begin using it as a park. By the 1890s visitors were arriving by streetcar to enjoy Point Defiance Park's beaches, gardens, and picnic areas.

There are dozens of temptations here, and it takes multiple visits to see everything. A great way to start is with a stop by the information kiosk immediately inside the main entrance, where you'll find a

Beachcomb in solitude along the northern shore at Point Defiance Park. To keep from being trapped by its high cliffs, check the tide tables before you visit.

map and brochures for different attractions inside the park. Then follow excellent signage that directs you to your destination. Or take a tour along Five Mile Drive, a scenic one-way roadway that loops through to offer peeks of most of the park's best features—and provides many opportunities to pull off into breathtaking viewpoints and quiet picnic areas. Note that certain hours of the day the drive is closed to cars so bikers and runners can exercise free of worry—and car fumes.

Even better is to explore the park by foot. Miles of superb dirt trails give you the chance to see some of the region's only urban old-growth forest. Well-placed trail markers and paths that crisscross in numerous places allow you to piece together your own tour of the park. One thing you won't want to miss is the 450-year-old Douglas fir (marked on maps as the Mountaineer Tree) at the north end of the park. Many animals live among the old firs, cedars, hemlocks, and madronas, including deer, bald eagles, owls, and bats. Seals and sea lions can sometimes be spotted in the waters nearby.

Another pleasant walk is an 0.8-mile stretch along the waterfront between the marina and Owen Beach on the northeast shore of the park. With both paved and unpaved tracks, it is a wheelchair- and stroller-friendly way to see some of Point Defiance Park's best views of Vashon Island, the ferries, and small boat traffic passing through Dalco Passage.

If you're looking for more solitude, it's possible to continue a walk along the sand north of Owen Beach toward the promontory, but consult tide tables first as it's easy to become stranded. This quieter section of the park has a flat shoreline with impressive cliffs, some stretching nearly two hundred feet overhead.

Point Defiance has several gardens with specific attractions, including a Japanese-inspired garden, a native plant garden, and gardens featuring roses, rhododendrons, and dahlias. Ebenezer Roberts was the park's first gardener—and its design mastermind. Beginning in the 1890s, he helped clear the land, established the rose garden with donated cuttings, and oversaw the creation of paths. He and his family lived in the Lodge inside the park, which then went on to house Tacoma parks superintendents for generations until 1980. Built in 1898, it is the oldest building still standing in the park and is now used as a summer visitors center.

You may need to plan a return visit to take in other features of the park, including the zoo (which opened more than one hundred years ago), an excellent wooded off-leash dog park with protection from rain and sun, a playground, the Nisqually Living History Museum, a 1914 pagoda built as a streetcar station, and well-furnished picnic areas scattered throughout the park.

Resources

WEBSITES

These great resources provide more information on city and regional parks, in particular the ones in this book.

Seattle Parks and Recreation: www.seattle.gov/parks
Port of Seattle Parks and Public Access: www.portseattle.org/parks-public-access
Seattle Department of Transportation Shoreline Street Ends Program:
    www.seattle.gov/transportation/stuse_stends.htm
King County Parks: www.kingcounty.gov/services/parks-recreation/parks
Washington State Parks: www.parks.wa.gov
Everett Parks & Recreation: www.everettwa.gov/149/Parks-Recreation
City of Shoreline: Parks, Recreation & Cultural Services:
    www.cityofshoreline.com/parks
City of Mercer Island Parks & Recreation: www.mercergov.org/parks
City of Renton Recreation Division: www.rentonwa.gov/recreation
Burien Parks, Recreation, and Cultural Services: www.burienwa.gov/parks
Metro Parks Tacoma: www.metroparkstacoma.org

FOR MORE ON SEATTLE HISTORY

I discovered quite a bit of inaccurate and contradictory historical information as I researched this book. Three of the best and most accurate sources on Seattle history are:

Historylink.org: www.historylink.org
Paul Dorpat, Jean Sherrard, and Bérangère Lomont's website:
    https://pauldorpat.com

Images of America book series with multiple titles highlighting Seattle history and Seattle-area parks, published by Arcadia Publishing:
www.arcadiapublishing.com/series/images-of-america-books

OTHER EXCELLENT RESOURCES

Jacobson, Arthur Lee. *Trees of Seattle*. 2nd ed. Seattle: printed by author, 2006.

Jaramillo, Jake, and Cathy Jaramillo. *Seattle Stairway Walks: An Up-and-Down Guide to City Neighborhoods*. Seattle: Mountaineers Books, 2013. More information available on authors' blog, www.seattlestairwaywalks.com.

Citizens for Off-Leash Areas (COLA) in Seattle: https://seattlecola.org

Friends of Seattle's Olmsted Parks: www.seattleolmsted.org

Seattle Parks Foundation: www.seattleparksfoundation.org

Year of Seattle Parks blog: www.yearofseattleparks.com

Acknowledgments

My brother-in-law, Matt Russell, gave me an education in skateboard parks, and I'm grateful for his helpful descriptions of the skate elements. Thanks to Scott Shinn of www.parents4sk8parks.org and Dan Hughes of www.northwestskater.com for checking my work on the skate parks.

Many people helped by checking my facts and adding important details to my research. Special thanks to Mike Westra from the Evergreen Mountain Bike Alliance; Jack Tomkinson from Urban Sparks; and Ellen Escarcega and Sharon LeVine of Citizens for Off-Leash Areas (COLA) in Seattle.

Thank you to Laura Shauger and Kate Rogers at Mountaineers Books for their guidance and enthusiasm and to Rebecca Jaynes for her careful copyediting. A big thank-you to Kirsten Colton for finding my blog and shepherding my book idea along.

Thanks to the Seattle Parks and Recreation department for their help, especially Christina Hirsch for nailing down many tedious facts for me.

A lot of our parks were developed because a small group of people living close by advocated, raised funds, and steered the process, working hand in hand with the city. Thanks to all the committed citizens who volunteer their time for our parks.

Seattle is fortunate to have a strong network of advocates for parks, nature, and recreation. Special thanks to Jake and Cathy Jaramillo for their leadership and inspiration.

The heroes of our region's parks are the maintenance crews who quietly mow the lawns, trim the bushes, pick up litter, make repairs, and much more. Thanks for making our parks a wonderful place to be.

I was lucky to have friends and family come along on park visits. Thank you especially to Kelsey Leighton, Lindsay Little, and Morgan McGinn for their companionship. My in-laws Jim and Carol McFeely have an abundance of good cheer and babysitting energy. My sister, Erika Krumbeck, is my cheerleader, and without her help, I would not have taken the steps that led me here.

My mom, Eva Sköld Westerlind, is my hiking buddy and plant-identification coach—thanks for your unending support and stellar proofreading. My sons, Liam, Evan, and Graham, patiently accompanied me to literally hundreds of parks over the past eight years. You are the best playground testers! My husband, David McFeely, is the most positive and adventurous person I know—your encouragement is the root of everything.

Index

A

Alki Beach Park and Playground 221–223
Andover Place 220
Atlantic (neighborhood) 149, 152, 195, 196, 198
Atlantic City Boat Ramp 180–183
Atlantic Street Park 195–196

B

Ballard (neighborhood) 102, 104, 105, 106, 108, 109
Ballard Commons Park 104–105
Ballard Corners Park 105–106
Ballard Locks. See Hiram M. Chittenden Locks
Ballard Playground 105
Bayview Playground 60
Bayview-Kinnear Park 68
Beacon Food Forest 189
Beacon Hill (neighborhood) 188, 191, 192, 194
Beer Sheva Park 180–183
Bell Street Park 36
Belltown 33, 35
Belvoir Place 119
Bhy Kracke Park 70–72
Boeing Creek Park 244–247
Bradner Gardens Park 202
Broadview (neighborhood) 81, 85
Burien 256
Burke-Gilman Trail 131

C

Cal Anderson Park 157–159
Camp Long 228–230
Capitol Hill (neighborhood) 156, 157, 159, 162, 163, 165
Carkeek Park 81–85
Cascade Playground 31–32
Centennial Park 27–29

Central District (neighborhood) 142, 145, 149, 152, 154
Central Park Trail 153
Charles Richey Sr. Viewpoint 220
Cheasty Boulevard 206
Cheshiahud Lake Union Loop 31, 77
Chinook Beach Park 183–184
City Hall Park 42–43
Colman, James 19, 202, 214
Colman Park 202–204
Columbia City (neighborhood) 207
Columbia Park 209
Cormorant Cove 220
Cottage Grove Park 230–232
Counterbalance Park 68–69
Cove Park 241
Cowen Park 120–122
Crown Hill (neighborhood) 108

D

Daejeon Park 194–195
Dahl Playfield 124–126
David Rodgers Park 76
Day Street Boat Ramp 151
Daybreak Star Cultural Center 55
Delridge (neighborhood) 230
Delridge Playfield 232
Denny Blaine Park 142
Denny family 18, 19, 33, 34, 88, 161, 221
Denny Park 32–33
Discovery Park 51–55
Don Armeni Boat Ramp 226
Downtown (neighborhood) 25, 27, 36, 38, 40, 42, 43, 45
Dr. Blanche Lavizzo Park 153
Dr. José Rizal Park 192–194
Duwamish Head 223

Duwamish Longhouse 234
Duwamish Waterway Park 234–236

E
East Louisa Street End (Eastlake Boulodrome) 167
East Montlake Park 172–173
East Portal Viewpoint 150–151
Ed Munro Seahurst Park 256–258
Eddie Vine Boat Ramp 111
Ella Bailey Park 58–60
Elliott Bay Marina 64
Elliott Bay Trail (Terminal 91 Bike Path) 29
Emma Schmitz Memorial Overlook 218–220
Ercolini Park 217–218
Everett 243

F
Fauntleroy Creek Ravine 241
Fauntleroy Park 240–241
Firehouse Mini Park 154–155
First Hill (neighborhood) 155
Flo Ware Park 149–150
Forest Park 243–244
Freeway Park 40–42
Fremont (neighborhood) 100
Fremont Peak Park 100–101
Frink Park 147–149
Froula Playground 124

G
Gas Works Park 96–97
Gene Coulon Memorial Beach Park 254–256
Genesee Park and Playfield 207–209
Georgetown (neighborhood) 187
Georgetown Playfield 188
Golden Gardens Park 109–111
Greg Davis Park 230–232
Green Lake (neighborhood) 91, 97
Green Lake Park 91–94
Greenwood (neighborhood) 89
Greenwood Park 89–91

H
Hamilton Viewpoint Park 225–226
Harborview Park 155–156
Herring's House Park 232–234

Highland Park (neighborhood) 236
Highland Park Playground 238
Hing Hay Park 49
Hiram M. Chittenden Locks (Ballard Locks) 102–104
Homer Harris Park 142–143
Howell Park 141–142

I
I-5 Colonnade 165–166
I-90 Trail 151, 195, 200
Interlaken Park 162–163
International District (neighborhood) 47

J
Jack Block Park 226–228
Jackson Park Perimeter Trail 87
Jefferson Park 188–191
Jimi Hendrix Park 200
John C. Little Sr. Park 187
Judkins Park and Playfield 152–154

K
Katie Black's Garden 194
Kenmore 247
Kerry Park 67–68
Kinnear Park 64–65
Kirke Park 106–108
Kobe Terrace 47–49
Kubota Garden 184–186

L
Lake City (neighborhood) 130, 131
Lake Union Park 29–31
Lake Washington Boulevard 137
Lakewood (neighborhood) 207
Laurelhurst (neighborhood) 118, 119
Laurelhurst Playfield 118
Lawton Park 56–57
Leschi, Chief 42, 147
Leschi (neighborhood) 145, 147, 150
Leschi Park 147–149
Leschi-Lake Dell Natural Area 149
Licton Springs Park 88–89
Lincoln Park 211–215
Little Brook Park 130–131
Llandover Woods Greenspace 85–86

Louisa Boren Park 161
Lowman Beach Park 216–217
Luther Burbank Park 252–254
Lynn Street Mini Park 166–167

M
MacLean Park 72–73
Madison Park 139–141
Madison Park (neighborhood) 139
Madison Park North Beach 141
Madrona (neighborhood) 141, 144
Madrona Park 144–145
Madrona Playground 145
Magnolia (neighborhood) 51, 56, 57, 58, 61, 62
Magnolia Boulevard 60
Magnolia Manor Park 57–58
Magnolia Park 61
Magnolia Playfield 60
Maple Leaf (neighborhood) 127
Maple Leaf Reservoir Park 127–128
Marra-Desimone Park 235
Marshall Park (Betty Bowen Viewpoint) 67
Martha Washington Park 179
Martin Luther King Jr. Memorial Park 206
Marymoor Park 249–252
Matthews Beach Park 131–133
Mayfair Park 74–76
Me-Kwa-Mooks Park 218–220
Mercer Island 252
Meridian Playground 94–95
Mineral Springs Park 89
Minor (neighborhood) 154
Montlake (neighborhood) 135, 162, 170, 172
Montlake Playfield 170–172
Mount Baker (neighborhood) 195, 196, 198, 200, 202, 204
Mount Baker Boulevard 206
Mount Baker Park 204–206
Mount Baker Ridge Viewpoint 200–202
Myrtle Edwards Park 27–29

N
Nora's Woods 147
North Passage Point Park 170
Northacres Park 86–88
Northgate (neighborhood) 86, 88, 128

O
Occidental Square 45–47
Olmsted Brothers firm 19, 23, 93, 100, 137, 148, 157, 159–160, 162, 177, 203–204, 206, 224
Olympic Sculpture Park 25–27
Othello Park 186–187
Oxbow Park 187–188

P
Parsons Gardens 65–67
Peace Park 170
Phinney Ridge (neighborhood) 97
Picardo (Rainie) P-Patch 126
Pinehurst Playground 130
Pinehurst Pocket Park 128–130
Pioneer Square 43–45
Plum Tree Park 143
Plymouth Pillars Park 156–157
Point Defiance Park 258–260
Powell Barnett Park 145–147
Pratt Park 154
Pritchard Island Beach 179–180

Q
Queen Anne (neighborhood) 64, 65, 67, 68, 69, 70, 72, 73, 74, 76, 77
Queen Anne Boulevard 66
Queen Anne Bowl Playfield 76

R
Rainbow Point 128
Rainier Beach (neighborhood) 179, 180, 183, 184
Rainier Beach Playfield 182
Rainier Playfield 209
Rainier Valley (neighborhood) 186
Ravenna (neighborhood) 120, 123
Ravenna Park 120–122
Ravenna-Eckstein Park 123–124
Redmond 249
Regrade Park 35–36
Renton 254
Roanoke Park 169
Rogers Playground 168–169
Roosevelt (neighborhood) 120

Rotary Viewpoint 230
Roxhill Park 238–239

S
Saint Edward State Park 247–249
Sam Smith Park 198–200
Sand Point (neighborhood) 113
Sandel Playground 90
Schmitz Preserve Park 223–225
Seacrest Park 226
Seattle Center 35
Seattle, Chief 34, 41, 44, 182, 221
Seattle Children's PlayGarden 196–198
Seward Park 175–179
Shoreline (city) 244
Shoreview Park 244–247
6th Avenue NW Pocket Park 108
Smith Cove Park 62–64
Solstice Park 215–216
Soundview Terrace 77–79
South Lake Union 29, 31, 32
South Park (neighborhood) 234
South Park Playground 235
South Passage Point Park 169–170
South Ship Canal Trail 77
Spruce Street Mini Park 155
Streissguth Gardens 163–165
Sturgus Park 195
Summit Slope Park 159
Sunset Hill Park 108

T
Tacoma 258
Terminal 105 Park 234
Terminal 107 Park 232–234
Terry Pettus Park 167
32nd Ave. W. Boat Launch 61–62
Thomas C. Wales Park 73–74
Tilikum Place 33–34

Trolley Hill Park 72–73
12th Ave. S. Viewpoint 191–192

U
University of Washington's Center for Urban
    Horticulture 119

V
Van Asselt Playground 187
Victor Steinbrueck Park 36–37
Viretta Park 142
Volunteer Park and Conservatory 159–161

W
Wallingford (neighborhood) 94, 96
Wallingford Playfield 95
Ward Springs Park 69–70
Warren G. Magnuson Park 113–117
Washington Park Arboretum 135–139
Waterfall Garden Park 47
Waterfront Park 38–39
Weather Watch Park 220
Wedgwood (neighborhood) 124
Wedgwood Rock 125
West Ewing Mini Park 76–77
West Montlake Park 172, 173
West Seattle (neighborhood) 211, 215, 216, 217,
    218, 221, 223, 225, 226, 228, 230, 232, 236,
    238, 240
West Woodland Park Playground 100
Westcrest Park 236–238
White Center (neighborhood) 238
Woodland Park 97–100
Woodland Park Rose Garden 100

Y
Yesler, Henry 19, 45, 143, 217
Yesler Terrace 155

About the Author

Linnea Westerlind is a Seattle-area native who grew up spending a lot of time outdoors with her parents and sister. In 2009 she started a project to visit all the parks in Seattle and write about them on her blog, www.yearofseattleparks.com, which is now a resource of nearly five hundred city, regional, and state parks. Linnea works as a communications and marketing consultant for nonprofits and businesses, and she also writes articles about parks and outdoor adventures for *ParentMap* magazine. Together with her husband and three sons, she enjoys skiing, hiking, biking, and camping throughout the Pacific Northwest. She lives in West Seattle.

MOUNTAINEERS BOOKS, including its two imprints, Skipstone and Braided River, is a leading publisher of quality outdoor recreation, sustainability, and conservation titles. As a 501(c)(3) nonprofit, we are committed to supporting the environmental and educational goals of our organization by providing expert information on human-powered adventure, sustainable practices at home and on the trail, and preservation of wilderness.

Our publications are made possible through the generosity of donors, and through sales of more than 600 titles on outdoor recreation, sustainable lifestyle, and conservation. To donate, purchase books, or learn more, visit us online:

MOUNTAINEERS BOOKS
1001 SW Klickitat Way, Suite 201 • Seattle, WA 98134
800-553-4453 • mbooks@mountaineersbooks.org
www.mountaineersbooks.org

Leave No Trace strives to educate visitors about the nature of their recreational impacts and offers techniques to prevent and minimize such impacts. Leave No Trace is best understood as an educational and ethical program, not as a set of rules and regulations. For more information, visit www.lnt.org or call 800-332-4100.

OTHER TITLES YOU MIGHT ENJOY FROM MOUNTAINEERS BOOKS

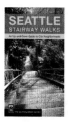

Seattle Stairway Walks
An Up-and-Down Guide to City Neighborhoods
Jake Jaramillo and Cathy Jaramillo
Full-color guide to 25 of the city's best neighborhood walks that feature public stairways

Turning Homeward
Restoring Hope and Nature in the Urban Wild
Adrienne Ross Scanlan
The journey of a newcomer to the Pacific Northwest who learns that home is where you create belonging

Day Hiking Snoqualmie Region
Cascade Foothills • I-90 Corridor • Alpine Lakes
2nd Edition
Dan Nelson with photography by Alan Bauer
An up-to-date edition to one of the easiest, most scenic regions for Seattle area hikers to visit

Biking Puget Sound
60 Rides from Olympia to the San Juans
2nd Edition
Bill Thorness
Includes downloadable cue sheets

Pacific Northwest Nature
Coloring for Calm and Mindful Observation
Lida Enche
An adult coloring book that will help you appreciate our natural world